Tennis Psychology:
200 + practical drills and the latest research

Written by Miguel Crespo, Machar Reid and Ann Quinn

Written by Miguel Crespo, Machar Reid and Ann Quinn.
© The International Tennis Federation, ITF Ltd, 2006.

Selected photo credits from Sergio Carmona, Marcelo Ruschel, Ron Angle and Paul Zimmer.

All rights reserved. No part of this publication may be reproduced, stored in a retrieval system, or transmitted in any form or by any means, electrical, mechanical, photocopied, recorded or otherwise, without the prior permission of the publisher.

Printed in Spain.

1-903013-28-3

Note: Throughout this book the pronouns "he", "him" and "his" have been used inclusively, and are intended to apply to both men and women.

International Tennis Federation, ITF Ltd,
Bank Lane,
Roehampton,
London SW15 5XZ,
England.
Tel: 44 (0) 208 878 64 64
Fax: 44 (0) 208 878 77 99
Web site http://www.itftennis.com
E-mail: itf@itftennis.com

Registered address:
PO Box N-7788
West Bay Street,
Nassau,
Bahamas.

PREFACES AND INTRODUCTION

"Sometimes my head goes away and doesn't come back. I have to get it back here." *Marat Safin*

PREFACE

The mental side of the game is considered to be one of the fundamentals for continued and successful tennis play. Achieving an optimal psychological state when playing tennis is not only crucial for performance but also for participation, since it is as relevant for the beginner player as it is for the touring professional.

A thorough understanding of the theoretical basis and the practical on and off-court application of the psychological components of matchplay is a must for players and coaches. By making this information user-friendly, an integrated approach to training that includes all elements of the game can be put in place to help players improve and reach the highest levels.

This book contains the most important information on the mental side of the game and I am convinced it will provide coaches around the world with the necessary practical information to help their players greatly improve their performance.

Francesco Ricci Bitti
President, International Tennis Federation

PREFACE

Over the past 20 years knowledge of the Sports Sciences has become increasingly important for the tennis coaches' work. The ITF commitment in this area has increased and in addition to producing approved syllabi for educating coaches which are now being used by over 80 ITF member nations, the ITF are also focusing on producing tennis specific sport science resources.

This psychology book includes not only extensive information on the mental side of the game but it also outlines practical on and off-court drills which can be used by tennis coaches to help their players to improve their competitive performance. On behalf of the Development Department of the ITF I would like to recognise the excellent work that has been done by Miguel Crespo, Machar Reid and Ann Quinn in producing this book. I would also like to recognise the work on this important project of our Development Research Assistant Patrick McInerney.

I hope that the practical information provided in this book will help coaches to be more effective in developing the necessary mental skills to improve their players performance.

Dave Miley
Executive Director, Tennis Development

INTRODUCTION

The professional game's ranking lists are replete with names. Behind those names are players' games; and behind those games are players' minds. Amongst the tennis playing elite, the mind ranks as their strongest competitive weapons. Post-match press conferences and interviews are rife with idioms that epitomise as much: 'The difference between winning and losing that match was between the ears' 'The game is 95% mental'... In light of this, under-estimating the importance of tennis' mental side or failing to spend the necessary time to develop the psychological skills needed for successful tennis performance, would be akin to losing a match before it has even started!

Emotions and cognitions directly influence the tactics, technique and physical condition of all tennis players. Consequently, the ability to learn, develop and optimise the use of psychological skills in different game situations on-court and at different times off it becomes vital to success.

The psychological challenge that tennis represents can be best appreciated by considering that a typical tennis match demands that players make approximately 800 decisions. To do this efficiently, players need to be motivated to play and to perform at their best. Appropriate goal-setting is one such means through which this can be achieved. Once players have this fundamental psychological skill, of motivation, they need to strive for an optimal performance state, a psychological construct related to flow state, and composed of an appropriate amount of many attributes such as calmness, activation, focus, and visual and mental 'clarity'. Tennis matches, of course, are not all plain sailing, and many things can affect the player's mental performance; bad calls, crowd behaviour and inclement weather to name but a few. Throughout, players are required to be positive, stay in the 'here and now', learn from mistakes, maintain their self-confidence and visualise their success. If not difficult enough, the game's uncertain match times, no substitutes or time-outs, changing surfaces and balls, and continuous travel certainly serves to add to the complexity of tennis psychological requirements.

While the tennis fraternity along with scientific and popular reading have detailed the mental intricacies of the game, documentation of practical drills to improve a player's repertoire of psychological skills, especially on-court, has been scarce. A wondrous anomaly given how important lucid mental function is perceived to be!

Most resources simply template the psychological skills needed for successful tennis performance, and in general provide infinitely more theory than practice; more general guidelines than specific, practical drills. We have thus tried to go about things a little differently... the necessary theory remains, but consistent with the research and recommendations of Gould et al. (1999b) it has been complemented by over 200 tennis-specific psychology drills to be practiced both on- and off-court.

The first part of **ITF Tennis Psychology** sets the scene by introducing the role of psychology in tennis play. It details the mental skills required for the game and their relationships with other tennis skills and training techniques. Motivation, emotional control (arousal, anxiety and stress), control of thoughts (self-confidence, self-esteem, self-efficacy, and attribution), concentration-focus, as well as other important considerations such as personality, gender, and disabilities are covered in depth. Additionally, values, sportsmanship, ethics, and moral issues, plus team psychology, the development of attitude, maturity and responsibility, and intellectual and social skills are discussed. The concept of mental skills training is also presented. Here, with the aid of applied research, we describe mental skills training, its features, and its primary goal: the achievement of an 'ideal performance state' or 'the zone'.

Part II is devoted to reviewing the most relevant mental training techniques for improved tennis performance: goal-setting, motivational climate, self-talk, arousal control techniques, visualisation, rituals, coping behaviours and routines, cognitive strategies, and attentional control. It also presents information on the characteristics, phases (assessment through to evaluation) and the implementation of mental skills training programmes for tennis.

One of the unique advantages that sets this book apart from other tennis psychology books, is Part III. This section introduces both on and off-court drills for the various psychological skills needed in the five game situations. That is, the provision of specific psychological on-court drills for the serve and return of serve, the baseline game, the approaching / playing at the net and passing the net player as well as for matchplay singles and doubles game situations. This has the potential to yield on-court psychological training that is better structured and more enjoyable. Equally, the examples of off-court training drills will assist the development of many other mental skills.

Finally, other factors including the fostering of positive psychological momentum, and specific mental considerations at select points in a player's career (i.e. as a junior, aspiring professional, or retired player; when experiencing a performance slump or suffering an injury) are expanded upon in Part IV. This part also includes information on the psychological benefits of tennis practice, as well as psychological strategies for the tennis coach, parents and officials.

Optimal player development requires that coaches organise and facilitate player practice of the mental skills needed for successful and enjoyable tennis play. **ITF Tennis Psychology** aims to firstly educate coaches about the theory behind the various psychological strategies to increase their understanding of the skills. Secondly and most importantly for the coach, this book provides many examples of mental skills and techniques they can apply to all players they coach from young juniors throughout the touring professionals.

INDEX

	PREFACES	5
	INTRODUCTION	7

PART I — MENTAL SKILLS FOR TENNIS — 13

- CHAPTER 1. ROLE OF PSYCHOLOGY IN TENNIS 15
- CHAPTER 2. MOTIVATION 23
- CHAPTER 3. EMOTIONAL CONTROL 31
- CHAPTER 4. CONTROL OF THOUGHTS 37
- CHAPTER 5. CONCENTRATION - FOCUS 45
- CHAPTER 6. OTHER PSYCHOLOGICAL CONSIDERATIONS 51

PART II — MENTAL TRAINING TECHNIQUES AND PLANS — 63

- CHAPTER 7. GOAL-SETTING 65
- CHAPTER 8. CREATING THE ADEQUATE MOTIVATIONAL CLIMATE 69
- CHAPTER 9. SELF-TALK 71
- CHAPTER 10. AROUSAL CONTROL TECHNIQUES 73
- CHAPTER 11. VISUALISATION 79
- CHAPTER 12. RITUALS AND COPING BEHAVIOURS 83
- CHAPTER 13. COGNITIVE STRATEGIES 87
- CHAPTER 14. ATTENTIONAL CONTROL 93
- CHAPTER 15. CHARACTERISTICS OF A MENTAL SKILLS TRAINING PROGRAMME 97
- CHAPTER 16. PHASES OF A MENTAL SKILLS TRAINING PROGRAMME 103

Tennis Psychology

PART III — ON- AND OFF-COURT PSYCHOLOGICAL DRILLS AND ACTIVITIES — 111

- CHAPTER 17. GETTING STARTED 113
- CHAPTER 18. SERVE AND RETURN OF SERVE 117
- CHAPTER 19. BASELINE GAME 125
- CHAPTER 20. PLAYING AT THE NET AND PASSING THE NET PLAYER 133
- CHAPTER 21. MATCH PLAY SITUATIONS 137
- CHAPTER 22. OTHER SITUATIONS 145
- CHAPTER 23. OFF-COURT MENTAL SKILLS PRACTICE 149

PART IV — OTHER IMPORTANT ISSUES — 165

- CHAPTER 24. PSYCHOLOGY OF MATCH PLAY: FOSTERING POSITIVE MOMENTUM 167
- CHAPTER 25. PSYCHOLOGICAL ASPECTS AT CERTAIN STAGES OF THE PLAYER'S CAREER 171
- CHAPTER 26. PSYCHOLOGY FOR THE TENNIS COACHES AND OFFICIALS 191
- CHAPTER 27. PSYCHOLOGY FOR TENNIS PARENTS 199

FINAL WORDS — 207
APPENDIX — 209

- SELF-ASSESSMENTS 209
- REFERENCES 233
- BIOGRAPHIES OF THE AUTORS 241
- USEFUL CONTACTS 243

PART I. MENTAL SKILLS FOR TENNIS

"I can't remember a time when I haven't been mentally tough out there." *Lleyton Hewitt*

ROLE OF PSYCHOLOGY IN TENNIS

In his 1975 book, '*The Inner Game of Tennis*', Gallwey coined the phrase, 'the most formidable opponent is often the one inside a player's own head'. Metaphorically appropriate decades on, it does beg the question 'how much have advances in sports psychology improved tennis coaching and playing?' While a case can be made for research facilitating talented players in achieving more consistent and better performances, equally, it could be argued that its contribution has been negligible. Somewhere in the middle, lies the suggestion that sports psychology has been effective in some capacities, yet not fully utilised in a large number of others. Its application throughout the course of a player's career, from child beginner to adult competitor, where coaches need to know what is appropriate and what is not; what is desired and what is required; epitomises the challenge confronting its more effective integration in tennis pedagogy.

Human life is characterised by various stages of development, each of which carries its own biological, sociological, and psychological idiosyncrasies. The boundaries of these stages are highly individual, and throughout, our sensitivity to different stimuli changes. Aptly named, 'sensitive periods', it is here where we fulfil certain developmental tasks (i.e. through play, learning, and work) along the way to establishing our own repertoires of cognitive, psycho-motor, and social skills.

With this backdrop in mind, we can appreciate why long-term tennis player development may also be considered to occur phasically. If, as research suggests, the development of elite skill takes approximately 10 years or 10,000 hours of deliberate practice and competition (Ericsson, 1996), logic dictates that this period will be punctuated by different stages of learning; different phases of emotional, physical and technical growth. As part of this process, key 'mental' qualities need to be nurtured.

> **REMEMBER:**
>
> Coaches and researchers have focussed on the study and practice of the mental skills needed for high performance, rather than the skills required to holistically best develop players over the course of their careers.

1.1. MENTAL SKILLS REQUIRED FOR TENNIS

Coaches, players, officials and fans all agree that the contribution of psychology to successful tennis play is significant. This consensus is borne out of game analysis, which highligths the psychological characteristics common to great players, the mental challenges inherent to the game (see Table 1.1) (Crespo, 2002), as well as the mental skills that players and coaches consider important for tennis play.

Key to the success of top 10 players, like Tim Henman, are robust mental skills.

GAME CHARACTERISTIC	PSYCHOLOGICAL IMPLICATION
Individual sport. No substitutions allowed.	Motivation and 100% effort are required in all matches.
No coaching during matchplay. No coaching allowed in the vast majority of tournaments.	Independent decision making. Self-confidence is a key ingredient for success.
Continuous game. No time-outs when desired, rather they relate to scoring, weather conditions, etc.	Time management and adaptation to the environment is essential.
Many play variations. Competition takes place on different surfaces (i.e. clay, hard, grass, indoors, outdoors), with different types of balls, scoring formats (i.e. 3 or 5 sets), and playing formats (singles, doubles, mixed doubles).	Players need to adapt to different game conditions. Control of emotions and thoughts are of paramount importance.
Open-skilled sport. Players will typically make between 800 and 1,000 decisions per match.	High levels of concentration are needed to make the right decisions at the right time.
Supreme co-ordination required. High-speed stroke production as well as fine racquet handling require significant dexterity.	Emotional control through relaxation or activation strategies are key.
Lots of dead time. Actual play time amounts to less than 20% of total match duration.	The 'stop-and-go' nature of the game places considerable demand on players' concentration skills.
Minimal off-season. The professional tennis calendar has virtually no off-season. Players can play all year round.	'Year-round' competitive calendars may increase the likelihood of players experiencing 'burn-out' problems.
Silent game. Play occurs while spectators are in silence.	Magnified feelings of 'being alone' and/or the implied comparison with another player in front of significant others may challenge a player's self-confidence.
Nº 1-year ranking. While attaining a high ranking is difficult, maintaining it may be more so.	Enhanced prospect of players sustaining 'performance slumps'.
To be followed by... irregular schedule. During tournaments, players will be uncertain as to their match times.	The importance of pre-match routines becomes even more apparent when match times are uncertain.
Match length dictated by score. Games are not played to time.	Players must stay in the 'here and now'. Strategical and tactical thinking, and control of thoughts should be high.
Knock-out competition system. In professional tournaments, there are no second chances.	As round robins are not common, no strategy other than winning the match can be adopted in most professional tournaments.

Table 1.1 Characteristics of tennis and the psychological implications.

MENTAL SKILLS THAT TENNIS COACHES CONSIDER TO BE IMPORTANT FOR TENNIS PLAY

Research has shown that coaches are gradually becoming more aware of the importance of mental skills for tennis performance and are more interested in understanding and applying mental training techniques in their daily work with players (Gould et al., 2001; Moran, 1995).

Interestingly, Table 1.2 lists the mental skills that coaches have indicated as the most important and most difficult to teach to players.

MOST IMPORTANT MENTAL SKILLS	MOST DIFFICULT MENTAL SKILLS TO TEACH
- Enjoyment - Self-confidence - Motivation / passion - Positive thinking / self-talk - Positive mistake management - Focus / concentration - Emotional control - Honesty / integrity - Practice intensity - Keeping competition in perspective	- Reframe pressure - Emotional control - Positive mistake management - Crisis-adversity management - Imagery / visualisation - Self-confidence - Time management - Motivation

Table 1.2 Mental skills that tennis coaches believe to be important for tennis play and those considered to be most difficult to teach. (Gould et al., 2001; Moran, 1995).

MENTAL SKILLS THAT PLAYERS CONSIDER TO BE IMPORTANT FOR THEIR TENNIS PERFORMANCE

Table 1.3 depicts the mental skills that players consider to be most important to their success (Jones et al., 2002; Terry, 1994; Young, 1998).

PRACTICAL APPLICATION:

Professional players who consistently play at high level, have strong mental skills and practice them regularly (Lubbers, 2001).

MENTAL STRATEGIES USED BY SUCCESSFUL PLAYERS	MENTAL SKILLS THAT PLAYERS CONSIDER AS IMPORTANT FOR THEIR TENNIS PERFORMANCE	MENTAL SKILLS THAT PLAYERS BELIEVE THEY LACK DURING 'LOST' MATCHES
- Practice a systematic pre-performance plan - Practice routines to deal with adversity/distractions before and during competition - Strong concentration skills; work on blocking out irrelevant thoughts - Don't worry about outcome; focus on what they can control - Develop detailed competition plans - Use imagery - Have learned to regulate arousal and anxiety	- Determination and commitment - Concentration, self-confidence - Belief in oneself - Ability to control one's nerves/anxiety - Love for, and interest in tennis	- Loss of concentration - Nerves - 'Choking' - Lack of motivation - Lack of confidence

Table 1.3 Mental skills used by successful players, those which are perceived as importat for both success and failure (Jones et al., 2002; Terry, 1994; Young, 1998).

1.2. RELATIONSHIPS BETWEEN MENTAL SKILLS AND TRAINING TECHNIQUES

Contemporary sports psychology delineates psychological processes, including mental skills and techniques; as underlying successful tennis performance (Weinberg and Gould, 1985). Yet, just as common to the literature, is the difficulty theorists encounter in distinguishing between what is a mental skill and what is a mental training technique to improve that skill (Thomas et al., 1999). For example, where Vealey (1986) described imagery as a technique, Hardy et al. (1996) considered it as a basic psychological skill.

Nonetheless, in this book, a clear distinction has been made. While by no means definitive, it does summarise the divergent research views, and thus allow for the convenient and intelligible grouping of related constructs. As illustrated in Table 1.4, there remains inter-relationships between the distinguished mental skills (motivation, concentration, emotional control, control of thoughts) and the training techniques (e.g. goal-setting, visualisation, attentional control, arousal control, self-talk, etc.) players and coaches can use to enhance them.

Indeed, one of the beauties of mental skills training is that the utility of some techniques (e.g. goal setting, visualisation, beathing) transcend more than one mental skill. Again, Table 1.4 highlights the relevance of all mental techniques to the training of the different skills as indicated (XXX= most relevant, XX= somewhat relevant).

		MENTAL SKILLS			
		Motivation (achievement, commitment, persistence, 100% effort)	Emotional control (arousal, anxiety, stress)	Control of thoughts (self-confidence, self-esteem, self-efficacy, attribution, positive thinking)	Concentration / focus, attention, anticipation
MENTAL TECHNIQUES	Goal-setting	XXX	XX	XX	XX
	Motivational climate	XX	XX	XX	XX
	Self-talk	XX	XX	XXX	XX
	Arousal, stress, anxiety control (activation / relaxation)	XX	XXX	XX	XX
	Visualisation (imagery)	XX	XX	XX	XX
	Rituals and coping behaviours (attitude)	XX	XXX	XXX	XX
	Cognitive strategies	XX	XX	XXX	XX
	Attentional control	XX	XX	XX	XXX

Table 1.4 Inter-relationship between mental skills and techniques in tennis.

1.3. RELATIONSHIPS BETWEEN MENTAL SKILLS AND OTHER TENNIS SKILLS

Like the inter-relationship alluded to above, mental skills can also be associated with other tennis skills (Figure 1.1). For instance, upon initial inspection the relationship between psychology and tactics may appear superficial, but closer examination reveals that almost every tactical decision or response has a psychological link. Similarly, when performing a mental skills on-court drill to train 100% effort, the player concurrently works physically and, potentially technically. This type of integrated physical-mental training drill is commonly used in high performance tennis training, and readers are referred to the book, *ITF Strength and Conditioning for Tennis*, for further examples.

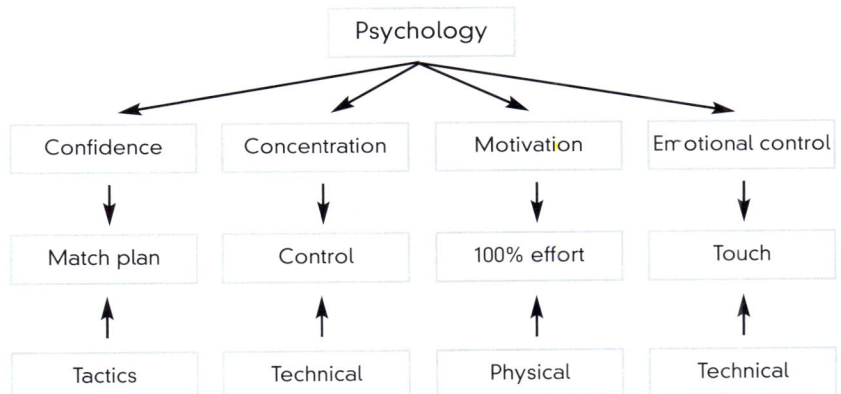

Figure 1.1
Relationships between selected psychological skills and other tennis skills.

1.4. WHAT IS MENTAL SKILLS TRAINING?

Mental skills training (MST) relates to the development of psychological skills that help maximise performance, enhance the sport experience, and foster personal development. It encompasses all of- but not only-cognitive, psychomotor, motivational, and psychoregulatory training and should see the player gradually learn to integrate mental skills into everyday life (Sledr, 2001).

As summarised in Table 1.5, MST also parallels other training modes, whether they be physical, technical or tactical, in a number of different ways (Dorsky, 1996; Duda, 2001a; Lubbers, 2001; Slder, 2001; Weinberg and Gould, 1995; Young, 1998; 2000). Ultimately, from a performance perspective, the most obvious parallel and the main goal of MST is to facilitate players' control of their performance which, if so done, will increase their chances of inducing an ideal performance state (Duda, 2001; Williams, 1986).

Mental skills training can help players to attend the most important task cues.

I. Mental skills for tennis

FEATURE	BACKGROUND
It is for ALL players	A common misconception is that great players are born with the necessary mental skills. More often than not however, they were practiced and learned as the players developed. Such is the efficiency with which they are integrated into these players' psyche's that they become automated and summoned into use on demand.
It is important	Mental factors primarily account for inter-day performance whereas technical, tactical or physical factors are relatively stable.
It is educational and develops life skills	The general objective of MST is to bring out the best in players and foster one's development rather than encourage winning at all costs. More specifically, from the coach's perspective it is likely to have three main, developmental goals: coaching to win, coaching to have fun and coaching to help players grow physically, psychologically and socially.
It entails initial assessment	MST incorporates two types of assessment: the player's psychological profile and a tennis-specific analysis where the player's on-court behaviour and match performanceis evaluated.
It respects individuality	The distinct developmental and maturation differences between players' demands that individual skill sets are identified and trained.
It is multi-dimensional	Practice does not make perfect; it makes permanent. That said, all of what players practice daily will have an effect on their mental states.
It is gradual and systematic	MST should be introduced regularly from the beginning of a player's career. Simply exposing players to exercises on an ad-hoc basis is inadequate. It is a long-term process and part of a year round training regime.
It requires action and training	Players cannot gain the confidence needed to win a Grand Slam by just attending a lecture or reading a book. While both forums may provide some valuable training tips, skill rehearsal stills needs to be performed on-court and whilst coaching.
It is performed both on- and off-court	Mental skills such as on-court routines, practice and match preparation, error management, positive body language and positive self-talk can and should be practiced on- as well as off-court.
It is structured according to training principles	The principles of overload and adaptation, which lead to steady, progressive growth, also apply to mental toughness. Through competition players should learn to improve their ability to relax, concentrate and overcome negative emotional responses.
It incorporates correct work:rest ratios	Playing enough matches complements mental training; while too much or too little competition will inhibit it. Players who compete in emotionally charged matches with little rest are likely to suffer in terms of emotional control, and may burnout. On the other hand, players who compete rarely will feel like they are mentally 'starting over' each time they step on court.
It requires evaluation	Mental skills need to be consistently challenged and periodically evaluated under competitive conditions.
It moves away from general guidelines	Traditional advice such as 'stay calm and relaxed' may not be appropriate for players who need to feel excited or 'on edge' to enter the 'zone'. Coaches must therefore identify the player's optimal emotional state prior to providing verbal stimuli to facilitate performance.
It is reversible	As happens with physical training, players that stop mentally working out will gradually lose the gains they have made. This is best illustrated by comments of tournament players who complain of lost match toughness after only 3-4 weeks without competition.
It works!!	Programmes that help players acquire and develop mental skills can improve their chances of becoming champions!

Table 1.5 Characteristics of mental skills training.

1.5. THE IDEAL PERFORMANCE STATE (IPS)

When tennis players experience the IPS, they feel totally immersed in their games, as if playing on automatic pilot with heightened mental acuity where everything seems to 'click'. Various terms are found in sport literature to describe these experiences, including 'flow' and 'surreal', but most commonly the 'zone' (Csikszentmihalyi, 1990).

CHARACTERISTICS OF THE "ZONE"

Jackson and Csikszentmihalyi (1999) described the following nine characteristics or dimensions of the zone:

1. **Balance between challenges and skills**: There is a match between players' skills and high situational challenges, which provides a high level of confidence, low anxiety and a sense of physical relaxation, but with unparalleled intensity.
2. **Effortless merging of action and awareness**: A sense of unity of body and mind is experienced such that players are aware of their actions but do not think consciously about them.
3. **Clear goals**: Goals are distinctly defined and meaningful to players.
4. **Unambiguous and immediate feedback**: Players can gauge how well they are doing from the feedback they receive.
5. **Total concentration**: Players' focus is only on the task at hand.
6. **A sense of control**: Players feel in control of play; automaticity; alertness.
7. **Loss of self-consciousness**: Players are not motivated by a fear of failure, nor do they entertain any negative thoughts.
8. **Altered sense of time**: Time often seems to slow down with players often unaware its passing.
9. **Rewarding experience**: A state of mind that is characterised by an intrinsic sense of personal fulfilment. When asked to describe the experience, players often use words like 'unforgettable' and 'out of this world'.

Other authors such as Loehr (1990), Young (2000) and Weinberg (2002) add the following characteristics:

— **Confidence**: High levels of self-confidence.
— **Physical relaxation**: Mental calmness and low anxiety.
— **Duration**: Temporary and relatively short.
— **Occurrence**: More frequent in training than in competition.
— **Performance**: Typically optimal, but not necessarily victorious.

While 'zoning' can occur by chance, research provides strong evidence to suggest that it is a state over which players have some control entering, and then maintaining (Jackson and Csikszentmihalyi, 1999). If so, this raises an obvious question for us as coaches ... how can we assist players maximise their chance of entering and ultimately staying in the 'zone'?

As aforementioned, this is the foremost goal of MST. And, if we delve into the research a little further, we can identify specific skills that need to be trained. For example, enhancing players' perceptions of their competence and control are reported to assist the achievement of the IPS, so Duda (2001a) recommends that coaches promote:

REMEMBER:

IPS is the optimal state of mental and physical arousal that allows for the execution of motor skills (Loehr, 1990).

WHAT RESEARCH TELLS US...
Players report playing in the zone more frequently in training than in competition during temporary and relatively short periods in which they see themselves playing their best tennis, yet not necessarily being victorious. They consider that this is a sensitive and volatile state influenced by an array of personal and situational factors, over which they have varying levels of control (Young, 2000).

- **Self-analysis**: Where players learn to analyse what factors lead to particularly good and poor performances. This precipitates the development of a plan for the mental factors that maximise the players' performance potential.

- **Self-monitoring**: Sees players learn to become more aware of their circumstances during training and competition. They then compare this information to that gleaned from the self-analysis to better understand the factors that lead to good performances.

- **Self-regulation**: The control over one's mental and emotional arousal levels to encourage the IPS.

PRACTICAL APPLICATION:

The presence of the IPS in training and competition cannot be guaranteed, but it can be made more likely, and coaches can help players reach this state more consistently. The IPS is strongly related to the concept of momentum which will be covered in Chapter 24.

Santos-Rosa et al. (2004) studied the effect of situational variables on the flow developed by competitive junior players and concluded that they could be used to predict the flow of a tennis match. Indeed, the variable identified to best predict flow was the players' perception of positive behaviours (e.g. praise, feedback) from the coach. That's to say, when the coach praised and gave positive feedback to the players before the match, they tended to experience flow. Additionally, an ego-oriented state (e.g. motivation towards winning) correlated positively with the development of flow; as did players' expectations of good results. There are however a number of factors perceived to affect the maintenance of flow or the zone, as highlighted in Table 1.6 (Young, 2000).

FACTORS RANKED BY ORDER OF IMPORTANCE THAT...		
Facilitate the zone	**Prevent the zone**	**Disrupt the zone**
Preparation (physical and mental).	Inappropriate focus.	Situational / environmental conditions.
Positive mood.	Problems with preparation.	Inappropriate focus.
Experience and control of arousal.	Sub-optimal mood.	Problems with motivation.
Motivation.	Inappropriate experience and control of arousal.	Sub-optimal mood.
Focus.	Problem with motivation.	Inappropriate experience and control of arousal.
Situational/ environmental conditions.	Situational/ environmental conditions.	Problems with preparation.
Positive feedback.	Negative feedback.	Negative feedback.

Table 1.6 Factors reported to facilitate, prevent and disturb the zone experiences of professional female players.

In summarising this chapter and providing a template for further discussion in the chapters to follow, the mental constructs most important for tennis performance can all be considered to belong to one of four main skills:

- **Motivation** - commitment - persistence - 100% effort - enjoyment.
- **Emotional control** - arousal, stress and anxiety control.
- **Control of thoughts** - self-confidence - self-efficacy - attribution - positive thinking.
- **Concentration** (focus) - attention - anticipation.

WHAT RESEARCH TELLS US...
The current state of research indicates that the zone should not be considered 'out of reach' or a chance event. Commitment and discipline are required but players can make it happen, and coaches can most certainly help (Young, 2000).

MOTIVATION 2

2.1. DEFINITION

In global terms, motivation defines the complex process that determines the direction (why tennis and not another sport) and intensity (why train and work so hard for the sport) of effort (Weinberg and Gould, 1995).

In studying these processes in tennis, researchers have been able to identify the following motives for participation:

— Participation of young tennis players is principally driven by a desire to improve playing level or skills, keep physically fit, and make new friends. Other less important motives include satisfying parents or friends, feeling important or popular and receiving extrinsic rewards (Balaguer and Atienza, 1994).
— Boys typically demonstrate a greater desire for competition, challenge and attaining status or rewards than girls (Balaguer and Atienza, 1994; González et al., 1999).
— Among players aged over 12, being popular, being with friends and satisfying parents and friends are less important motives than for younger players (Balaguer and Atienza, 1994).
— As compared to players aged over 12, it is more important for younger players to like their coaches (Balaguer and Atienza, 1994; González et al., 1999).
— Reasons for participation while mainly intrinsic (González et al., 1999; Puig and Villamarín, 1995), do become increasingly extrinsic with age (Lesko, 1992).
— Age, gender and club atmosphere were agents influencing both personal control and motivation. Personal control (i.e. perceived competence) appears to exert significant influence over the motivational profiles of beginner tennis players (Villamarín et al., 1998).
— No differences exist in the perceived competence and intrinsic motivation between beginner and intermediate players (Lesko, 1992).
— More successful Davis Cup players show greater motivation for participating and competing in tennis than less successful players (Butt and Cox, 1992).

While indications are that players therefore possess performance-oriented motives, to further understand the intricate and very individual nature of motivation, it is also important to dispel some common misconceptions:

— **Motivation is synonymous with arousal:** Coaches often think that pre-game talks 'motivate' players to better performance. However, Roberts (1992) has shown that motivation and arousal are independent entities.

— **Motivation is related to positive thinking or the 'you can do it!' principle:** Again, research indicates that if expectations are not realistic, they are of little benefit (Roberts, 1992).

— **Motivation is an inherent trait:** Rather it can be improved and enhanced in sportspeople of all ages and skill levels (Balaguer and Atienza, 1994).

PRACTICAL APPLICATION:

Coaches need to appreciate what 'drives' their players. Within any playing group, each player will have different motives and therefore respond more or less positively to different forms of motivation. Coaches that can tailor their approach to connect with players in this fashion, are best positioned to help all players reach their potential.

WHAT RESEARCH TELLS US...
Research has shown that reasons for drop out vary between professional players: injuries, travel, media, season length, and issues with agents (WTA, 2004), and amateur players: difficulty of the game, lack of time, lack of suitable playing partners, and insufficient improvement (USTA, 2003).

I. Mental skills for tennis

2.2. TYPES, THEORIES AND MODELS OF MOTIVATION

Four main theories have evolved over the last 40 years to explain motivation's role in sport. The ways in which the need achievement, attribution, intrinsic and extrinsic motivation, and social cognitive theories view motivation in sporting contexts are discussed below.

NEED ACHIEVEMENT THEORY

This approach believes that there are two motive states: to achieve success and to avoid failure which interact with environmental cues (e.g. pride and shame) to arouse affective states and action (McClelland, 1961). While contributing significantly to the enhanced general understanding of motivation, research has failed to provide conclusive proof of the application of need achievement in sport. Individuals driven by the motive to achieve success have indeed been shown to select challenging tasks and demonstrate improved performance (Roberts, 1992). Unexpectedly however, the fear of failure, which motivates other individuals, has not been related to increased risk aversion and poor performances (Maehr, 1974). Nonetheless, one consistent and significant finding is that achievement motivation varies among cultures and between men and women (McClelland, 1961).

ATTRIBUTION THEORY

This theory suggests that individuals' perceptions of success and failure are affected by need achievement. In other words, individuals who are high or low on need achievement are likely to think differently about success and failure. This is borne out of the development of attributional patterns whereby the manner in which individuals attribute the causes of results (winning and losing) affects expectancies of future success and failure, and is assumed to affect achievement striving (Heider, 1958).

Coaches should help players make the correct attributions for their wins and losses. That is, players should endeavour to make attributions centered on internal and stable factors that they have under their control. Equally, it is important that players avoid the phenomena of 'learned helplessness' which will be elaborated on in Chapter 4.

INTRINSIC AND EXTRINSIC MOTIVATION THEORY

REMEMBER:
Intrinsically motivated players play tennis because they love the game and want to achieve a desired level of competence and be successful. Extrinsically motivated players play tennis in the search for tangible (e.g. trophies and money) or intangible (e.g. recognition and adulation) rewards.

Individuals participate in sport for different intrinsic or extrinsic motives. Individuals are considered intrinsically motivated if they perform an activity, without an external reward; while the opposite applies to extrinsically motivated individuals (Deci and Ryan, 1985).

Study of this theory in sport has shown that external rewards that fail to provide information (how players perform the task) and control (how much players can dictate the outcome of their performance) can negatively affect intrinsic motivation as the reward becomes more important than the internal reason (i.e. the pleasure) for completing the task. On the contrary, if these rewards help individuals develop the perception of competence and personal responsibility, they will enhance intrinsic motivation (Deci and Ryan, 1985).

WHAT RESEARCH TELLS US...
Research evaluating the attribution theory in sporting contexts has shown that individuals that attribute positive results to internal (skills, effort, practice) and not external factors (luck, easy match, referee) increase their feelings of pride and satisfaction, and thus motivation (Roberts, 1992). Alternatively, negative results attributed to internal factors cause negative feelings, dissatisfaction and a lack of motivation (McAuley and Duncan, 1990). Positive results attributed to stable factors (skill, task difficulty) are associated with expectancy of future success, while negative results attributed to these same factors correlate with expectations of future failure (Kim, 1990). Studies have additionally shown that females tend to use more external attributions, and that attribution patterns change with age (Hewitt and Jackson, 1986).

Coaches at all levels need to understand the consequences of any reward system they use with their players. As part of this review, it is also important to evaluate how the competitive structure and tournament system of tennis may influence the intrinsic motivation of your players.

SOCIAL COGNITIVE THEORIES

This group of theories are built around the expectations and values that individuals attach to different goals and achievement activities. Each with their own nuances, the three theories considered to fall under sport's 'social cognitive' banner are self-efficacy, perceived competence and goal achievement motivation.

Theory of self-efficacy

Self-efficacy is the conviction one needs to successfully execute the behaviour necessary to produce a certain outcome (Bandura, 1977). The motivational mechanism of this theory is the principle that having mastery expectations influences performance.

It is not concerned with the ability of individuals, but rather the individuals' assessments of what they can do with their ability. For this reason, the term self-confidence is often used interchangeably.

The relationship between motivation and self-efficacy in tennis was studied by Puig and Villamarín (1995). These researchers were able to show that players who possessed greater self-efficacy were more intrinsically motivated, and that self-efficacy seemed positively related to a player's percentage of matches won and years of playing experience.

Theory of perceived competence

The underlying assumptions of this theory are that perceived competence is a multidimensional concept (cognitive, social and physical) and that individuals are motivated to show competence in achievement domains such as tennis. Within this approach, success and failure are evaluated by significant others, and produce contrasting amounts of intrinsic pleasure, perceived competence and achievement (Harter, 1978). Other factors such as extent of sports participation and age have also been shown to affect how competent performers perceive themselves (Roberts et al., 1981). Indeed, in some instances as when young players play competitive tennis, self-worth may be wrongly equated to achievement:

— Win <=> Success <=> Good person.
— Loss <=> Failure <=> Bad person.

Successful on-court experiences are important in assisting players develop their self-efficacy. Practices and matchplay should not result in repeated failure, but instead expose players to attainable yet challenging exercises to foster their self-confidence.

Goal achievement motivation or goal perspective theory

A contemporary theory in achievement psychology (including sport), goal achievement motivation helps explain some of the mechanisms behind certain players' seemingly endless motivation to train and compete, and others' apparent lack of motivation or even withdrawal from tennis. By extension, the importance of goal-setting in tennis and other sports is emphasised (Duda, 2001b).

This theory assumes that a player's main goal is to display competency. In turn, such competency must be assessed and success defined. Players' goal orientations refer to their concepts of ability and more broadly describe how most players assess competence and define success. To this end, players can be considered task-oriented, ego-oriented or a combination of the two, while the extent to which players are ego- or task-oriented is

PRACTICAL APPLICATION:

Specific practices and drills need to be planned so that players of different ages and abilities are able to show their competence. Similarly, as significant others may play prominent roles in assessing competence, coaches need to carefully consider the appropriateness of any feedback given.

MEASUREMENT TESTS FOR MOTIVATION:

Research evaluating motivation in tennis has largely focussed on its role in participation and goal achievement motivation. In doing so, investigators have made use of measurement tools such as the COI (Competitive Orientation Inventory, Vealey, 1986), SOQ (Sport Orientation Questionnaire; Gill and Deeter, 1988), POSQ (Perception of Success Questionnaire; Roberts and Balagué, 1989) in addition to TEOSQ and the PMCSQ mentioned in the text.

measured in terms of quantity (high or low). Researchers have developed questionnaires to determine the extent to which both players (TEOSQ, Task and Ego Orientation in Sport Questionnaire; Duda and Nichols, 1989) and training environments (PMCSQ, Perceived Motivational Climate in Sport Questionnaire; Walling et al., 1993), may be task- and/or ego-involved.

The impact of goal achievement motivation and motivational climates on tennis performance has been extensively researched in recent years. Table 2.1 highlights the general characteristics of both types of orientations and provides a summary of the most important research findings of goal perspective theory applied to tennis (Berlant and Weiss, 1997; Duda et al., 1995; Fry and Newton, 2003; Harwood and Swain, 1998, Newton and Duda, 1992, 1993, 1995; Solmon and Boone, 1993; Williams, 1994). Chapter 8 expands upon the intricacies of motivational climates in tennis.

	TASK-ORIENTED	EGO-ORIENTED
Concept of ability	Self-referenced.	Subjectively-referenced, normatively defined.
Causes of tennis success	Trying hard (exerting effort), task mastery (meeting the demands of the task), do not hesitate to experiment with and learn new skills, personal improvement, collaborating with others to foster learning.	Showing superior ability, beating others, and/or demonstrating superior competence.
Motives for participation	Players play tennis for fitness, development and competition. More prone to be intrinsically motivated. Associated with the perception that tennis is satisfying and enjoyable (overall intrinsic interest).	Players play tennis to gain recognition, status, and competition. Less likely to be intrinsically motivated. May perceive tennis as boring (overall extrinsic interest).
Perceived purposes of sport	Tennis should teach players the value of hard work, show them how to co-operate, and help them develop as people.	Tennis has to improve one's popularity, feelings of importance, and potentially aid players in earning considerable money.
Means used to reach the goals	Associated with endorsement of sportsmanlike behaviours.	May perceive cheating in tennis as legitimate or "fair game".
Stress	Low levels of anxiety and stress. Concentrated and feeling good about the match.	High levels of anxiety and stress. Worries and expresses outcome or performance concerns; may withdraw.
Learning strategies used	Effective strategies.	Ineffective strategies.
Effort	Will give 100%.	Reduce exerted effort.
Interpretation of mistakes	Recognises mistakes and problem solves to improve.	Downplays the significance of the task.
Preferred processing strategies and feedback	Deep-processing strategies, prefers objective/task feedback.	Superficial strategies. Rejects task performance related feedback, preferring normative feedback.
Coping strategies employed	Active problem solving: effective long and short term.	Emotional / avoidance / withdrawal: May be effective in the short term but not long term.
Questions posed by players to themselves	How do I do this? How can I get better?	How am I doing (compared to others)? How can I show I am better…or "not worse"?
Task selection	Positively related to the selection of challenging tasks.	No data available.

Table 2.1 The principles and research findings of goal perspective theory applied to tennis.

WHAT RESEARCH TELLS US...
The development of task and ego goals rest on a complex interaction of cognitive-developmental and social-environmental factors. In tennis, these factors can be summarised as: cognitive-developmental skills and experiences, motivational climate conveyed by significant others, structural and social nature of the game, and the match context (Harwood and Swain, 2001).

ORIENTATION	ABILITY	MOTIVATIONAL PATTERN
TASK	High/Low	Positive / Adaptative
EGO	High/Confident	Motivated achievement
	Uncertain competence	Maladaptative pattern

Table 2.2 Relationships between goal orientations, ability and motivational patterns.

Goal perspective theory has determined the effect of the different goal orientations on players' motivational patterns such that important inferences can be drawn. As highlighted in Table 2.2, players high in task-orientation will show positive/adaptative motivational patterns independent of their perception of ability (high or low). Conversely, players high in ego-orientation will show motivated achievement patterns when they have high and confident perceptions of their abilities. However, their motivational patterns will be maladaptative when they doubt their competence.

2.3. BURNOUT

DEFINITION

A phenomenon closely related to motivation, burnout can be considered as the exhaustive psycho-physiological responses that result from frequent, sometimes extreme, and largely ineffective efforts to meet excessive demands (Weinberg and Gould, 1995).

REMEMBER:
Avoid doing too much, too soon, too fast, too often - before it is too late. Sometimes we learn how much is enough by observing how much was too much.

CAUSES OF BURNOUT

It is generally assumed that burnout is caused by chronic, high levels of stress and dissatisfaction that stem from environmental stressors such as overtraining, too much stress, staleness, inadequate recovery, the external pressure to win, travel commitments, disagreements with management or parents, and/or trying to juggle multiple roles (Weinberg and Gould, 1995). These demands however, do not automatically translate to burnout. Rather, an 'out of sync' and maladaptive interaction between the player and the situation is most commonly at fault. That is, the underpinnings of burnout seem to relate to how players perceive the stressors or demands, how well equipped they consider themselves to meet these demands, and how they view the consequences associated with failing to do so. Here, players that feel ill-equipped or uncertain in their ability to meet any important and personally meaningful demands, are at greater risk of burning out (Smith, 1986). Furthermore, if the players in question do not possess the necessary coping skills to deal with the stress from such appraisals, burnout becomes increasingly likely.

Several models of sport-specific burnout have been developed emphasising aspects such as the cognitive-affective process (Smith, 1986), the negative-training stress response (Silva, 1994), and identity development and external control (Coackley, 1992). Authors such as Kuipers (1996) have also distinguished sympathetic overtraining (increased sympathetic tone in the resting state, elevated resting heart rate, increased blood pressure, poor appetite, weight loss, disturbed sleep, and mental irritability) from parasympathetic overtraining (increased parasympathetic tone in the resting state, low resting heart rate, low blood pressure, good appetite, and normal sleep).

MEASUREMENT TESTS FOR BURNOUT:
Researchers have used different tests for assessing burnout such as: the Eades Athletic Burnout Inventory (Eades, 1991), the POMS - Profile of Mood States (McNair et al., 1971) or the Maslach Burnout Inventory (Maslach and Jackson, 1981).

WHAT RESEARCH TELLS US...
Duda et al., (2001) found that players high in task-orientation and whom perceived a task-involving tennis environment, were less likely to report psychological withdrawal from tennis and exhibited lower total burnout. When the motivational climate was deemed more ego-involving, players reported greater devaluation by the coach and teammates.

BURNOUT IN COMPETITIVE JUNIOR TENNIS PLAYERS

In Garcés' 1995 study almost 50% of the sample of young tennis players had suffered burnout symptoms on at least one occasion, with their incidence increasing along with age and competitive demands. Not surprisingly, these same players expressed greater dissatisfaction with tennis play than the remainder of the sample. A course of studies by Gould et al. (1996a, 1996b, and 1997) built on Garcés' earlier work and identified a variety of personal and situational predictors of burnout, and in the process, suggested a close link between perfectionism and the incidence of burnout in tennis. Their findings are summarised in Table 2.3 while Table 2.4 provides advice for players, coaches and parents so as to minimise the prospect of players burning out.

Note: Burnout is not only limited to tennis players. Tennis coaches have also been reported to suffer from the condition and tell-tale signs of its onset as well as coping strategies are outlined in Chapter 26.

CHARACTERISTICS OF "BURNOUT" PLAYERS	CHARACTERISTICS OF BURNOUT		FACTORS LEADING TO BURNOUT
- Gave less input in training. - More likely to have played up an age division. - Lower in extrinsic motivation. - More apathetic and withdrawn. - Less likely to use planned coping strategies, especially positive interpretation. - Perceived their parents to have very high expectations and be more critical. - Displayed greater perfectionism and concern about making mistakes. - Practiced fewer days.	**Mental symptoms** - Low motivation. - Negative outlook. - Feelings of isolation. - Concentration problems. - Frequent emotional highs and lows. - Low physical and mental energy.	**Physical symptoms** - Symptomatic: Injuries, lack of energy, illness. - Asymptomatic: No physical symptoms, no lack of energy, no sign of illness.	- Physical problems and poor play. - Overtraining physically, emotionally or mentally. - Inadequate recovery, sleep, nutrition or rest. - Time demands of tennis. - Travel concerns. - Difficulties in adjusting to school. - Dissatisfaction with social life. - Negative parental influence. - Unfulfilled, inappropriate expectations. - Lack of enjoyment. - Lack of motivation. - A want to pursue other interests. - Personality not conducive to competitive tennis. - Perceived failure or lack of perceived success.

Table 2.3 Characteristics of, and factors contributing to burnout.

ADVICE FOR PLAYERS	ADVICE FOR COACHES	ADVICE FOR PARENTS
- Play for 'your' reasons. - Balance tennis with other past-times or pursuits. - No fun, no play: try to make it fun. - Relax. - Take time off. - Set challenging and realistic goals and reward yourself.	- Cultivate personal involvement and two-way communication with players. - Value and act on players' input. - Endeavour to understand players' feelings. - Encourage players to be task-oriented and foster a training environment to facilitate that.	- Recognise optimal amount and type of encouragement. - Gradually lessen involvement. - Reduce importance of outcome. - Show support/empathy. - Separate/clarify parent/coach role. - Solicit player input. - Schedule and partake in non-tennis activities with children.

Table 2.4 Advice for players, coaches and parents on how to avoid burnout (Gould et al., 1996a, 1996b, 1997; Duda et al., 2001; Loehr and Striegel, 1994).

2.4. QUALITIES RELATED TO MOTIVATION

Coaches will have a 'working familiarity' with several of the concepts closely associated with motivation. Qualities such as commitment, persistence, effort and competitiveness are important aspects which contribute to motivation but should not be mistaken as motivation (Table 2.5).

QUALITY	WHAT IT IS	HOW IT CAN BE FOSTERED
COMMITMENT	Commitment is more than giving 100%. It is dedication to the pursuit of a goal through good and bad times, following excellent or poor performances.	Weinberg (2002) identified the following factors as likely to increase a player's commitment: - History of making promises a reality. - Recent 'peak performance' experiences. - Mastering difficult skills. - Being around others who make commitments to change. - Understanding the benefits of commitment.
PERSISTENCE	The ability and willingness to persevere in the pursuit of a goal in spite of obstacles or in the face of failure. Persistent players are those that work harder when the going gets tough.	Create a training atmosphere in which the idea of 'fighting' and being a smart court 'warrior' is highly emphasised.
100% EFFORT	The (maximal) intensity with which one pursues goals.	Instil and assist players understand training principles such as 'no two bounces', 'play the best possible shot', etc.
COMPETITIVENESS	"A disposition to strive for satisfaction when making comparisons with some standard of excellence in the presence of evaluative others" (Martens, 1976, p.3). Tennis professionals have demonstrated more sport and interpersonal competitiveness than amateur players (Houston et al., 1997). It develops in 3 stages: - <u>Autonomous</u>: Before approximately four years of age, children focus on mastering the environment. It is punctuated by self-evaluation/assessment, devoid of comparison to others. - <u>Social comparison</u>: From the age of approximately five, children begin to compare themselves with others. - <u>Integration</u>: No typical age. It is the combination of previous two stages, and not everybody reaches it.	Coaches and parents should nurture the right balance between competition and cooperation, especially at the early stages of development, to ensure that players are challenged and have fun. Brown (1988), for example, found that beginner players that participated in tennis classes where cooperation was encouraged improved more than those in classes where instruction was based around individual tutelage. Coaches can enhance cooperation during lessons by maximising participation and opportunities to learn and experience success through the provision of positive feedback as well as through suitable score-keeping.

*Table 2.5
Concepts that help shape the role of motivation in tennis.*

2.5. MOTIVATIONAL PROBLEMS

Motivational problems are not uncommon in tennis. Coaches should be aware that they can arise from:

- **Incorrect attributions:** Always attributing the causes of defeats to external factors (i.e. the opponent, the weather, etc.).
- **Inappropriate self-rewards/self-punishment:** When players reward themselves undeservedly, or constantly and negatively criticise themselves during or after matches.
- **General lack of motivation:** Due to poor tournament or practice planning (i.e. inappropriate tournament selection, boring practices, performance 'slumps', etc.).
- **'Over-motivation':** Leading to exuberance and excessive self-confidence.
- **Misplaced motivation:** Where players compete just for external rewards (i.e. money, trophies), or as a result of negative motives (i.e. fear of losing).

2.6. GUIDELINES FOR IMPROVING MOTIVATION

PRACTICAL APPLICATION:

Self-motivation is a motivational technique with which coaches should be familiar. Players, unknowingly, use it almost everyday and Samulski (2004) has made a distinction between three different types of self-motivation:
- **Motoric:** Energising exercises, isometric exercises, focussing on inspiration and dynamic and rhythmical movements.
- **Cognitive:** Individual goals, knowledge of one's own capabilities, anticipation of positive reinforcements, causal attribution, self-reward and verbal self-reinforcement.
- **Emotional:** Pleasure while moving, feeling of success, feeling of flow and emotional identification with the group.

The three primary strategies to motivate players – setting correct goals, developing appropriate motivational climates, and using rewards wisely – will be detailed in Chapters 7, 8, and 26. However, other guidelines that can help coaches in their roles as 'facilitators of performance' are outlined below (Loehr and Striegel, 1994; Weinberg and Gould, 1995).

- **Get familiar with the reasons why players play**. The coach can ask players: What motivates you to play tennis? What causes your motivation to drop? What do you like/dislike about playing tennis? What do you prefer... winning or playing well?
- **Understand that some players may participate in tennis for more than one reason**. Motives vary greatly, are likely to be unique to each individual and may change over time. Appreciate that players may be motivated both by their needs and traits as well as the characteristics of the situation.
- **If possible, adapt the characteristics of the situation to the needs of the players**. This may require coaches to provide appropriate competition or recreation, individualise coaching and training (differentiation), and be creative with workouts to keep them fun and challenging.
- **Emphasise the benefits of playing tennis** and help players to find its humorous side, while encouraging them to have fun.
- **Be aware that your behaviours influence the players' motivation**. Learn which type of feedback is most effective, and communicate to players that you believe in them.
- **Reward players if they achieve what they set out to achieve**.
- **Try to bring about change in players' motives for involvement if they are misplaced**. This can be pursued through the appropriate use of behaviour modification techniques.

EMOTIONAL CONTROL 3

3.1. INTRODUCTION

The control of one's emotions during tennis play is of paramount importance both for high performance and enjoyment of the game. There are several terms that are related to maintaining an emotional equilibrium such as arousal, anxiety and stress.

AROUSAL

Arousal is a state of physiological and psychological activation, which runs along a continuum from deep sleep to intense excitement. Herein, degrees of activation can be identified and, in general terms, high arousal implies over-excitation, while low arousal is associated with a state of apathy. Indicators of over- and under-arousal are outlined in Table 3.1. It then follows that arousal, also referred to as activation or excitation, needs to be optimised if maximum performance is desired. Finding and maintaining a state of optimal physical and mental activation is highly individual and by no means easy, and when confronted with high-stress environments, players skilled in doing so come to the fore.

REMEMBER:

Arousal control is the skill that enables players to find the right balance of relaxation, calmness and intensity within the stressful environment of competition.

TYPICAL SIGNS OF OVER-AROUSAL/EXCITATION	TYPICAL SIGNS OF UNDER-AROUSAL/EXCITATION
- Muscles become tight and rigid. - Accelerated heart rate, shallow and irregular breathing, elevated sweat response, and high blood pressure. - Concentration difficulties (everything can appear a blur). - Inability to think clearly and accurately. - Attention gets compromised (e.g. bad line calls, personality of opponent, crowd noise, etc.) and refocussing becomes difficult. - Feelings of high anxiety and/or fear. - The onset of fatigue occurs earlier than normal and produces co-ordination deficits. - Increased negativity and self-criticism. - Decreased emotional control. - Increased nervousness and fear.	- Feel devoid of energy or 'fire'. - Feel slow and heavy. - Poor concentration and highly distractable. - Minimal patience and a 'don't really care' attitude. - Noticeable absence of tension or anxiety. - Poor sense of timing or anticipation. - Appear bored and lazy. - Feel a sense of helplessness ('nothing I do works'). - Demonstrate bad temper, aversion to play, lack of enthusiasm, poor anticipation, or mental apathy.

Table 3.1
Symptoms of over- and under-arousal.

ANXIETY

Anxiety is a negative emotional state; a form of arousal triggered by fear or the perception of danger. It is generally accepted to have two components: **cognitive anxiety** (i.e. worry, nervousness) and **somatic anxiety** (i.e. degree of perceived physical activation). However, psychologists may also refer to **state anxiety**: a temporary change in mood state and feelings of tension, or **trait anxiety**: a personality characteristic leading to the objective perception of non-dangerous circumstances as threatening thereby resulting in disproportionate state anxiety responses (Spielberger, 1966). A link between state and trait anxiety has been substantiated such that individuals with high trait anxiety typically experience more state anxiety in highly competitive situations (Martens, 1977).

I. Mental skills for tennis

STRESS

MEASURING TESTS FOR AROUSAL, ANXIETY, ETC.:

The most common instruments for measuring constructs such as arousal, anxiety, pressure, mood states and stress are: the STAI (State Trait Anxiety Inventory; Spielberger et al., 1970) which is the self-evaluation most used, the SCAT (Sport Competition Anxiety Test; Martens, 1977) which measures the competitive trait anxiety, and the CSAI (Competitive State Anxiety Inventory; Martens et al., 1990), and the CSAI-2 (Martens et al., 1982) which measures the competitive state anxiety.

Stress is an imbalance between demand and response capability. It is a process or sequence of events that starts with the presentation of psychological and/or physical demands (Table 3.2). These demands are then perceived as *'threatening'*, producing a physical and psychological reaction. If this reaction triggers a poor performance or outcome, it will become an additional demand, and the cycle of heightening stress and poor performance engulfs the player.

Exacerbating this is the fact that situation specifics and indeed the personality characteristics of individual players are likely to contribute or predispose some players to higher levels of stress:

— **Situational contributors** to stress include the degree of event importance (i.e. the more important the event, the more stress provoked), and the uncertainty of the situation (i.e. the greater the uncertainty, the greater the stress).
— **Personal factors** contributing to stress include trait anxiety and self-esteem. Research in tennis has consistently shown that high trait anxiety and low self-esteem are associated to more extreme state anxiety reactions (Perry and Williams, 1998).

PHYSICAL STRESSSORS	MENTAL STRESSORS
- Playing in long matches. - Playing in poor weather conditions (e.g. windy, rainy, cold, and hot). - Playing on poor courts (e.g. cracked surfaces, etc.). - Not being able to relax between shots. - Attempting to master shots that call for high precision.	- A lack of confidence due to insufficient or poor training. - Inability to be coached during a match; players are on their own. - Fear of failure (especially as related to self-worth issues). - Inability to keep the game in perspective. - Focussing on things that cannot be controlled, such as an umpire's decision. - Focussing on the outcome rather than the performance. - Coping inappropriately with mistakes, rather than learning from them. - Using negative self-talk. - Envisioning poor performance. - Failure to eliminate peripheal distractions.

Table 3.2 Sources of physical and mental stress.

3.2. THEORIES TO EXPLAIN THE EFFECT OF AROUSAL AND ANXIETY ON PERFORMANCE

Numerous researchers have attempted to explain the relationships between anxiety/arousal and sports performance. The prevailing theories are discussed below.

— **Drive / social facilitation theory** proposes a linear relationship between arousal and performance, where the more activated or 'psyched up' players become, the better they will perform, and vice versa. Obviously the personal experiences of many players and coaches tell a different story, and the fact that many competitors perform very poorly when overly-excited or anxious provides little support for this theory (Martens et al., 1990).

> **WHAT RESEARCH TELLS US...**
> Most relevant studies on anxiety and related management strategies in tennis have concluded that:
> - Anxiety is detrimental to tennis performance as it typically causes players to become more vulnerable (El Gammal, 1993; Farouk, 2003).
> - There are no gender differences between the effects of anxiety and tennis performance (Perry and Williams, 1998).
> - Winners have significantly lower cognitive anxiety prior to competition than losers (Terry et al., 1996).
> - Significant reductions in somatic anxiety and cognitive anxiety and significant increases in self-confidence can be realised with proper training (Terry et al., 1995).
> - Coach support and strategies that focus on helping young players to differentiate their self-worth from their tennis abilities can assist their emotional development and well-being as well as reducing their anxiety (Ryska, 1992; Saferstein, 1989).
> - Stress illness was the most pervasive health problem identified in junior elite tennis players (Dunlap and Berne, 1991).

Tennis Psychology

The social facilitation theory states that the audience will help players perform well on well-learned or simple skills and will decrease performance on unlearned or complex tasks (Zajonc, 1965). This theory however, presents no clear explanation of the choking processes that some top players experience when playing under pressure.

— **Inverted-U theory** contends that players will experience poor performance when their arousal levels are either very low or very high. Maximum or best performances will be sustained when players attain optimal levels of arousal, as represented by the zone around the top of the inverted-U (Landers and Boutcher, 1986). While embraced by much of the high-performance sports community, there are suggestions that optimal performance does not necessarily occur at the centre of the arousal curve (Hardy, 1990).

— **Individual zones of optimal functioning (IZOF)** describes players as having individual zones or ranges of optimal state anxiety in which best performances are more likely to occur. Some will perform maximally at lower zones of state anxiety, while others will reach peak performance at medium (as hypothesised in the inverted-U theory) or higher zones (Hanin, 1993).

— **Multidimensional anxiety theory** suggests that state anxiety is multidimensional and its two components (cognitive-worry and somatic-physiological) influence performance differently:

  — Worry is negatively related to performance: the more worry, the worse performance.
  — Physiological responses are related to performance in Inverted-U fashions.

— **Two alternative models;** In an effort to more comprehensively account for anxiety's effect on performance, Hardy (1990), with his **catastrophe model,** suggested that physiological arousal is related to performance in an inverted-U fashion, but only when the player is not worried (low cognitive anxiety). If worried, players are likely aroused beyond their optimal arousal zones, causing 'catastrophic' decreases in performance.

Martens (1987), on the other hand, linked the influence of arousal on performance to **player interpretation of arousal level**. That is, a positive interpretation of arousal would affect performance positively, and a negative interpretation, negatively.

PRACTICAL APPLICATION:

According to the drive / social facilitation theory when players are learning new or complex skills coaches should eliminate audiences and limit situations perceived as evaluative.

REMEMBER:

Coaches should help players identify and then reach their individual zone of optimal functioning.

Even the game's very best players suffer from, and need to learn to minimise fluctuations in the anxiety-arousal levels.

WHAT RESEARCH TELLS US...
Competition typically produces higher stress than pre-competition, practice or rest (Krahenbuhl, 1971), however no differences have been shown in stress levels between junior players' practice and competition (Pantelidis et al., 1997). Players of different skill levels have also been noted to experience similar pre-season or pre-match stress levels (Aronson, 1986).
Post-match stress generally manifests as initial anger, followed by shame, and depression, and while match evaluation is necessary, should not be completed immediately after the match (Davis, 1991; Dunlap and Berne, 1991).

I. Mental skills for tennis

3.3. PRESSURE

REMEMBER:
Pressure does not automatically cause poor performance, but the player's interpretation of pressure is likely to trigger one of two sensations. That is, excitement and challenge will be met with players responding positively, while nervousness and heightened anxiety would perpetuate a probable negative response.

Pressure is a term often used when coaches and players are asked to define stress. All players feel it, lots fear it, and some try to ignore it. Whatever the circumstance, it's clear that for a player's potential to be fulfilled, a plan for pressure management is essential (Gould, 1997).

Specifically, the negative reactions to pressure include; exploding, holding it, rushing, not thinking, catastrophising, wandering or day-dreaming. During matchplay, responses to pressure include: tanking, anger, fear and fighting. The characteristics of these emotions and the physical and mental aspects are depicted in Table 3.3.

EMOTIONAL RESPONSE DURING MATCHES	ASPECTS	CHARACTERISTICS
TANK	PHYSICALLY	Head, hands, arms, and racquet hang low; demonstrable and visible heaviness.
	MENTALLY	Switches off, stops trying, seeks excuses, complains continuously, may believe they are better than the other player.
	COMMENT	Is it worth playing like this?
ANGER	PHYSICALLY	Exhibited physically (racquet abuse) or verbally (negative self-talk).
	MENTALLY	Blocked due to pent up frustration with oneself, the opponent, the umpire, the crowd, etc.
	COMMENT	It is difficult to play like that!
FEAR	PHYSICALLY	Suffocation and paralysis or, at the other end of the spectrum, everything happens at 100 km/hr.
	MENTALLY	May be tentative, indecisive, tries to avoid responsibility.
	COMMENT	Fear can at least be interpreted positively as it is indicative of a player that cares.
FIGHT	PHYSICALLY	Ready for the match.
	MENTALLY	Optimal activation state.
	COMMENT	This is how the champions play!!

Table 3.3 Typical responses to pressure during a match play.

Players need specific techniques to cope with those situations that can make or break their games. Often termed mistake management strategies, these interventions can help to channel pressure correctly, and thus lead to superior play, and will be covered in Chapter 13.

THE CHOKING PROCESS

Despite the best mental competitors' efforts to concentrate on performance over and above outcome, there will likely be occasions when specific results or goals mean so much that pressure will inadvertently mount. Whether it be winning a tournament, beating a nemesis, or reaching a

WHAT RESEARCH TELLS US...
According to Hardy (1990), coaches should be aware of their players' ideal arousal levels, but also be cognisant of the extent to which they experience cognitive state anxiety (worry).

ranking goal, perceptions are that there is a 'bit more than normal' riding on the result. Failure of competitors to perform in such circumstances gives rise to speculation that they 'choked'; speculation, which is magnified by subsequent, similar performances. The process of choking during a tennis match is illustrated in Figure 3.1, and the physical and psychological sensations that players are likely to encounter are outlined in Table 3.4.

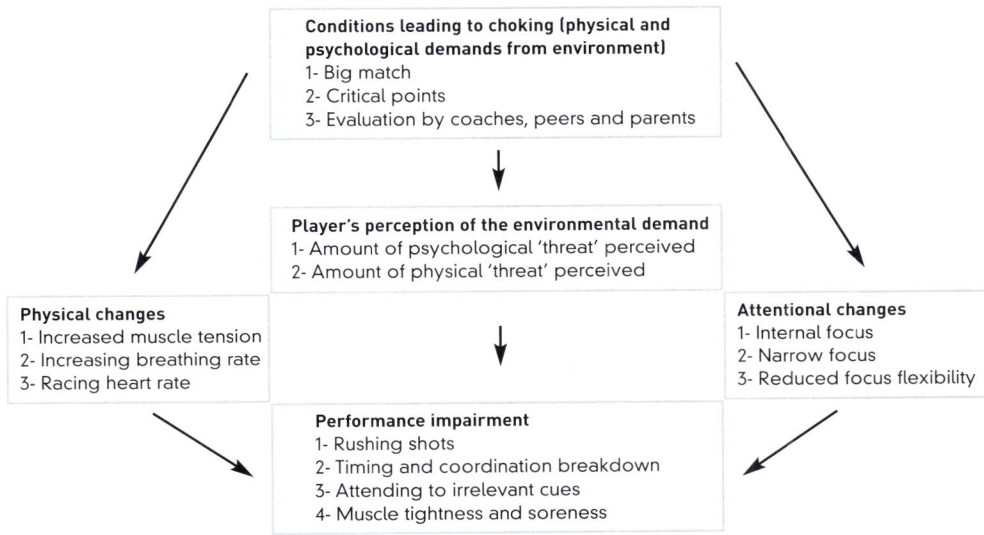

Figure 3.1
The process of choking (adapted from Weinberg, 2002).

PHYSICAL FEELINGS		PSYCHOLOGICAL FEELINGS	
THE ZONE	CHOKING	THE ZONE	CHOKING
Loose	Tight	Controlled	Beaten
Relaxed	Tense	Confident	Scared
Solid	Shaky	Powerful	Weak
Balanced	Unsteady	Commanding	Dominated
Strong	Weak	Calm	Upset
Light	Heavy	Tranquil	Panicked
Energetic	Tired	Peaceful	Worried
Effortless	Rigid	Easy	Rushed
Fluid	Jerky	Clear	Confused
Smooth	Awkward	Focussed	Overloaded

Table 3.4
Comparison of feelings associated with the zone and choking (Nideffer, 1992).

3.4. GUIDELINES FOR IMPROVING EMOTIONAL CONTROL

There is no shortage of on and off-court psychological techniques to improve the emotional control of players. They range from methods of activation or energising (breath control, visualisation, self-talk, music, etc.) to relaxation techniques, cognitive restructuring, stress inoculation, cognitive-affective stress management, and bio-feedback, and will be expanded upon in Chapter 13. Fundamental to all techniques however, are the following guidelines put forward by Weinberg and Gould (1995):

I. Mental skills for tennis

- Help players identify the zones of optimal arousal needed for peak performance and learn how to use different strategies to achieve them.
- Assist players in becoming aware of the interaction between personal (trait anxiety and self-esteem) and situational (importance and uncertainty) factors in determining the level of state anxiety and arousal.
- Practise strategies to assist players recognise the aforementioned signs of arousal by asking them and making it easy for them to express and talk about their feelings.
- Individualise teaching and coaching and vary levels of state arousal or anxiety accordingly.
- Facilitate player confidence through positive practice and competition environments. Encourage mistakes to be viewed as productive building blocks for on-going and future success.

CONTROL OF THOUGHTS 4

Controlling the cognitive aspects of behaviour is fundamental for successful tennis play. In this chapter we summarise the different mental skills related to these aspects: self-confidence, self-esteem, self-efficacy and attribution.

4.1. SELF-CONFIDENCE

In a tennis context, self-confidence can be considered the belief or degree of certainty that players have in their ability to be successful in executing a skill or series of tasks. It is proven to be one of the best predictors of competition success (Bandura, 1977). Indeed, some authors refer to a positive self-fulfilling prophecy, where expecting something positive to happen actually helps it to happen. On the contrary, if players possess little self-confidence, they may expect to fail... and this expectation, in part, causes them to fail (Weinberg, 2002). Research collectively suggests that self-confident players are characterised by or benefit from:

— Being more positive (Lee et al., 1992).
— Enhanced concentration (Weinberg and Gould, 1995).
— More fighting spirit (Weinberg and Gould, 1995).
— More challenging goal-setting (Weinberg, 2002).
— Being more successful during practice and matches (Jaenes, 1995).
— Lower cognitive and somatic anxiety levels, and lower total mood disturbance (Covassin and Pero, 2004).
— Not being as affected by negative events (i.e. losing a match) (Covassin and Pero, 2004).
— Performing better under pressure and adversity (Jaenes, 1995).
— Positive flow-on effects to physical endurance (Weinberg and Gould, 1995).

RELATIONSHIP BETWEEN SELF-CONFIDENCE AND PERFORMANCE

Possessing self-confidence does not guarantee optimal performance and nor can it overcome incompetence. However, in its absence, optimal performance does become infinitely more difficult to achieve. The relationship between self-confidence and performance is depicted in Figure 4.1, and resembles the "inverted-U" that Landers and Boutcher (1986) proposed to describe the interaction between arousal and performance. That is, performance improves as levels of self-confidence increase up to an optimum. Either side of this point, where self-confidence is too high or too low, affects performance adversely. Optimal self-confidence is individual and multifactorial.

MEASUREMENT TESTS FOR SELF-CONFIDENCE:

Self-confidence can be evaluated through a variety of measures. Vealey (1986) developed the TSCI (Trait Self-confidence Inventory), the SSCI (State Self-confidence Inventory) and the COI (Competitive Orientation Inventory), while Weinberg (2002) created a specific confidence inventory applied to tennis.

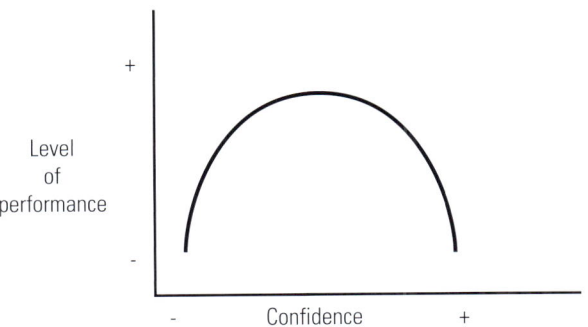

Figure 4.1
Relationship between self-confidence and performance.

I. Mental skills for tennis

PROBLEMS WITH SELF-CONFIDENCE

> **REMEMBER:**
> Players who have high expectations are more likely to receive more of their coach's time / attention, which in turn positively affects player performance and ultimately serves to confirm the coaches' expectations (Weinberg and Gould, 1995).

The number one problem players encounter with self-confidence is not having enough! Enough in a shot (the backhand, the second serve, etc.); enough in pressure situations (tie-breakers, match points); enough against certain opponents (good friends, long time adversaries); or enough in certain matchplay situations (easy shots, rain delays)! A lack of self-confidence triggers self-doubts which negatively affect performance, increase anxiety, hamper concentration and undermine decision-making.

Ranked closely behind having insufficient confidence, is problem number two: having too much! Over-confidence can be appreciated in players who possess more confidence than their abilities warrant, and can present as poor match preparation, a blasé attitude, wavering concentration, and a lack of intensity and effort.

Problems with self-confidence may also manifest in or contribute to an inability to let go of past performances, focussing on outcome rather than performance goals, the inappropriate development of skills (i.e. slow down the learning process), poor recovery, and even overtraining.

GUIDELINES FOR IMPROVING SELF-CONFIDENCE

Confidence is not an inherited trait. It can be developed through planned and purposeful practice, using tools such as goal-setting, specific training and competition measures (performance accomplishments, physical conditioning and preparation), control of thoughts and self-talk (thinking confidently), control of behaviours and body language (acting confidently), visualisation, cognitive restructuring, problem solving, fostering independence and defining success appropriately. These and other techniques are expanded upon below, as well as in Part III.

— **Set goals to develop self-confidence:** Players need to understand where they are 'at' and what beliefs, if any, may be holding them back (Girod, 2001; Quinn, 2003). They should establish an agreement with themselves, and in doing so, a plan of attack. It should see them giving their best and maximum effort at all times, maintain their worth as a person and avoid comparisons. They should accept imperfection, yet not doubt themselves.
— **Train smartly:** Players should practice with intensity. Solidifying strengths, improving weaknesses and increasing technical and tactical effectiveness (preparation) are crucial for self-confidence, and should be done daily.
— **Get in great shape:** To feel confident on the court and ready to perform, players should be in fantastic physical shape. Fitness is the key to a positive mindset, to being sharper in their mind and on their feet, to accepting that extra challenge and to being their best. Their confidence increases exponentially, and with it they can hit harder, move faster, think quicker and last longer than their opponents. They go into a match knowing they will not fade when the going gets really tough.
— **Improve other mental skills:** As players' mental skills improve, they start to truly believe that they do possess self-confidence and control necessary to perform well.
— **Plan competition carefully:** Competing against better players while winning more matches than losing is important for the developing player (2:1 win:loss ratio). Players' tournament and competitive schedules should be guided by realistic and attainable weekly and daily goals. That is, a steady diet of perceived success is virtually assured if proper goals and sub-goals are established.
— **Become body language aware:** As the self-fulfilling prophesy would suggest, acting and

> **WHAT RESEARCH TELLS US...**
> - Players who have skill / technique-related thoughts are more likely to be successful during practice, while negative self-evaluations may adversely affect the players' ability to successfully execute a technique (Lee et al., 1992).
> - Winners displayed significantly higher self-confidence, lower cognitive and somatic anxiety levels, lower total mood disturbance scores, and were not as affected by negative events as losers (Covassin and Pero, 2004).

looking confident is vital to improving self-confidence. Players should look strong, together and in control, even if they do not always feel it. Some examples of positive body language include: correctly imitating a shot just missed, standing tall, and walking powerfully.

- **Increase self-discipline:** Compelling as it is observable, self-confidence levels steadily increase as players exercise a higher degree of self-discipline in training and practice. Self-discipline provides additional evidence that 'I am in control'.
- **Develop independence:** Players cannot simply rely on their coaches, parents, partners or trainers all the time. Players should be independent, not dependent. Acknowledgment and praise should thus come from within and this will further increase self-confidence. And when players acknowledge themselves, they have to make sure they talk to themselves like they mean it. They have to say things with passion! The stronger the feeling, the greater the excitement and energy, the quicker the manifestation.
- **Teach self-belief:** Teaching a player to believe in himself is crucial to success because winners radiate a positive, confident attitude. These players refuse to entertain the possibility of failure. They think they can, and know they will achieve the goals they set themselves.
- **Foster positive thinking:** The average person has between 60,000-80,000 thoughts a day, many of which are repeated thousands of times, and many of which are negative. Remember the self-fulfilling prophesy, 'what you focus on is what you become'. We are exactly what we think we are. Encourage players to view events as positive challenges, and welcome them as a step on their paths toward greatness.
- **Acknowledge oneself:** It is very important that players compliment themselves on all those great shots and hard work that they are doing daily.
- **Memorise experiences of success:** Players should try to memorise each shot they perform well during practice. This may serve as the first link in the confidence chain. Each point that players win in a match, each victory, especially in difficult conditions, should also be lodged in the memory bank. To do so, players can use the following four methods:
    a. Use positive self-talk after each significant success (e.g. 'great play/shot!'). They can also say the word aloud.
    b. Use rituals after each significant success (e.g. pump their fist, Hewitt's sign).
    c. Take 'mental pictures' of the successes experienced.
    d. Develop post-match routines: Document all the significant successes experienced in the match in a notebook to facilitate future performance.

Lleyton Hewitt rarely fails to display positive body language on court.

- **Use self-persuasion at all times (especially when in doubt).** For instance, players can decide on positive beliefs to rehearse, and repeat time and time again, when serving or returning serve. Cues like, 'my serve is my real strength', or 'my backhand return is a weapon' can be used to good effect.
- **Pretend:** Players can ask themselves: If I had confidence in myself, how would I feel? What would my attitude be like? How would I walk? The trick is to reproduce the aspects of confidence by adopting the stance (i.e. head up, eyes looking straight ahead, shoulders back and broad, straight position), the gestures (i.e. confident steps, sure movements), the respiratory rhythm and amplitude, as well as the muscular tone which characterises confidence. Players need to identify themselves with the characters that they want to be: Tennis players who believe in themselves.
- **Understand expectations:** Expectations from both player and coach can help overcome psychological barriers to performance. Coaches shape their expectations from the personality characteristics and performances of their players. These expectations then influence coach behaviour as they spend more or less time with players, provide varying amounts of reinforcement and praise, and give more or less feedback depending on the expectations the players have of themselves (Girod, 2001; Quinn, 2003).

4.2. SELF-ESTEEM

Self-esteem is the evaluation people make and customarily maintain with regard to themselves. 'Self-esteem' expresses an attitude of approval or disapproval and indicates the extent to which individuals believe themselves capable, significant, successful, and worthy. In short, an individual's self-esteem is a judgement of worthiness that is expressed by the attitudes they hold toward the self. It is a subjective experience conveyed to others by verbal reports and other overt, expressive behaviour.

Positive self-esteem supports the self-confidence required to be process-oriented in the pursuit of new goals and areas of mastery. It's essential to success in pressure situations, and contributes to persistence, independence, and impulse control among other variables associated with productivity and success.

DEVELOPING SELF-ESTEEM

Dent (2002) suggests that coaches and parents can help players develop their self-esteem through:

- Performance accomplishments.
- Vicarious experience - the…'If he can do it, I can do it!' principle.
- Verbal persuasion - by self or others.
- Fostering and rewarding strong work ethics.
- Facilitating the development of sound stroke technique.
- Assisting them become physically fit.
- Ensuring that they hit a lot of balls.
- Developing them as people.
- Telling them 'what they can do' rather than 'what they cannot do'.

4.3 SELF-EFFICACY

The concepts of confidence and expectations were brought together by Bandura (1977) to develop his self-efficacy theory in the late 1970's. Put simply, self-efficacy is the perception of one's ability to perform a task successfully, and is largely considered a specific form of self-confidence. While Bandura's theory was outlined in Chapter 3, Table 4.1 reinforces the four principal sources of self-efficacy.

MEASUREMENT TESTS FOR SELF-EFFICACY:

Several research efforts have evaluated self-efficacy in tennis. The most common method of its measurement has been the Physical Self Efficacy Scale (PSE) Ryckman et al. (1982).

SOURCES OF SELF-EFFICACY IN SPORT	DESCRIPTION
PERFORMANCE ACCOMPLISHMENTS	Successful experiences raise the level of self-efficacy whereas defeats produce the opposite phenomena.
VICARIOUS EXPERIENCES / DEMONSTRATIONS / MODELLING	Observing demonstrations following the process of: - **Attention:** Dependent on the respect for the person observed, interest in the activity, and how well the demonstration can be seen and heard. Best demonstrations focus only on a few key points, are repeated several times, and direct the observers to what to look for. - **Retention:** Can be achieved through mental practice techniques, analogies or by verbally repeating the key points of the action. - **Motor reproduction:** The coordination of the muscle actions with thoughts through physical practice with optimal repetition and progression. - **Motivation:** Facilitated by praise, rewards, using appropriate models and persuasion. Observing how others perform can increase the perception of self-efficacy, while past experiences of the player and the characteristics of the model, will also influence demonstrations.
VERBAL PERSUASION	Persuasive verbal techniques to influence behaviour can be used to foster self-efficacy. Deception is a technique that can also be employed but recommendations are for it to be used cautiously. Factors that influence verbal persuasion include credibility of the individual who persuades (usually the coach) and how realistic the goal behaviour is.
EMOTIONAL AROUSAL	Perceptions of arousal can affect behaviour by altering self-efficacy expectations. Negative to positive changes in arousal will enhance self-efficacy and vice versa.

Table 4.1 Sources of self-efficacy in sport.

In two separate papers, Weinberg et al. (1992) and Weinberg and Jackson (1990) highlighted several strategies that coaches have used to reasonable effect to foster self-efficacy in players (Table 4.2).

METHODS TO IMPROVE SELF-EFFICACY	
MOST USED AND EFFICIENT STRATEGIES	**OTHER SUPPLEMENTARY STRATEGIES**
- Encourage positive talk from the player. - Act confidently (modelling). - Ensure performance improvements through instruction and drilling. - Liberally use rewarding statements.	- Verbally persuade the player that they can do it. - Emphasise improvements in technique while downplaying match outcome. - Ensure performance improvements by setting specific performance goals. - Emphasise that failure results from a lack of effort or experience and not from a lack of innate ability. - Have players imagine themselves succeeding. - Employ hard physical conditioning drills. - Reduce feelings of anxiety by employing relaxation techniques. - Highlight similar players to have achieved great success. - Emphasise to players that feelings of anxiety are not fear but a sign of readiness.

Table 4.2 Strategies coaches commonly employ to enhance player self-efficacy.

WHAT RESEARCH TELLS US...
The magnitude and strength of players' self-efficacy has been positively associated with tennis performance (Barling and Abel, 1983; Theodorakis et al., 1993).

I. Mental skills for tennis

4.4. ATTRIBUTION

MEASUREMENT TESTS FOR ATTRIBUTION:

Sport psychologists have used several instruments to evaluate attribution. Most used, has been the self-evaluation, where players are simply asked to answer questions about the cause of the match result. Performed over time, this process may lead to the identification of specific attributional patterns among players. An example of an attributional self-evaluation specific to tennis can be found in the Appendix, while the Causal Dimension Scale II (CDS II; McCauley et al., 1992), the Modified Attributional Style Questionnaire (Prapavessis and Carron, 1988), the Sport- attributional Style Scale (SASS; Hanrahan et al., 1989), the POS (Performance Outcome Survey; Leith and Prapavessis, 1989) and WSARS (Wingate Sport Achievement Responsibility Scale; Tenenbaum et al., 1984) are other commonly used assessment tools.

Attribution, as emphasised in Chapter 2, is a cognitive process used by individuals to explain the cause, origin and sense of events or behaviours. In tennis, it is best understood as players try to explain their successes or failures, wins or losses. Players use attributions in unusual and unexpected situations, when they have failed or not achieved the proposed goals, and when they need to explain their feelings in different situations. Attributions allow players to control their environment, keep, improve and protect their self-esteem, and to retain a positive, social front to thus influence expectations of future success or failure.

In the last half of the 20th Century, several models were proposed to account for the process of attribution in tennis (Heider, 1958; Weiner, 1985; Roberts and Pascuzzi, 1979). For example, Weiner (1985) defined three categories of attributions: **stability** (if the causes are permanent or unstable over time), **causality** (internal or external influences), and **controllability** (extent to which factors are under the player's control), while Roberts and Pascuzzi (1979) presented an alternative attributional model (Figure 4.2). In Weiner's model, he considered stable factors to be the player's talent or ability, an unstable factor to be luck, internal cause to equate to effort, external cause as the opponent, the match plan to typify a controllable factor, and weather to represent a factor over which players have no control. Guallar and Balaguer (1994) subsequently linked these different categories of attributions to variation in emotional reactions, self-confidence, and expectations of future success or failure. Attribution to internal or external factors (so called 'locus of causality') affect players' feelings toward the results achieved, whereas attribution to stable or unstable causes (stability) helps to determine the future expectations of players.

STABILITY	LOCUS OF CAUSALITY	
	INTERNAL	EXTERNAL
STABLE	Ability / Skill	Practice Match difficulty
UNSTABLE	Effort Practice Condition	Luck Umpire

Figure 4.2 An attributional model in sport (Roberts and Pascuzzi, 1979).

Table 4.3 summarises the consequences of attributions after wins and losses (Guallar and Balaguer, 1994).

RESULT	ATTRIBUTED TO	CONSEQUENCE
SUCCESS	Internal factors: effort or skill.	Produces feelings of pride and self-confidence.
	External factors: luck or easy match.	Decreases self-confidence feelings.
	Stable factors: skill.	Strengthens expectations of future success.
	Unstable factors: effort.	Does not determine similar expectations in the future.
FAILURE	Internal and stable factors: lack of skill.	Negative feelings.
	Internal and unstable factors: lack of effort.	Improvement expectations.
	External factors.	Protects the self-esteem.

Table 4.3 Consequences of attributions after wins and losses.

WHAT RESEARCH TELLS US...

Winners as compared to losers...1. Attribute their performance to more internal or personal, (effort) and stable (effort, difficulty of the match) factors and less to internal debilitating factors (e.g. lack of practice) (Forsyth and Schlenker, 1977; Hewitt and Jackson, 1986; Kim, 1990; Spink and Roberts, 1980); 2. Associate the expenditure of high effort more to internal and less to personally controllable causes (Kim, 1990); and 3. Attribute convincing wins to skill and effort, but ambiguous wins to the difficulty of the match (Spink and Roberts, 1980).

Interestingly, older players have been noted to give more internal attributions for their satisfaction and more unstable attributions for the result than younger players (Balaguer et al., 1993). Guallar et al. (1993) also showed that some players will focus on their performance rather than the outcome of the match, and therefore be more or less satisfied (with their performance) irrespective of the result.

LEARNED HELPLESSNESS

After a series of losses, players may begin to develop negative and apathethic responses. Otherwise referred to as 'learned helplessness', players start to feel that irrespective of what they do, nothing will influence the result of the match, and that defeat is inevitable. Largely a by-product of players who make internal and stable attributions (e.g. primarily based on their skill), this and other undesirable attributional patterns can be addressed through attributional re-training. Research has shown that players classified as helpless attributed failure performances to internal, persistent, and recurrent factors more than other players (Prapavessis and Carron, 1988). Here, players are assisted in re-directing their attributions to internal and unstable factors but above all, to factors they can control (e.g. effort, practice, physical condition).

PRACTICAL APPLICATION:

There is a tendency for players to attribute successful results to internal causes, and defeats to external factors. This is typically done in an effort to protect their self-esteem, and can often be observed when reading the post-match interviews of some professional players.

GUIDELINES FOR IMPROVING ATTRIBUTION

Coaches can guide players to appropriate perceptions of success and failure as a precursor to helping them optimise their attributions. Some guidelines to facilitate this process are:

— Assist players perceive success based on effort, practice and the learning of the game's skills.
— Help players to develop optimal and realistic expectations by asking them to analyse and evaluate their goals.
— Understand the fact that children under 10 do not understand the difference between skill and effort. Thus, with small children coaches should foster their natural enthusiasm for learning by reinforcing satisfaction with behaviour, independent of the outcome.
— Coaches should be aware that expectations of their students will influence their performance.
— Guide players in performing realistic post-match analyses of their performances.
— Understand that occasionally, internal attributions following a success or a win help to maintain motivation for future performances.
— Analyse the complex relationships between attributions and emotions by taking into account both the characteristics of the situation and the players' perceptions of those characteristics.

REMEMBER:

Players with the right attribution patterns see winning as a consequence of their abilities and losing as a lack of effort, thus increasing their motivation to try harder. Conversely, players that attribute incorrectly see winning as a consequence of luck or poor opposition. Oftentimes, they believe that irrespective of how hard they try, they will lose, thus leading them to create a stockpile of readymade excuses.

CONCENTRATION-FOCUS 5

5.1. DEFINITION

Concentration is a skill consisting of several elements (Boutcher, 1992; Guallar and Pons, 1994):

— **Selectivity:** Ability of a player to attend to what is important during play (relevant cues) and tune out what is not, while also being able to selectively direct attention (from one cue to another). This process evolves as players learn the sport and sees players variably and selectively attend specific stimuli (internal or external). Initially, players are consciously very attentive (control processing), yet as they master more of the game's technical skills, their attention shifts to become more automated (automatic processing). Attending to the most relevant stimuli requires that player interest and mental predisposition are sound.
— **Duration:** The ability to maintain attention over time.
— **Capacity:** The amount of (internal and external) information that players can process at any one time. Attending to more than one source of information has been noted to impair the performance of some players.
— **Clarity:** The efficiency of one's attention along the attention continuum (from maximum alertedness to coma state).
— **Width:** Spectrum of attention.

> **REMEMBER:**
> Concentration is the ability to direct and maintain focus on relevant cues.

THEORIES OF ATTENTION

As inferred above, attention and concentration are closely related. In general terms, there exist four theories to explain attention in sport.

— **Social-psychological theories:** Researchers have focussed on distraction theories (i.e. loss of attention caused by factors that attract attention to task-irrelevant cues), automatic execution of skills, and attentional styles. These styles will be detailed in the pages to follow.

— **Psychophysiological theories:** Use encephalogram or heart rate to study attention and its relationships with performance.

— **Integrated-information processing approach** (Boutcher, 1992): Considers attention to involve both **control** and **automatic processing**. Control processing, which involves the analysis of novel or inconsistent information, places high attentional demands on the performer. In having to make tactical decisions relating to shot selection each and every point, tennis players are regularly challenged in this fashion. Just as comprehensive in its use, automatic processing is responsible for the performance of well-learned skills. However, under no direct conscious control, it occurs effortlessly and requires little attention on behalf of the performer. The execution of tennis skills by the game's elite personifies this type of processing.

— **Attentional focus model** (Nideffer, 1976): Defines two different dimensions of attentional focus: direction, which can be external (directed outside the player, e.g. environment) or internal (e.g. a player's emotions), and width, which accounts for the number of stimuli being attended (e.g. attention to a high number of stimuli requires broad attentional focus, while a narrower attentional focus would be used to hone in on fewer stimuli). When considered holistically, direction and width produce four different types of attentional focus, as shown in Figure 5.1.

> **REMEMBER:**
> Tennis, as an open skill sport, requires a combination of both control and automatic processing.

I. Mental skills for tennis

```
                            EXTERNAL
                               ▲
        Assess                 │        Act / React
Used to evaluate the           │   Effective for focussing on objects
environment, allows players    │   when performing a movement or
to read the game               │   action (e.g. visual cueing of the ball
(e.g. anticipating the         │   prior to hitting it).
opponent's movements,          │
ball direction, etc).          │
BROAD ◄─────────────────────── ┼ ─────────────────────► NARROW
                               │
Assists analysis / review of   │   Permits mental rehearsal (e.g. using
past information and           │   imagery to simulate a positive
decision-making                │   emotional state).
(e.g. analysing a point,       │
evaluating match strategy).    │
        Analyse                │        Rehearse
                               ▼
                            INTERNAL
```

Figure 5.1 The four types of attentional focus applied to tennis (adapted from Nideffer, 1976).

REMEMBER:

The activation level of players influences their ability to shift attentional focus. Low activation states are associated with low motivation and poor focus on relevant cues, whereas high activation states impair one's ability to maintain attention on the same cues.

While players will have preferred attentional styles by virtue of genetic, biochemical and learned differences, they should be able to shift from one to another depending on the demands of the situation or environment (Nideffer, 1976). Players themselves see concentration as a multidimensional process, consisting of a scanning and a focussing component (Van Schoyck and Grasha, 1981). So, rather than one type of attentional focus prevailing for the entire duration of a match, Balaguer (1993) generalises the following attentional foci as applicable to different game situations:

— **Before the match:** Players tend to use internal-broad attentional foci to plan strategies and review their opponents' games.
— **Before the point:** When preparing to serve, players first adopt an external-broad focus in observing their opponents and attending to any external factors that may affect the point. Players will then shift to an internal-broad focus to determine point strategy, whereby once finalised, they will become more internally and narrowly focussed to adjust tension levels to control the ball.
— **During points (when rallying):** Recommendations are that players use an intense, external-narrow focus (e.g. on the ball).
— **Between points:** A relaxed, internal-broad attentional focus should be used by players.

FACTORS AFFECTING CONCENTRATION

REMEMBER:

Some researchers consider to choking fundamentally be a concentration problem (Nideffer, 1992; Weinberg and Gould, 1995; Weinberg, 2002).

Distractions to performance can manifest in a variety of ways. Physiologically, players may experience heightened muscle tension, elevated heart rates, increased perspiration and irregular breathing. Concentration is likely to be similarly affected, with uncharacteristic rushing, disrupted rhythm, poor decisions and increased unforced errors being more frequently displayed (Prapavessis, 1993).

> **WHAT RESEARCH TELLS US...**
> Players' abilities to focus appear to remain unaltered after periods of intense physical activity and they are still able to focus on relevant cues without eye and head movements (Castiello and Umiltà, 1988). During matchplay, competitive junior players who predominantly use an external-narrow attentional style, tend to get distracted due to external and internal factors, and lack attentional flexibility (Solanellas et al., 1996).

To this end, Figure 5.2 highlights factors that are believed to affect concentration during tennis play, and that may lead to the observation of these symptoms.

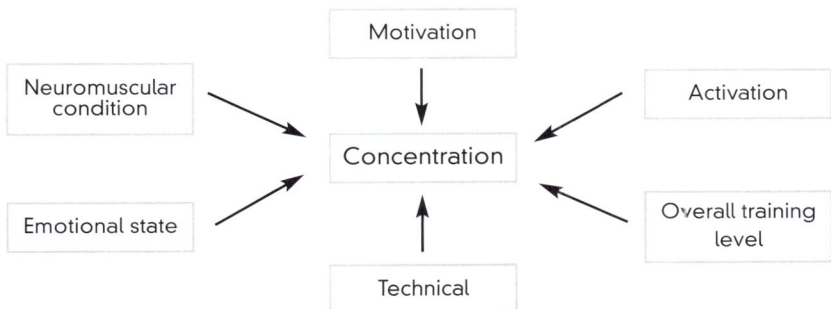

Figure 5.2
Factors affecting concentration (adapted from García Ucha, 2001).

5.2. CONCENTRATION PROBLEMS IN TENNIS

First and foremost players and coaches need to understand that it is impossible to concentrate for 100% of the time during a tennis match. Additionally, the ability to concentrate is commonly affected in three broad ways, which in turn also approximate the types of distractions that permeate the game (Table 5.1). Players' typical physiological, attentional and behavioural responses to these distractions are outlined in Table 5.2 (Prapavessis, 1993).

EXTERNAL DISTRACTIONS	INTERNAL DISTRACTIONS	PERSONAL DISTRACTIONS
- Boredom. - Apathy. - Anger. - Rush. - Too many cues. - Noise. - Spectator movement. - Over-awareness of the opponent.	- Disassociation: Attending to past or future events. - Lack of confidence. - Too many cues (over-analysis): 'Paralysis by analysis'. - Excessive stress. - Choking. - Being overly relaxed. - Fear of failure. - Fear of social /peer evaluation. - Embarrassment.	- Inadequate food intake, sleep, and/or rest. - Poor hydration. - Low physical fitness. - Other relationship problems.

Table 5.1
Different distractions present during tennis play.

REACTIONS TO DISTRACTIONS		
PHYSIOLOGICAL	ATTENTIONAL	BEHAVIOURAL
- Increased muscle tension. - Increased heart rate/ perspiration. - Irregular breathing.	- Narrow attention span. - Internal focus of attention.	- Rushing. - Poor timing and rhythm (e.g. miss hits). - Irregular breathing. - Decreased movement speed. - Compromised decision- making. - Transfer of weight, rarely moves forward. - Increase in unforced / forced errors (cannot control).

Table 5.2
Physiological, attentional, and behavioural responses to distractions in tennis.

GUIDELINES FOR DEALING WITH DISTRACTIONS

When dealing with distractions, players and coaches may want to consider these useful tips:

— Players should be prepared for everything: wind, bad line calls, noisy crowds, gamesmanship, cheating... and automate appropriate mental and emotional responses through practice.
— Coaches should schedule practices that present players opportunities to overcome such distractions.
— Players should most certainly address those situations that have proved problematic and adversely affected their performances in the past.
— Players should learn from lapses in concentration by reviewing their affected behaviours.
— Players should make a habit of practicing these strategies.

REMEMBER:

Audiences generally improve performance good shots per rally) in more-skilled players but impair performance in less-skilled players (Dube and Tatz, 1991).

5.3. GUIDELINES FOR IMPROVING CONCENTRATION IN TENNIS

Coaches can play a vital role in improving a player's concentration. However, practice is needed and improvements tend to be more qualitative than they are quantitative (Burke, 1988). Like the training of the game's other skills, training to improve concentration must be tailored to the individual player. In doing so and in enlisting some of the off- and on-court concentration interventions detailed in Chapter 14, it is worth considering some of the suggestions spawned from the empirical work of those sport psychologists in the field (García Ucha, 2001; Girod, 1999; Moran, 1994, 1996; Young, 2003):

— **Identify and focus on task relevant cues:** A coach can assist players to identify (or revise) key task relevant cues and the times at which players should attend to those cues. Players should understand the game's attentional demands and potential attentional problems they may encounter.

Through practicing eye control, players can improve their ability to focus during point play.

WHAT RESEARCH TELLS US...
According to Hunfalvay (2004), examination of the visual attention of expert wheelchair tennis players when returning a serve revealed two distinct eye movement patterns. One group of expert players predicted the ritual and preparatory phases of the serve ahead of time, while a second group watched the motion of the serve as it occurred in 'real time'.

- **Control emotions:** Anxiety and tension can break player concentration by diverting attention to pounding hearts, sweaty hands and rapid breathing. To minimise the chances of this occurring, a coach can work with players to identify their optimal arousal zones and the means of attaining and maintaining it under pressure.
- **Set goals:** Players will generally concentrate better if challenged to perform well. A coach can assist players to set specific goals that are 'parked' in their subconscious minds as they attend to the requirements inherent in achieving the goals.
- **Control thoughts:** Promote action driven by positive thought, and control thoughts which are irrelevant to the task.
- **Use instructional self-talk, 'triggers' and cue words:** A useful means of maintaining focus, or re-focussing when concentration is broken, is for players to use 'triggers' or cue words. Players should select some that are meaningful (e.g. 'hit early', 'move in', 'attack', 'hit the lines').
- **Think about that one point:** Concentration can be dramatically improved if a coach is successful in training players to think about playing one point, and only one point, at a time. Worrying about missed shots or thinking ahead to winning / losing is the downfall of many players. A coach needs to instil in players that each point should be played to the best of a player's ability regardless of the score.
- **Practice concentration both on- and off-court:**
    a. Hold practices in noisy places that may present additional distractions.
    b. Schedule simulated matchplay with distractions.
    c. Players can keep concentration logs of factors that assist their concentration.
    d. Practice at upcoming tournament sites to simulate the elements that may disrupt concentration.
- **Develop, practice and use pre-, during- and post-match routines:** Most top players use a specific warm-up ritual to help them focus their minds on the pending match. This helps players concentrate only on what can be controlled, reduces distractibility, increases the likelihood of processing task-relevant cues, and limits worry or speculation about the outcome. Similar to a pre-match routine, a routine during play can trigger players to focus on the task at hand, or refocus if concentration has been lost (serve and return of serve rituals are examples of this). The routine can be quite simple or involve a series of activities. A coach can work with players to develop appropriate routines to be used at pertinent times during matchplay.
- **Enjoy the game:** Having fun relates positively to concentrating well. In this sense, it is important for coaches to put competing / winning / losing in perspective. That is, the essence of competing is to perform to the best of one's ability in an on-going process of self-improvement.
- **Attend to physical fitness:** Since a loss of concentration can be due to a lack of conditioning, a coach needs to address the level of physical fitness of their players. Coaches can work with players to ensure that their fitness exceeds the demands of successfully competing.
- **Perfect technical skills:** Player concentration can be adversely affected if concerns exist over technical proficiency.
- **Develop match strategies:** Prior to competing, players need strategies that address how they: (a) plan to play important points and the match, and (b) will effectively deal with potential distractions (e.g. bad calls, windy conditions, spectator support for the opponent). Here, a coach can provide invaluable input through 'scouting' the opposition while being simultaneously cognisant of the strengths and limitations of their players.
- **Practice eye control:** Players can fix their eyes on the court, focussing on a piece of equipment, on a given spot somewhere (the back fence, the net, etc) on- and off-court.
- **Use visualisation:** Visualisation is a powerful concentration technique. By visualising what to do next, often players will then do it.
- **Learn to shift focus when needed.**

REMEMBER:

Training to improve concentration should be designed to direct, or redirect, player attention to task relevant cues. Next time you are tempted to instruct players to 'concentrate', think again!; It is far more pertinent and helpful to say: 'Concentrate on...'.

MEASUREMENT TESTS FOR CONCENTRATION:

Various instruments can be used to measure concentration including both off-court tests: TAIS (Test of Attentional and Interpersonal Styles; Nideffer,1976), concentration questionnaires (Orlick, 1986), analysis of thoughts and grid tests (Harris and Harris, 1984), and on-court tests: notational analysis of non-verbal behaviour during the match-practice. Of added note is that Van Schoyck and Grasha (1981) have developed a tennis-specific version of Nideffer's Test of Attentional and Interpersonal Style (T-TAIS) to assess a player's ability to concentrate.

OTHER PSYCHOLOGICAL CONSIDERATIONS 6

In this chapter other important mental features of tennis are detailed. Key issues such as the personality of tennis players as well as psychological implications of gender and disability, values, sportmanship, ethics, and the psychology of doubles play will be discussed.

6.1. PERSONALITY AND TENNIS

Personality can be defined as the set of unique characteristics that describe an individual (Weinberg and Gould, 1995). Analysis of its structure reveals that it takes shape on a continuum from internal to external and from consistent to dynamic; and is composed of:

— **A psychological core:** Attitudes, aptitudes, abilities, knowledge, skill, temperament, values, interests, motives and beliefs. They are the most internal, stable and consistent aspect of personality.
— **Typical responses:** The individual behaviours in response to the changing conditions of the environment.
— **Role-related behaviours:** The most external and dynamic aspect of personality, they reflect the individual's perceived socialisation (e.g. the roles played by the person).

Sledr (1996) further expands upon the primary functional subsystems that he considers to comprise a player's psychological core:

— **Aptitudes** are generally understood as the innate neurophysiclogical and kinesthetic characteristics of an individual.
— **Abilities** are mental dispositions of personality and are limited by and developed from aptitudes. They infer that players possess specific knowledge or motor skill, are relatively stable yet can be difficult to objectively measure. They are needed to succeed in an activity, but do not guarantee success. Where 'aptitudes' imply that futher learning is required, abilities provide for immediate task performance.
— **Knowledge** and **skills** are formed through activity repetition; without which they are forgotten. Abilities are more general and permanent mental prerequisites, which facilitate knowledge development and skill acquisition.
— **Temperament** can be defined as the emotional profile of a person. It is inborn and virtually permanent but can be modelled through learning and education. It can be observed as players behave and respond, and is largely considered to fit one of four temperament types (Sledr, 1996; Unierzisky, 1996):

  - **Sanguine:** A sanguine player is mentally stable, extroverted, lively, active, cheerful and adapts easily to change.
  - **Choleric:** An unstable extrovert, who lacks self-control and is impetuous, with a short-temper that can make co-operation with others difficult.
  - **Phlegmatic:** Individuals that are placid and generally well adapted to life.
  - **Melancholic:** Melancholic players are unstable introverts who are highly sensitive.

The idiosyncracies of the above temperaments do not imply that one is better than another. In fact, players will regularly exhibit characteristics of different temperament types: of variable stability and extro/introversion.

REMEMBER:

Coaches, players and sport psychologists consider personality to be very important in sports performance. In fact, knowledge of tennis player personalities provides coaches and psychologists an insight into players' motives and behaviours which can in turn assist goal-setting and programme development.

MEASUREMENT TESTS FOR PERSONALITY:

There are instruments available to measure how personality affects player behaviours, including the Eysenck Personality Inventory (Eysenck and Eysenck, 1968), the Cattell 16PF (Cattell, et al., 1983) and the Minnesota Multiphasic Personality Inventory, MMPI (Minnesota Univ., 1930).

— **Intelligence** is comprised of three well-defined and balanced capacities:
  - **Analytic:** Diagnosis of the situation and / or problem.
  - **Creative:** Presentation of resourceful problem-solving strategies.
  - **Practical:** Selection and implementation of appropriate interventions based on diagnosis and previous experience.

— **Character,** a combination of relatively stable personality traits formed during life, can be observed in how players relate to themselves and their surrounds. Character is shaped through education, self-development, experience, and other social influences, and tends to represent the maturity of the individual.

— **A trait,** is a distinguishing feature of a person's character.

RESEARCH ON PERSONALITY IN TENNIS

A primary objective of any tennis coach is to assist players reach their 'potential'. In doing so, coaches must try to understand and cater for a tennis player's mental 'make-up'. Unfortunately, research provides us little guidance here, and we have to look toward investigative data on moods, intelligence, and personality traits and profiles for insights into the tennis player psyche (Table 6.1).

PRACTICAL APPLICATION:

In applying standard coaching principles, coaches should respect the temperament type and other personality idiosyncrasies of the player.

MOOD STATES	INTELLIGENCE	PERSONALITY
State anger relates negatively to winning percentage (Collins, 1990).	Minimal relationship, if any, exists between general intelligence and success in tennis competition when players are considered to have 'normal' intelligence (Thorpe, 1967).	Singer (1969) noted no significant personality differences between tennis players of different playing levels, yet Daino (1985) found significant differences in personality traits between tennis players and non-players.
In relative terms, vigour mood states increase with age, while all other mood states decrease (Wughalter and Gondola, 1991).	The intelligence of the players aged under 12 does not positively influence the results they achieve (Unierzyski, 1996).	The personality of tennis players cannot be considered a unidirectional absolute, and is likely comprised by varying degrees of dependence need, aggressiveness, perception of control, personal efficacy, masculinity, independence, competitiveness and intolerance (Conforto and Marcenaro, 1979; Paulhus et al., 1979).
Players with strong temperaments (high force of excitement and low reactivity of the nervous system) are better equipped to problem solve, manage stressful situations, and fight to the end, while high reactivity negatively affects tennis performance (Orawiec and Dañczyk, 1994; Czajkowski, 1995; Unierzyski and Gracz, 2002).	A wide range of tennis teaching strategies should be used to foster the players' eight multiple intelligences: verbal / linguistic, visual / spatial, bodily / kinaesthetic, naturalistic, musical / rhythmic, mathematical / logical, and inter / intra personal (Mitchell and Kernodle, 2004).	Compared to sedentary individuals of the same age, tennis players have more self-confidence, ambition, optimism, suspicion, and anxiety, and are characterised by higher levels of energy and dynamism, antagonism, autonomy, self-sufficiency, and intelligence (Fox, 2000; Marrero et al., 2000; Schubert and Vanfraechem-Raway, 1986).

Table 6.1 A summary of research findings into moods, temperament, intelligence and personality traits and profiles among tennis players.

WHAT RESEARCH TELLS US...
The **trait approach** assumes that the core units of personality are traits, which are relatively stable and endure over time. The **situational approach**, however, largely considers behaviour to be determined by the environment. The **interaction approach** better explains personality since it argues that both situation and traits determine behaviour (Weinberg and Gould, 1995).

6.2. GENDER AND TENNIS PSYCHOLOGY

According to Gill (1992) where sex differences refer to biologically based differences between males and females, gender differences relate to social and psychological characteristics and behaviours associated with males and females. To this end, gender roles are the patterns of beliefs, attitudes, behaviours, skills and interests that cultures identify to reflect feminity or masculinity (Weinberg and Gould, 1995). In tennis, research has shed light on some specific gender differences between male and female players, as presented in Table 6.2.

REMEMBER:

Anderson (1982) examined the role of each player in professional mixed doubles matches. Analyses showed that success of the teams was more highly related to the ability of the female player than to the ability of the male counterpart.

FACTOR	FEMALE	MALE
Attributions of good performances (Heath, 1982).	Effort	Skill
Level of competitiveness (Houston et al., 1997).	Very high	High
Main stressors in professional tennis (WTA, 2004).	1. Injuries, 2. Travel, 3. Season, 4. Expectations, 5.Competition	No data available

Table 6.2 Gender differences between male and female tennis players.

Interestingly, research has unveiled more psychological 'similarities' between genders than it has differences. This suggests that culture and socialisation patterns rather than biology play lead roles in shaping behaviour. That males tend to be encouraged from a very early age to participate in 'games', while females are often discouraged is an example of such divergent socialisation. Several myths describing potential 'side-effects' of female participation in sport (e.g. complications in childbearing, damage to reproductive organs, menstrual problems, undesirable body shapes, diminished feminity, etc.) have also fostered a certain gender inequity.

From a mental standpoint, both female and male players are equally well-equipped to deal with the demands of tournament play.

I. Mental skills for tennis

PSYCHOLOGICAL IMPLICATIONS OF THE FEMALE ATHLETE TRIAD

The Female Athlete Triad is a set of medical conditions that decreases athletic performance (Otis, 2001). It consists of the interrelated problems of disordered eating, amenorrhea and osteoporosis. These disorders lead to medical and psychological problems and decreased athletic performance, and may be linked to overtraining. They do so because of inadequate nutrition, loss of lean muscle mass, dehydration, decreased bone strength, increased risk of injuries, and heart problems.

The Triad begins with pressures to lose weight, which often leads to disordered eating practices such as fasting, bingeing and purging, and the use of laxatives. If women frequently use disordered eating practices, they are in states of energy drain. This can lead to amenorrhea, the absence of regular menstrual cycles, which is a serious sign of the underlying medical problems of disordered eating or overtraining. When females do not have regular menstrual cycles, they lack the hormones necessary to build bone. The result is a lack of bone formation and actual irreversible bone loss, leading to osteoporosis: 'old bones in young women'.

Female players face not only the pressures from society, but also pressures from the game. Although there is no evidence that being thinner equals better performance, most women are told to lose weight to be faster. Recall that during puberty, females gain more body fat while males gain muscle mass. However, different messages are given to men and women to improve athletic performance after puberty. Men are told to 'bulk up' whereas women are told to lose weight. Athletic women also are expected to fit into form-fitting revealing clothing.

REMEMBER:

From a psychological perspective there are two key points that may lead to the onset of the Triad. These are the pressures on female players due to unrealistic goal-setting and the 'need' for them to have a low body weight.

For most women in modern developed societies, thin is not only in, but thinner is viewed as better. However, healthy bodies come in all sizes and body types are inherited. For tennis, many different body types can be successful. Most female players have muscular (mesomorphic) body types whereas the 'ideal' woman is a tall thin ectomorphic body. Pressures on women to be unrealistically thin come from the media, parents, advertising, peers and coaches. There is inadequate scientific evidence to support the notion that the thinnest player, especially in tennis, is the best. Rather, genetic body types, training habits, nutriton, and technical-tactical skills, most likely play a larger role in athletic performance.

GUIDELINES WHEN COACHING FEMALE PLAYERS

Coaches should be cognisant of the fact that generally speaking, as compared to males, females…

— Have a higher desire to learn during practices.
— Are more disciplined.
— Require more emotional support from their coach and others.
— Are more open and are more grateful for the advice.
— Are more diligent and meticulous.
— Are more emotional.
— Are more affected by external factors.
— Mature 2-3 years earlier.

PRACTICAL APPLICATION:

Coaches can play critical roles in preventing, recognising, and referring females with one or all aspects of the Triad, and are strongly encouraged to consider the following guidelines (Otis, 2001):
- Understand the Female Athlete Triad and signs of disordered eating.
- De-emphasise weight as a performance issue. Concentrate on speed, strength, recovery, and technique.
- Refer weight and medical issues to local medical professionals.
- Model healthy eating behaviour.
- Help females build a healthy self-image with positive feedback about their strengths and abilities no matter their body type.
- Emphasise the diversity in tennis, where many different body types, sizes, and shapes are successful.

So, in turn, coaches should deal with specific situations (e.g. menstruation) carefully and considerately; encouraging girls to develop independence, while also providing opportunities for girls and boys to train together and learn from each other (Otis, 2001).

6.3. PLAYERS WITH DISABILITIES

While able-bodied tennis has been around for well over a century, the game in its various other forms (wheelchair, deaf, mentally impaired...) is in its formative years. Broadly labelled Disabled Tennis, the wheelchair game is the most visible of its devotees. Indeed, in assuming wheelchair players to be representative of the wider disabled playing population, researchers have shown tennis participation to significantly improve disabled players' perceptions of their physical competence as well as positively affect their mood states (Greenwood et al., 1990; Hedrick, 1984). Leitao and Machado (2003), and Leitao and Do Lago (2003) have emphasised the profound effect a player's family can have on disabled players, especially when those players present certain cognitive traits. Equipped with this knowledge, it becomes all the more important for coaches to educate families as to the need to appreciate the disabled players' efforts over and above any result.

PRACTICAL APPLICATION:

With the correct introduction to the game, all players can play tennis well and enjoy the game. So when working with disabled players, practices should be varied, challenging and fun.

Involvement in tennis has been shown to positively affect wheelchair players' mood states and perceptions of physical competence.

6.4. VALUES, SPORTMANSHIP, ETHICS AND MORAL ISSUES

Tennis has a social and educational role whereby it can positively contribute to a player's personal well-being as well as instil an appreciation of societal values. Values are defined as desirable goals, varying in importance, that serve as guiding principles in sport. They are many and varied, and have been described as either being terminal, instrumental, motivational or utility-oriented (Schwartz,1992).

Values can be learned through familial experiences, education and socialisation, among other processes. Socialisation broadly describes the process of learning one's culture. It entails the learning of skills, traits, dispositions, values, and attitudes for the performance of societal roles. Different influences blend together to facilitate this process. Involvement in sport, and more specifically in tennis, is one such influence. For example, participants can be socialised into sport (e.g. various agents of socialisation influence attitudes towards sports) as well as socialised via sport (e.g. participation impacts on skill, personality, social relationships, etc). Indeed, Table 6.3 summarises the values most likely to be learned, challenged or realised through sports (and tennis) participation (Gutiérrez, 1995).

I. Mental skills for tennis

VALUES	
SOCIAL	INDIVIDUAL
- Respect - Cooperation - Social interaction - Friendship - Teamwork and sense of belonging to a team - Competitiveness - Solidarity, social justice and responsibility - Group cohesion - Equity - Tolerance (affirming diversity) - Social inclusion (inclusiveness) - Fairness - Gender equality - Constructive challenge and competition - Expression of feelings - Comradery - Care for others	- Creativity - Enjoyment - Personal challenge - Self-discipline - Self-awareness and self-control - Achievement - Reward - Adventure and risk - Sportsmanship, honesty, integrity - Spirit of sacrifice - Hard work, dedication, commitment - Independence and autonomy - Time management - Delayed gratification - Moral reasoning and ethical behaviour - Leadership - Decision-making - Self-esteem - Toughness - Courage - Compassion - Open mindedness - Respect and recognition (social image) - Humility - Obedience - Impartiality

Table 6.3 Values that can be learned through tennis.

Coaches should help players develop a positive and responsible attitude to their own physical, mental, emotional and social well-being. On- and off-court coaching practices present excellent opportunities to introduce concepts such as respecting the rights and views of others, and the need to be open-minded. Similarly, the rules and structure of drills and competitions should endeavour to develop a sense of justice through fairness, inclusiveness and non-discriminatory practices, as well as a concern for other people and for the environment through cooperation, care, compassion and constructive challenge.

GUIDELINES TO FACILITATE THE LEARNING OF VALUES IN TENNIS

To further facilitate the learning of values through tennis, coaches, parents and officials can selectively consider the following recommendations as well as those presented in Table 6.4 (Crespo and Reid, 2004).

Coaches should:

— Act as role models for their students.
— Identify values to be developed in the tennis lessons, and use progressive and inclusive drills to do so.
— Promote equity and be coherent at all times.
— Advertise a Code of Conduct that is to be applied and respected.
— Always promote tennis as a healthy activity that players can partake in for life.
— Try to help players understand that respecting other players as well as the rules of the game largely contributes to its meaningfulness and to player satisfaction.
— Be creative so that games are presented in such a way that they are cooperative and fun but also retain that element of healthy competition toward the achievement of a goal.
— Do not hesitate to help players recognise, understand and deal with any difficult or controversial situations that may arise in a game.

- Use role-playing and specific drill scenarios to present players with choices as to appropriate behaviours and conducts in the face of moral and ethical dilemmas that may manifest in tennis.
- Never lose sight of the fact that the individuals are more important than their tennis game!

TENNIS LESSONS PROVIDE	
OPPORTUNITIES TO...	ENHANCING...
Self challenge and achieve mastery	Feelings of competence and self-worth
Develop self-determination	Responsibility for participation and achievement
Give appropriate encouragement and feedback	Honest social support systems
Experience fun and excitement	Attitudes of pleasure
Reflect on competition and comparison	Attitudes of tolerance and open-mindedness

Table 6.4 Opportunities that tennis lessons provide to learn values.

Parents should:

- Reinforce the principles of sportsmanship and fair play in tennis.
- Involve their children in tennis programmes that focus on the person and not on the player or prospective champion.
- Place more value on the performance and the effort of their child during a match than its outcome.
- Assist their child appreciate opponents as individuals who are cooperating in the game, and without them, the match would not go ahead.

Officials should:

- Make educational and sports organisations aware of the need for cooperation.
- Organise conferences, produce resources and conduct promotional campaigns to disseminate the educational and social values of tennis.
- Cooperate with the media to promote the theme of learning societal values through tennis.
- Publicise examples of good practice.
- Encourage tennis in the sport/school curriculum and promote player exchanges between schools/clubs.
- Promote the voluntary work in tennis events and stress its positive contribution to tennis and society.

PRACTICAL APPLICATION:

Coaches can enhance sportsmanship in their players by explaining it in their programmes; by demonstrating, reinforcing and encouraging its associated behaviours; and by regularly challenging players with moral dilemmas and choices in practice (Weinberg and Gould, 1995).

Sportsmanlike behaviours also need to be fostered in players. To do so, players should first understand how (good and poor) sportsmanship is conveyed (Table 6.5). Then, with the help of the coach, they should recognise that sportsmanlike behaviours can and should transcend tennis and be displayed in other, non-sporting contexts.

AREAS OF CONCERN	SPORTSMANLIKE BEHAVIOURS	UNSPORTSMANLIKE BEHAVIOURS
BEHAVIOUR TOWARD OFFICIALS	Questioning officials in the appropriate manner.	Arguing with or swearing at officials.
BEHAVIOUR TOWARD OPPONENT	Treating all opponents with respect and dignity at all times.	Arguing with, making sarcastic remarks to or gesturing aggressively at opponents.
BEHAVIOUR TOWARD TEAM-MATES	Providing constructive comment and positive encouragement.	Remarking negatively or sarcastically. Swearing or arguing irrationally.
BEHAVIOUR TOWARD SPECTATORS	Making only positive comments to spectators.	Arguing, commenting negatively or swearing at spectators.
RULE ACCEPTANCE AND INFRACTIONS	Obeying all rules.	Attempting to manipulate or take advantage of the rules.

Table 6.5 Summary of sportsmanlike and unsportsmanlike behaviours during tennis play (Weinberg and Gould, 1995).

I. Mental skills for tennis

6.5. TEAM PSYCHOLOGY: GROUP DINAMICS, TEAM COHESION AND DOUBLES PLAY

REMEMBER:

A group is a collection of individuals who have a collective identity, common goals, structured modes of communication and a certain degree of interdependence (Weinberg and Gould, 1995). Groups evolve into teams that have both formal (e.g. coach, players, etc.) and informal roles (e.g. those that comprise group dynamics). To optimise group or team dynamics, these roles should be clarified and accepted by all members. Minimising status differences among roles and emphasising the importance of each member's contribution to team success is likely to facilitate this process.

Tennis is mostly an individual sport but players practice in groups, play doubles events and may, at some point, employ a support team, so group dynamics needs to be duly considered. Indeed, during team events such as Davis Cup or Fed Cup, coaches and players often attribute success or failure to the cohesion of the team. This can be operationally defined as the unity of a team around common goals and is affected by leadership, environmental or team factors (e.g. history) (Carron, 1982).

In building on this concept, researchers regularly distinguish between task cohesion (i.e. players have the same goals) and social cohesion (i.e. players like each other). In doubles play, although the two are not mutually exclusive, a high degree of task cohesion is a must since research indicates that team-cohesiveness is more important than the doubles teams' technical prowess (Manili and Pase, 1986; Rota et al., 1986).

ROUTINES PERFORMED BY THE TEAMS	TYPES OF COMMUNICATION USED	FREQUENCY OF POSITIVE COMMUNICATION	PERSONALITIES
1) Response: - At the same time. - As a team. - Same response.	Non-Verbal: - Walking together and rituals. - Hand signal. - Eye contact before each point. - Smiling face.	Service: Pros: 96% (5.1 sec). College: 78% (3.6 sec). Amateur: 14% (1.9 sec).	Personalities: - Not uncommon to see different personalities in a team. - One player assumes leadership of the team. This player is not necessarily the better player, but may be the better tactician or more experienced or more supportive team member.
2) Relaxation: - For shorter time. - Not as crucial (physically, psychologically). - Walk together.	Verbal: - Tactics (who calls the serve?, type of return, formation, game plan, etc.) - Emotional support, truth, synergy.	Return: Pros: 71% College: 58% Amateur: 17%	
3) Preparation: - Longer. - Very important. - Decide the serve.	Rescue: - Agreement between players on what to say if partner is struggling.	Overall: Pros: 83% College: 59% Amateur: 17%	
4) Rituals: - Each player follows his own rituals.			

Table 6.6 Summary of psychological characteristics of doubles play (adapted from Cayer, 1991; and Loehr, 1991).

REMEMBER:

In doubles, hand signals behind the back, can become too impersonal and non-communicative when things are not going to plan.

Other factors known to characterise the psychology, and more particularly communication, of doubles play are highlighted in Table 6.6. Indeed, indications are that on the serve, not only do professional players communicate more often, but also for a longer period of time than lesser level players. This suggests that professional players better fulfill the common coaching cue that verbal communication and visual contact be established after each point so as to maintain a strong positive rapport between the players.

WHAT RESEARCH TELLS US...
Social support from the coach, family, friends, team mates, sports medicine staff and significant others has a positive effect on performance and in shielding players from negative stressors (Quinn, 2001b; Rees and Hardy, 2001; Rees et al., 1999).

With positive, cooperative team environments largely in the interests of everyone, coaches and players can put in place measures to increase the likelihood of them being fostered. For example, according to Weinberg and Gould (1995) it is important for coaches to clearly communicate each individual's role while setting challenging team goals and encouraging a team identity. Similarly, for coaches to best negotiate barriers to team cohesion it is recommended that they:

— Be available to provide social support.
— Set rules that are positive, fair, agreed and reinforced.
— Maintain close contact with players.
— Promote team distinctiveness (e.g. uniforms) and fairness.
— Minimise status differences among roles.
— Emphasise the importance of each player's contribution to the team.

To facilitate the creation and maintenance of a true team environment, players should be encouraged to give 100% effort at all times; help, praise, and get to know team-mates; resolve problems immediately and not be a source of conflict (Weinberg and Gould, 1995).

PRACTICAL APPLICATION:

Here are some mental 'pointers' for players to maximise the enjoyment of the doubles experience (Braden and Burns, 1996; Perlstein, 1995; Weinberg, 1988; 2002):
- Find a partner with whom you can communicate well, enjoy being with, and that may complement you psychologically.
- Be wary of the appropriateness of your non-verbal communication (e.g. body language).
- Give honest feedback to your partner, but first determine how your partner likes to receive it (e.g. timing, directness …)
- Praise and encourage your partner when appropriate.
- Simple things like sitting down and standing up together at change overs, communicating after each point, and leaving the court together regardless of the result are important to reinforce team cohesion.
- Have fun.

6.6. DEVELOPING ATTITUDE, MATURITY AND RESPONSIBILITY

The emotional experience of tennis is an important part of most players' life. Pleasure / displeasure, tension / relaxation and a plethora of other feelings are inextricably linked to the game and exact their own unique influence on each player's emotional experience. As detailed in Chapter 3, the 'art' of controlling one's own emotions is central to both enjoyment and high performance tennis success.

Nevertheless, success in tennis is about much more than just winning matches; it is also about developing the right attitudes, which if done successfully can accelerate learning and improve competitive performance. Wilson (2001) has summarised some of the key attitudes of successful junior players:

— Vision to develop realistic ambitions.
— Long-term perspective to progress steadily and consistently.
— Action-oriented to commit to hard work and training.
— Independence to face difficulties in the world of professional tennis.
— Attention to detail in expecting high standards of themselves.
— Responsibility to make progress and not excuses.
— Approach competition positively and face the demanding nature of the game.
— Resiliency to cope with failure.
— Confidence to be 'performance-oriented'.

Zlesak (1995) recommends that players of different ages set basic goals to guide them in developing a professional attitude (Table 6.7).

REMEMBER:

By gradually giving increased responsibility to young players, coaches build up and create their independence and self-confidence, which in turn very naturally moulds a professional attitude.

AGE GROUPS	CHARACTERISTICS
UNDER 10	- Be on time for the lesson. - Bring their racquet, water, etc., to the court. - Bring the necessary equipment for the lesson (balls, cones, etc.). - Collect balls when indicated. - Behave on court. - After the lesson collect all the equipment used.
UNDER 12	- Prepare things themselves. - Packing their bags before practice (racquet, balls, spare shirt, bottle of water etc.). - Always be on time for practice. - Learn basic tennis rules (how the game is scored, the time between points and changeovers etc.).
UNDER 14	- Warm-up correctly before practice and matches, without being asked or supervised by the coach. - Develop a correct drinking regime (stick to it even when practising). - Send in entries for tournaments themselves. - Find their doubles partner themselves. - Deliver their racquets for restringing, ask for required tension, etc., themselves.
UNDER 16-18	In practice: With or without the coach present, the player should: - Practice with quality and intensity at all times (full concentration and best effort). - Maintain emotional control (both in practice and matches). During tournaments players should: - Book practice courts and get practice balls themselves. - Arrange different practice partners (not only team mates). - See schedule of play. - Scout opponents. - Maintain good eating habits. - Prepare the bag, string own racquets, understand tournament regulations.

Table 6.7 Basic goals that players of different ages can set along the way to developing a professional attitude.

By the age of 14, players should be finding doubles partners for themselves.

INTELLECTUAL AND SOCIAL SKILLS

The development of intellectual and social skills is another very important aspect of any psychological training plan. Coaches should include the development of these skills as part of successful training and competition.

In the most simplest of terms, intellectual skills (i.e. practical and verbal intelligence) can be practised by emphasising the importance of 'thinking' both on-court during practices and matches as well as off-court. Where possible, coaches can also link players' academic activity to their tennis careers (e.g. when travelling encourage players to read books, participate in cultural visits, etc.).

Social interaction with other players, coaches and officials is of considerable importance for the tennis player. Players practise not only to improve their games, but also to increase their social status and prestige (i.e. they perceive the social and economic influences common to tennis).

Peer relations are crucial for the child or adolescent player, while the influence of significant others also increases throughout puberty. Player rivalry should also be kept in perspective so as to not interfere with their development (Sledr, 1996).

Coaches also play a vital role in shaping players' attitudes to competing, winning and losing. Those players who find the 'zone' on a consistent basis are those who love to compete and define winning in terms of how well they utilise their abilities in the pursuit of a worthwhile goal. Coaches need to believe, and instil in their players, that enjoyment and doing one's best is the essence of tennis. In this context, a 'successful' coach is one whose players relish matches (or practice sessions) as a time to test themselves to the fullest in an on-going process of self-improvement (Young, 2000).

Crespo (1995) has shown that the coach's leadership dimension of social support is an important ingredient in the players' perceptions of training and coach satisfaction, and thus in their overall player development. Other skills that tennis coaches should possess and that are also related to the intellectual and social development of players will be elaborated on in Chapter 26, while the role of the parents will be discussed in Chapter 27.

PART II.
MENTAL TRAINING: TECHNIQUES AND PLANS

"Just be positive. Go out there and play your game and be tough. Just keep saying positive things to yourself." *Maria Sharapova*

GOAL-SETTING

7.1. BACKGROUND

Goal-setting is the comprehensive and systematic planning process used to achieve a goal. Achieving a goal means attaining a specific level of proficiency in a task, usually within a specified time limit. The importance of goals lies within the fact that the primary reason for setting them is to provide direction and focus. Goals are of considerable functional importance because research has shown that they influence performance in three distinct ways (Weinberg, 2003; Weinberg et al., 1997):

— **Directing attention to tennis' task relevant cues**, which helps to focus attention on the task at hand (e.g. improving their shot selection or backhand cross-court).

— **Mobilising effort and increasing persistence** by providing feedback in relation to one's own performance. For example, some tennis players may not feel like working hard day in, day out or feel bored with the repetitive routine of practice. However, by setting short-term goals and seeing progress toward the achievement of their long-term goals, motivation can be maintained on a daily basis as well as over time.

— **Developing relevant learning strategies to enhance performance**. This point is best illustrated by considering that a tennis player aiming to reduce their unforced errors from 15 to 10 per set would likely hit with more topspin, aim closer to the centre of the court (away from the lines) or hit more cross-court shots to increase his margin for error. Irrespective of the tactic used, a new problem solving strategy is developed to help the player become more consistent and reduce unforced errors.

> **REMEMBER**
>
> Goal-setting can be considered predominantly a motivational technique or strategy. However, it can also be applied to improve self-confidence, concentration and emotional control.

While all goals do indeed share some common characteristics, Table 7.1 distinguishes between, and highlights the characteristics of some different types of goals.

TYPE OF GOAL	CHARACTERISTICS AND MODE OF MEASUREMENT	EXAMPLE
OBJECTIVE	Quantifiable	"Improving one's first serve percentage from 55% to 60%".
SUBJECTIVE	Less quantifiable	"Increasing satisfaction as a member of a team".
OUTCOME	Usually use winning and losing as their reference. Here, the achievement of the goal depends, at least in part, on the ability and play of the opponent.	"Winning the National Championships".
PERFORMANCE	Refers to one's actual performance in relation to their own standards of excellence. They are under the control of the performer.	"Reducing unforced errors from 20 a set to 15 a set".
PROCESS	Usually concerned with how tennis players perform a particular skill and thus these are often the focus of goals in practice or training.	"Placing the ball toss at 11 o'clock when serving".
SHORT-TERM	Daily commitments during the next three to six months.	"Visualise the return of serve 15 times a day, five days a week for the next 4 months".
MEDIUM-TERM	Six months to five years.	"Improving the crosscourt, topspin forehand deep into the corner this season".
LONG-TERM	Players' dreams and aspirations.	"To win a Grand Slam".

Table 7.1 Types of goals.

These different types of goals do share some things in common. For example, typically they are <u>S</u>pecific, <u>M</u>easurable, <u>A</u>ction-oriented, <u>R</u>ealistic, <u>T</u>imely, <u>E</u>valuated, <u>R</u>ecorded, and <u>S</u>elf-determined. Represented as the acronym SMARTERS, these characteristics are elaborated on in Table 7.2.

CHARACTERISTIC	DESCRIPTION	EXAMPLE
SPECIFIC	Specific goals produce higher levels of task performance than no goals or general 'do your best' goals (Weinberg, 2003). Contrary to popular belief, 'going out and doing your best' is not as powerful in enhancing motivation and performance as encouraging players to go out and achieve a specific goal.	As performance goals, 'improving the percentage of first serves from 52% to 65% by July 1st' will work better than simply 'improving the serve'.
MEASURABLE	Greater motivation is provided when players have a way to measure the progress they are making toward achieving their goal.	If players set a goal to improve forehand consistency, how do they know that they are improving this aspect of their games unless they have a way to measure their performance and progress? Setting a goal to hit 20 forehands in a row in practice between the service line and the baseline and then recording their performance will provide them with a regular measure of their improvement.
ACTION-ORIENTED	Unfortunately, goals are often set without a solid series of strategies identified to achieve these goals.	If tennis players set a goal to improve their first serve percentage from 55% to 60%, they need to develop strategies to accomplish this goal (e.g. practice 100 ball tosses at 12 o'clock position 3 times a week or hit 50 topspin serves 4 times a week) and set both short and medium-term goals as described in Table 7.1.
REALISTIC AND CHALLENGING	Goals should be challenging and difficult, yet attainable (Locke and Latham, 1990). Goals that are too easy do not present a challenge to the individual, which leads to less than maximum effort. Conversely, setting goals that are too difficult and unrealistic will often result in failure. This can lead to frustration, lowered self-confidence and motivation, and decreased performance.	"Winning Wimbledon at 12" is obviously an unrealistic goal which players will fail to achieve.
TIMELY	All goals should have a specific time frame attached to them. That is, the players need to know by when they want to achieve each goal.	"I will reduce the number of unforced errors in a serving game by 20% by August 12".
EVALUATED	Goals should be evaluated both by the player and the coach in the time frame scheduled.	Schedule evaluation and re-evaluation meetings in individual and group formats.
RECORDED	Recording goals (i.e. writting them down) formalises player commitment.	"I (name of the player) commit myself to put my best effort into the achievement of the following goals..."
SELF-DETERMINED	Tennis players should have a lot of input into and ownership over their goals. The tennis coach should guide players in shaping their goals so they are 'SMARTERS'.	If a player has a 1:5 winner to error ratio and wants to set a goal for a 1:1 ratio, then the coach may suggest that a 1:3 ratio is more realistic. If the player reached this goal (by a specific date), the 1:1 ratio could then be pursued.

Table 7.2 Characteristics of goals - the SMARTERS acronym.

MISTAKES IN GOAL-SETTING

One common misconception among tennis coaches and players is that the mere fact that one sets goals automatically makes them effective. Similar 'mistakes' impeding the effectiveness of goal-setting include setting too many goals at the same time, employing goals that are too general, failing to adapt goals that are not achieved, and only using outcome goals.

7.2. HELPING THE PLAYERS TO SET GOALS

A player might have a long-term goal (i.e. being selected for the national team), which might be a few years away and still difficult to envisage. To ensure that the player remains motivated and interested in its pursuit, daily practices need to be made enjoyable, and appropriate daily goals set. The following three steps are an undertaking by coaches (and players) to set the wheels in motion, while examples of a questionnaire to facilitate goal-setting can be found in the Appendix.

1. Planning.

— Player self-evaluation.
— Coach evaluation of the player.
— Coach determines the methodological approach to be adopted.
— Set goals.
— Prioritise goals.

2. Communicate and agree the goals with players. Explain the process to the parents.

— Outline the importance of goal-setting and highlight how each goal will be achieved.
— The player, parents and the coach should sign a contract to formalise the goals and commit to the process.

PRACTICAL APPLICATION:

Coaches should:

- Use a combination of process, performance, and outcome goals that are challenging yet realistic (moderately difficult). Process and performance goals should receive the greatest emphasis as they are under a player's control (Weinberg et al., 1997).
- Promote the utilisation of both short-term goals, that provide motivation, and medium and long-term goals, which provide direction.
- Help players prioritise goals in order of importance.
- Make players aware of the most common barriers to achieving goals such as lack of time, stress, fatigue, academic pressures and social relationships.
- Set action plans to facilitate goal-setting.
- Formalise and commit to goals by putting them down on paper.
- Give players feedback as they progress toward their goals. This results in better performance than either goals or feedback alone (Weinberg, 2003).

Goal-setting should involve, to varying degrees, players, coaches and parents.

WHAT RESEARCH TELLS US...
Even with lower level players, self-efficacy, goal-setting, and commitment to achieving goals have been shown to influence performance (Theodorakis, 1996). Among young players, the primary reasons for setting goals are to focus attention, problem-solve, and increase effort, while the most effective goals appear to relate to physical condition, practice and technique (Weinberg et al., 1997). Season-long player, parent, and coach intervention programmes on goal involvement responses have revealed positive behavioural changes in all players (Harwood and Swain, 2002).

> **REMEMBER:**
>
> Goal-setting should not be limited to mental training but used for technical, tactical and physical work as well. Periodisation and planning are practical ways of goal-setting.

3. Follow-up.

— Evaluate goals and progress regularly.
— Respect goals (player + coach + parents) and their timelines.
— Encourage player feedback and do not hesisate to adapt goals if necessary.

To summarise this Chapter in a sentence... goal-setting, when used consistently and systematically, is a proven enhancer of performance, satisfaction, fun, and intrinsic motivation (Harwood and Swain, 2002).

CREATING THE ADEQUATE MOTIVATIONAL CLIMATE

8.1. DEFINITION

The motivational climate are the training and competition goals created by significant others (coach, parents, peers) and perceived by the players. This climate appears in tennis sessions, tournament venues or at home. Unfortunately, until recently the impact of significant others on player motivation had attracted minimal research interest (Duda, 2001b).

Children and adolescents develop their preferences for task- and ego-oriented goals through repeated interactions with significant others. They also perceive a situational goal structure in tennis, which is, largely created by these same individuals.

The terms task- and ego-oriented are also applied to describe motivational climates in tennis. Their main characteristics, corroborated by research findings in tennis are depicted in Table 8.1.

CHARACTERISTIC	TASK-INVOLVING	EGO-INVOLVING
Rewards and perception of improvement (Balaguer et al., 1997, 1999; Kavussanu and Roberts, 1996).	Reinforces effort and progress. Players focus on the intrinsic reward of learning and perceive increased improvement.	Reinforces results and outcome. Players perceive minimal improvement.
Recognition (Duda, 2001b).	All feel they have an important role.	Only for talented.
Cooperation / Cohesiveness (Balaguer et al., 1997, 1999).	Valued and encouraged. Players value their coach.	Breeds players rivalry within the team or squad.
Mistakes and learning process (Balaguer et al., 1997, 1999).	Accepted as part of learning. Players focus more intently on the process.	Often the source of punishment.
Success, flow state, perceived competence and self-confidence (Cervelló et al., 2002; Kavussanu and Roberts, 1996).	Fosters strong work ethics, (Trying hard), and higher perceived competence. Positive and significant predictor of self-confidence.	Promotes out-doing others, and achieving without effort.
Enjoyment, satisfaction, effort and persistence (Balaguer et al., 1997, 1999; Kavussanu and Roberts, 1996; Yi-Hsu et al., 2005).	Relates positively to player enjoyment, persistence, effort, and satisfaction. Players also commonly display higher satisfaction with their coaches.	Detracts from player enjoyment and sees players less satisfied with their coaches.
Tension, anxiety, pressure (Cervelló et al., 2002; Hatzigeorgiadis and Biddle, 1999; Kavussanu and Roberts, 1996; Yoo, 2003).	Players anxiety responses and 'toughts to scape' likely reduce.	Players tend to feel more pressure (somatic and cognitive anxiety).

Table 8.1
Main characteristics of task- and ego-involving motivational climates.

PRACTICAL APPLICATION:

Some parents and significant others seem to project a more ego-involving motivational climate in tennis (focussing on winning and being better than others) than their children hold by themselves. Emphasising the idea that success is not only winning, congratulating good effort and not only ability, and asking parents to have realistic goals for their children, are some simple ways of encouraging a more task-involving climate.

II. Mental training: Techniques and plans

8.2. FOSTERING A POSITIVE MOTIVATIONAL CLIMATE IN TENNIS

REMEMBER:

Motivational climate in tennis becomes more ego-involved as we move from beginner's tennis to competition tennis. At the beginner level, task-oriented motivational climates are important to enhance the motivation and enjoyment of all players. At advanced levels, an ego-involving motivational climate may prevail, yet coaches should be task-involving in their interactions with players during training and before and after competition.

As mentioned in Chapter 2, the impact of motivational climates on tennis performance has attracted increasing research interest in recent years. In providing overwhelmingly support for task-oriented learning environments, findings suggest that these environments correlate well with positive perceptions of improvement, and player satisfaction with their performance and coach (Duda, 2001b). While accepting that ego-oriented motivational climates become more prevalent as 'stakes' increase, players' perceptions of these climates produce more anxiety and pressure, and are less conducive to learning as well as less enjoyable (Kavussanu and Roberts, 1996). With this in mind, it's clear that coaches should, where possible, create high task-involving environments (Duda, 2001b). To do so, and therefore foster positive motivational patterns in players, they may find merit in asking themselves:

What does success mean to players?
— How am I explaining success and failure to players?
— How do I react when players make mistakes/perform poorly?
— What role do extrinsic variables play in the players' training?
— What is the players' self-esteem built on?

Having done so, other handy tips coaches may use to help engage players in more rewarding task-involving environments include:

— Use optimal challenge to fit skill / drill difficulty to the ability of the players (adapting drills and equipment).
— Keep practices stimulating by using a wide variety of drills than are more co-operative than competitive to improve relationships between players.
— Keep everyone active emphasising effort, learning and improvement of new abilities.
— Do not instruct or evaluate your players constantly.
— Recognise the limitations of each player as well as individual progress and improvement.
— Help players set individual, realistic and measurable short-term performance goals that are based on improvement and effort rather than on results and skills.
— Involve players in decision-making and leadership roles by providing them some autonomy in drill selection during practices.
— Use flexible, multiple and heterogeneous grouping arrangements.
— Encourage players to self-evaluate, and ask for feedback.

Table 8.2 summarises different ways of creating a task-oriented or mastery motivational climate using the TARGET strategies (Harwood and Biddle, 2002).

Table 8.2
The TARGET strategy for task-oriented motivational climate.

TARGET	STRATEGIES
Task: Coaching activities	Have variety and individually challenging activities; have the players set process rather than outcome goals.
Authority: How the coach operates with the players	Let players have a 'say' in matters such as leadership roles, decisions, practices, etc.
Recognition: What is rewarded?	Recognise personal progress and improvement in rewarded? players.
Grouping: Use of groups	Be flexible over groupings in practice, avoid always having the most or least skilled players together.
Evaluation: Use of feedback	Evaluation based on improvement and effort; allow players to evaluate themselves as well as be evaluated by others; avoid public evaluation.
Time: Scheduling	Allow time for practice and improvement; help players with time management to encourage practice.

SELF-TALK 9

9.1. DEFINITION, TYPES AND BENEFITS

Put simply, self-talk is the collection of thoughts or statements (audible to others or not) players make to themselves regarding their performance. These 'conversations' are crucial for moulding attitudes and beliefs. Indeed, they are among the most powerful tools in eliciting behaviour change (Johnston, 1994).

There are various types of self-talk. That is according to the content, it can be considered situation appropriate-positive, inappropriate-negative, and behavioural (Weinberg, 2002). Inappropriate-negative has been observed the most common form of self-talk used by players, while behavioural self-talk (i.e. a combination of both positive and negative thoughts) is less prevalent. Behavioural self-talk can be motivational (used by more than half of the players), or instructional (best used during practice). As per its duration, self-talk can vary from single cue words (the most used) to phrases and long sentences (Van Raaltke et al., 1994).

Obviously, the most beneficial form of self-talk is that which is appropriate-positive. Positive self-talk is noted to improve concentration ("Watch the ball!") and technique ("Bend your knees!"); help initiate action and reaction ("Move!"); create positive expectations and confidence ("I can win!"); foster more successful competitive outcomes; aid pressure management ("Need to improve this!"), motivation ("Come on!") and fighting spirit ("Go for it "); and alleviate fear and choking ("Just relax!").

9.2. GUIDELINES TO IMPROVE SELF-TALK

For self-talk to be of benefit, players must learn to control it at all times. Needless to say, the game's greats learn to do just that, and for the most part only entertain positive thoughts. Affirmations (i.e. "Good shot!") are probably the easiest and simplest technique to influence and affect the conscious mind, and are a great tool to facilitate positive thoughts (Quinn, 2001a). In encouraging players to use affirmations among other similar modes of positive self-talk, factors to consider are (Weinberg, 2002; Weinberg and Gould, 1995):

— **Commitment:** Players should ask themselves "Do I really want to eliminate negative self-talk?".
— **Practice** should be undertaken with insight, effort and persistence.
— **Self-monitor content:** Players should document their thoughts and the resultant performance consequences post-match. This first step in self-monitoring will assist players in acknowledging the events that trigger negative self-talk. To this end, Table 9.1 provides some examples of the consequences of positive and negative self-talk commonly experienced by players.
— **Encourage players to create a success file** that details their achievements, strengths and aspirations. It may include awards, footage of great matches, or even articles on role models.
— **Body language**: Agree to a signal or gesture to be performed each time players play a great point. This is a great way to also complement self-talk.
— **Help players to ask** powerful questions at the end of each day. For example, "What did I learn today? What did I do really well today? What could I do better to improve?"

REMEMBER

Players should speak with confidence to create it on and off the court.

I. Mental training: Techniques and plans

SITUATION	EXAMPLE OF SELF-TALK	CONSEQUENCES (EMOTIONAL, PHYSIOLOGICAL, BEHAVIOURAL)
PRE-MATCH	"I am not feeling very confident".	Takes too much time to get into the match.
	"I am really looking forward to playing this match".	Tough match, great performance, big win!!
BEFORE SERVING	"Come on, go for it".	Optimism, motivation, increased effort.
BEFORE RECEIVING	"It is impossible for me to get my backhand return in".	Hopelessness, anger, frustration.
AFTER MISSING AN IMPORTANT SHOT	"I will never win".	Hopelessness, increased muscle tension or even apathy.
	"Keep your eye on the ball".	Promotes concentration, optimism, calmness.
FOLLOWING A BAD CALL	"Focus on the next point".	Enhanced concentration.

Table 9.1 Situation, description and consequences of self-talk (adapted from Weinberg and Gould, 1995).

— **Promote self-assessment** so that players examine when self-doubt occurs and what they say to themselves. They also need to understand how they recover from mistakes and react to adversity. Are they afraid to hit certain shots?, Do they really expect to play well; if their confidence fluctuates throughout a match, or do they sometimes feel overconfident? Do they enjoy tough, tight matches?
— **Help players ackowledge and counter irrational thougths like**: "My performance on the court reflects my worth as a person", "Playing poorly early in a match means playing poorly later", "Being critical to myself helps my performance on the court", "External circumstances are responsible for my losing" (Weinberg, 2002).
— **Use STOP (thought or negative self-talk)** or another appropriate cue word to cease any negative or irrational thoughts and allow players to re-focus on the task at hand.
— **Sandwich comments** referring to areas in need of improvement between positive comments. For example: "My serve is improving (positive comment), my topspin serve is usually a little bit short (area to improve), I will work hard to play it deeper (finishing on a positive note)".
— **Change vocabulary.** Table 9.2 highlights some important, though slight, changes to a player's vocabulary that have the potential to re-direct thought (Whittam, 1994).

WORDS CHARACTERISTIC OF...	
NEGATIVE SELF-TALK	POSITIVE SELF-TALK
Always	Often
I must	I want
I cannot	It may be difficult
Never	Rarely

Table 9.2 Reframing negative self-talk into positive self-talk.

> **WHAT RESEARCH TELLS US...**
> Losing players have been observed to use more negative or inappropriate self-talk than winning players, but with comparable amounts of positive self-talk (Johnston, 1994; Van Noord, 1984; Van Raaltke et al., 1994).

10 AROUSAL CONTROL TECHNIQUES

10.1. DEALING WITH PRESSURE

Players need techniques to control their level of arousal and to improve their performance in stressful situations. Pressure abounds in tennis, but it by no means necessitates that players will play poorly as a result. Indeed, champion players learn how to use pressure to their advantage by employing a variety of stress-busting strategies (Gould, 1997). As part of any effective strategy is the need for players to:

— Develop an appropriate perspective.
— Manage energy efficiently through:
  - Control of breath.
  - Activation techniques.
  - Relaxation techniques.
— Use positive self-talk.
— Build their confidence.
— Develop routines.

In this chapter we will describe some of the most used arousal control techniques applied to tennis. Additional information on these or other techniques can be found in the references of the Appendix.

> **REMEMBER**
>
> Poor performances under pressure have long been and mistakenly considered a result of mental warfare. However, research indicates that players need a combination of **physical** (movement, hydration, nutrition, fitness), **emotional** (self-awareness, self-regulation, mistake management, breath control, body language), and **mental** (concentration, goal-setting, visualisation, mental preparation, time management, self-talk) skills to be able to perform at their best under pressure (Loehr and Gullikson, 2001).

10.2. DEVELOPING AN APPROPIATE PERSPECTIVE

As simple as this may sound, the first step for players to handle stress is for them to become aware of it. Then, by understanding that not all individuals are affected in the same way, they should identify the situations or stressors that adversely affect their play the most. In doing so, players will begin to appreciate that they can exhibit varying levels of control over these stressors. Ultimately, the key for players is to hone in or focus on what they can control (see Table 10.1).

FACTORS THAT PLAYERS CAN CONTROL	FACTORS THAT PLAYERS CANNOT CONTROL
- Mental state. - Feelings. - Responses to situations. - Intensity levels. - Thoughts. - Actions. - Confidence. - Training. - Pre-match preparation (such as stretching and warming-up). - Game plans for a particular opponent. - Nutrition and fluid intake before and during matches. - The ability to stay calm and focussed, etc.	- The weather. - Parent's (coach's) actions. - Opponent's action, performance, and luck. - String breakages. - Court surface. - Dubious calls by opponent or linesman. - Tournament draws. - The umpire. - State of the court. - Spectators' behaviours. - Luck.

*Table 10.1
Factors over which players have varying levels of control.*

II. Mental training: Techniques and plans

Understanding that mistakes are part and parcel of the game, that no player is immune to them, and that they form a part of an on-going learning process is also important in developing and maintaining an appropriate perspective. Players who dwell on mistakes spiral into continual second-guessing, failing to ever properly prepare to win the next point. Focussing on performance rather than outcome goals is likely to be similarly beneficial in helping players to keep tennis in perspective.

10.3. BREATHING

Breath control can be a very useful technique in manipulating arousal levels. Simply by adjusting their depth and rate of breathing, players can begin to have an immediate effect on their psychological and physiological states. That is, shallower, quicker breaths tend to heighten arousal levels, while breathing that is deeper and slower is likely to trigger the opposite effect. In general terms, four types of breathing can be used.

PRACTICAL APPLICATION:

Centered breathing is a practical breathing technique that can be used both on- and off-court, with the process for off-court centered breathing as follows: Find a comfortable place and close your eyes. Breathe in: Slowly take in air, filling the diaphragm and then the upper lungs counting from one to seven. Hold: Hold the breath for that same period. Breathe out: Then, let it out for the same count. Repeat this two to three times. When using centered breathing on-court players can shorten the time to a few seconds when breathing in, holding and breathing out. If players feel that theyneed to increase their arousal, they can use short, quick breaks to elicit an increase in their breathing rate (Girod, 2004).

1. **High breathing** ('clavicular' or 'collarbone breathing') refers to what takes place primarily in the upper part of the chest and lungs. It involves the raising of the ribs, collarbone and shoulders, and engages the lungs' upper lobes, which have a limited air capacity. For this reason it is the least desirable form of breathing.

2. **Low breathing** ('abdominal breathing' and 'diaphragmic breathing') predominantly occurs in the lower part of the chest and lungs, shifting the abdomen in and out, and manipulating diaphragmic position. It is far more effective than high or middle breathing. To perform low breathing, players should 'expand' their stomachs sligthly forwards (with no strain) as they inhale, before allowing their stomachs to return to their resting state as they exhale.

3. **Middle breathing** (thoracic, intercostal or rib breathing) fills the middle lungs with air, and while considered better than high breathing, is inferior to low breathing and the 'complete breath technique'. With this form of breathing, the ribs and chest are expanded sideways.

4. **The "complete breath"** is a combination of high, low and middle breathing, designed to expand the lungs to their fullest capacities. It involves the entire respiratory system and expands the lungs so as to take in more air than the amounts inhaled by all of the three kinds of breathing mentioned above.

Different types of breathing can be employed to control arousal levels between points and during changes of ends.

Tennis Psychology

10.4. ACTIVATION TECHNIQUES

While breathing can play a role in helping players to feel more activated or 'pumped up', several other techniques can also be used. Some more conventional and commonly used, some that require equipment other than just a racquet and ball, and others more suited to training than competition! Among these alternative strategies are:

— Body movement: jumping or 'bouncing' up and down between points.
— Using a power walk.
— Alternating muscle contraction and relaxation.
— Listening to energising music.
— Biofeedback: heart rate monitors, electromyography, etc.
— Visualising challenge and success.
— Using positive self-talk.

10.5. RELAXATION TECHNIQUES

In high-pressure situations, players' hearts often beat more than 180 times per minute, their brains process information they did not know to exist and their once supple musculature takes on an almost statue-like appearance. It is here, in the face of this mounting inner (and outer!) torment that arousal levels need to be mediated. Table 10.2 summarises some relaxation techniques that can be employed by tennis players on- and off- court.

ON-COURT	OFF-COURT
- Control of breath (centered breathing). - Vision control: Close eyes and relax or focus the attention on one point. - Relaxation: progressive muscle relaxation, autogenous, sophrology. - Visualisation/imagery. - Bio-feedback. - Smile when confronted with difficult situations. - 'Shake' / loose hands, arms, shoulders and neck. - Take time between points.	- Control of breath (centered breathing). - Vision control. - Hypnosis and self-hypnosis. - Yoga. - Meditation. - Progressive desensitisation. - Cognitive restructuring. - Self-instruction / talk. - Relaxation, sophrology. - Music. - Humour. - Bio-feedback.

Table 10.2 On-court and off-court relaxation techniques that can be used by tennis players.

VISION CONTROL

One of the most common relaxation methods is the use of vision control, which can be achieved by performing one or more of the following relaxation routines:

— **Eye closing:** Simply closing your eyes and letting go, possibly aided by counting numbers each time you breathe out.
— **Palming:** A relaxation technique wherein you cover each eye with the palm of each hand. As this excludes a maximum amount of light, it can be very relaxing.
— **Sunning:** A high intensity light bulb shines on closed eyelids, to create a relaxation experience that many compare to sunbathing on a beach.

REMEMBER:

Most stress or arousal management techniques (breathing, vision control, muscle relaxation, visualisation, bio-feedback, time management, hypnosis, self-hypnosis, yoga, meditation, progressive desensitisation, etc.) can be used both on- and off-court.

MUSCLE RELAXATION

There are several methods of muscle relaxation, yet the two most extensively used and therefore those that will be discussed are **Progressive Muscle Relaxation (PMR)** and Autogenic or Autogenous Training. Progressive muscle relaxation, developed by Jacobson in 1938, is a two-step self-administered process that encourages deep muscle relaxation through the alternate contraction and relaxation of the body's muscles.

— **Step One (Tension):** First, players should focus their minds, for example, on their right hands. Then, while inhaling they maximally contract the muscles in their hand as hard as they can and hold to the count of five.

— **Step Two (Releasing the Tension):** After the count to five, players gently release (letting go of all tightness) their muscles as they simultaneously exhale. Staying relaxed for about 15 seconds, they then repeat this contraction-relaxation cycle, and progress from the muscles of the hands to the arms, shoulders, feet, legs, thighs, bottom, stomach, back, chest, shoulders, neck, mouth and jaw, eyes, scalp, and face.

There are two versions of the PMR that vary in duration (from one to 30 minutes) and suitability for on-court and off-court use. The shorter method, which can be more suitably applied on-court is expanded upon in the Appendix.

Autogenic training – created by Schultz and Luthe in 1959 – comprises of six exercises that help players progressively achieve a state of complete physical and psychological relaxation and the release of anxiety and tension. Following an introductory breathing warm-up, phase one, termed heaviness, would see players repeat statements ("My (limb) is getting heavy, heavier and heavier, completely heavy… I feel supremely calm"), while inhaling and exhaling. Phase two, or warmth, sees players repeat the process but with the word warm substituted in place of heavy, while calm heart (Phase three) would end with a command on the calmness of the players' hearts. Breathing is introduced in Phase four ending with a mention of one's calmness of breath. Phase five emphasises the softness and warmth of the stomach. Phase six directs players to cool off their foreheads. All phases culminate with the statement: "I feel supremely calm."

> **PRACTICAL APPLICATION:**
>
> Some suggestions for the off-court practice of the PMR include:
>
> - Practice in a quiet place, alone, with no distractions.
> - Remove your shoes and wear loose clothing.
> - Avoid eating, smoking, or drinking, immediately beforehand.
> - Sit in a comfortable chair if possible.
> - If you fall aslevvccxxep, give yourself credit for the work you did up to the point of sleep.
> - When you finish a session, relax with your eyes closed for a few seconds, and then get up slowly. Count backwards from five to one, while breathing slowly and deeply, and then say, "Eyes open. Supremely calm. Fully alert."

HYPNOSIS

When induced correctly, hypnosis sees players enter states of heightened awareness and focussed concentration whereby they become more receptive, better able to manipulate perceptions and behaviours, and more attentive to changes that can be made to improve performance (Liggett, 2000). In effect, their attention is withdrawn from the outside world and is centred on mental and somatosensory experiences. The techniques used to induce hypnosis share some common features such as the need for receptive, willing and cooperative players that are able to relax, trust, and concentrate on the voice of the hypnotist while closing their eyes excluding all else. Self-hypnosis can also be learned by players to achieve similar results. Its basic stages are relaxation (PMR), deepening (count down technique, metronome, etc.), suggestions (thinking about or verbalising them), and termination (count and finish).

> **REMEMBER**
>
> Believing that you can be hypnotised is key to it being induced.

CENTERING

Centering, a martial arts concept now commonly applied in sport, sees players become increasingly aware of the movement of their body's centre of mass and how this can be affected by heightened calmness, relaxation and clarity. Many of the refocussing techniques covered in Chapter 14 can assist players internalise this process.

YOGA

Yoga has multiple uses in life and in sport. Indeed, in tennis it can play a vital role in player development, especially if introduced early on. The empirical work of many practitioners indicates that the breathing techniques essential for all yoga asanas (exercises) are learned with greater ease in childhood (Singh, 2003). As aforementioned, the ability to control breath can help players' bodies and minds function optimally during matchplay. Furthermore, by facilitating the development of specific components of physical fitness with meditation and concentration techniques to relax and focus the mind, yoga's integration into tennis training can complement other physical, technical and tactical training protocols (Singh, 2003).

MEDITATION

The goal of meditation is to calm the storm of ideas that go through a player's mind by focussing on the here and now. Closely related to one's philosophy of life and religious orientation, it can be interpreted differently through vipassana (concentration on one object), transcendental (mantra repetition - e.g. "omm"), shamadi (focus on vital rhythm - e.g. heart beats), zen (breathing exercises), and while walking. Irrespective of which variation is used, the physiological effects remain the same with players likely to produce more theta waves to enhance relaxation, more serotonin (a neurotransmitter that counters depression), and more endorphins, which promote happiness (Solberg et al, 1995). In general, the following directives can be applied to all forms of meditation:

— Needs to be practiced regularly (i.e. as part of a daily routine).
— Focus should be shifted to turn attention away from everyday events. Concentrating on a higher power or special word may help here.
— Breathe deeply to slow down heart rate, and disengage from activities.
— Sit on the ground or on a chair, or walk.
— Dedicate at least 10 minutes to each meditation session.
— Make sure the performance environment is calming and relaxed.
— Incorporate mantra: Repeat the word "omm" or focus on a single object or point in the environment.

BIOFEEDBACK

Biofeedback helps players to increase their body and mind awareness by reducing habitual, psychological and physiological stressors. Here, the underlying assumption is that players can learn to control certain involuntary processes (heart rate and blood pressure) that increase under stress. In effect, players are provided physiological feedback from which they can begin to regulate their arousal levels or facets of their stress response. There exist several means,

---

WHAT RESEARCH TELLS US...

Butler (1996) recommends a mnemonic tool called PRESSURE for those players who have a hard time coping in competitions. The word can be broken down as follows:

— **P**repare - Athletes must psychologically prepare for what they will face during the competition.
— **R**elax - Diaphragmatic breathing exercises, may be necessary prior to competition in order to prevent over arousal which would result in a deterioration in performance.
— **E**xternalise - This involves the belief that problems are not within yourself. This can be of assistance when athletes feel that there are too many demands placed upon them.
— **S**tay Positive - Acknowledgement of the importance that individuals should have confidence in their abilities.
— **S**ingle Minded - Stay focussed on the task at hand. This can be used both in training and competition.
— **U**nite - Particularly useful within the framework of teams sports, this component encourages athletes to consider what roles others will fulfill and the importance of working together as a team throughout the competition.
— **R**e-evaluate - How important is this event in the real world?
— **E**xtend yourself - Give your best performance every time no matter how important, or unimportant, the competition is.

requiring varying levels of technical equipment and expertise, through which biofeedback can be provided to players, including:

— **Temperature biofeedback:** A common thermometer to measure the warmth of players' hands can indicate the extent to which they are relaxed. In general, the warmer the hands, the more relaxed the players.
— **Electromyography (EMG):** Measurement of the electrical activity of muscles can provide information regarding the appropriateness and intensity of muscle contraction.
— **Using a heart rate monitor:** Heart rate can be used to guage stress levels.
— **Galvanic skin response (GSH) or Electrodermal response (EDR):** Determines the electrical conductivity of the skin, which is associated with sweat gland activity and, indirectly, stress response.

HUMOUR

Humour can be a powerful tool to reduce stress, enhance well-being, break tension, view matches from a different perspective, boost confidence, and release negative energy.

It can be practiced naturally by looking for humour in the players' own behaviours and performances, and also by approaching tennis as it was intended...as a game!

SOPHROLOGY

This technique, developed by Colombian neuropsychiatrist Alfonso Caycedo in the mid 1970's, is a combination of therapeutic hypnosis, Jacobson's PMR, Schultz's autogenic training, phenomenology psychiatrics, zen and yoga. It is called 'the science of harmonious consciousness' and involves three basic somatosensory progressions that emphasise the perception and achievement of particular body postures and breathing patterns.

OTHER AROUSAL CONTROL TECHNIQUES

Techniques such as hydrotherapy, phytotheraphy, aromatheraphy, homeotheraphy, musicotheraphy, massage and self-massage, tai-chi, chi-kung, reflexology, acupunture, and flotation can also be used to successfully control arousal.

Note: Building confidence, using positive self-talk, and following routines double as effective arousal control techniques and are covered in Chapters 4, 9, and 12 respectively.

PRACTICAL APPLICATION:

To most effectively deal with pressure on-court, players are likely to need some sort of practical 'action plan' that encourages them to (Moran, 1995b):

- **Understand body signals:** Players should learn to welcome signals of body alertness, viewing them as essential for good performances.
- **Take control:** Slow down and breathe deep: Pressure can cause players to accelerate their behaviour so efforts to regain rhythm and a more desirable tempo are important.
- **Stay in the here and now:** One of the best ways to counteract pressure on-court is for players to simply ask themselves, 'What is that I have to do right now in this point?' Using short, specific and positively-phrased questions or instructions is a powerful way of dealing with pressure.
- **Focus on what they can control:** When under pressure players tend to focus their minds on things which lie outside their control (e.g. 'What will the coach think of me if I lose?'), further affecting decision-making and their sense of control.
- **Think constructively and positively:** Focus only on positive thougths and powerful self-talk.
- **Train your players to encourage themselves and use positive self-talk.**

WHAT RESEARCH TELLS US...
Reductions in pre-competition state anxiety can be realised through a variety of intervention strategies: centering (a somatic intervention strategy), imagery rehearsal (a cognitive intervention strategy), a combination of both, and the concentration grid (a control intervention) (Coakley and Terry, 1994; Knisel, 2001). Coping stress strategies have also been linked to significantly improved tennis performance (Anshel,1990; Anshel and Wrisberg, 1993), although relaxation and hypnosis along with instructions for mentally practicing tennis strokes through visualisation have been shown as no more effective for teaching skills to beginners than traditional instruction (Greer and Engs, 1986).

Tennis Psychology

VISUALISATION

11.1. DEFINITION, BENEFITS AND MECHANISMS

Visualisation, also called imagery or mental rehearsal, is the process whereby internal images are produced consciously. It accesses as many modes of expression (sight, smell, sound, touch, and taste) as possible, and in doing so is proposed to elicit many benefits. While research evaluating its merits for tennis performance has been inconclusive, suggestions are that it can help players reduce anxiety, decrease errors, heighten anticipation, coordination and concentration, enhance self-confidence, accelerate learning, improve stroke precision and performance, and facilitate an injured player's rehabilitation.

The literature offers three main mechanisms - the Carpenter effect, the symbolic theory, and the psychological skills hypothesis - to explain how visualisation works (Girod, 2003; Weinberg and Gould, 1995). The 'Carpenter effect' suggests that watching a tennis match can actually stimulate the muscles and areas of the brain that are activated during competition. Players can therefore learn vicariously, unconsciously imitating the models that they observe. Pete Sampras, for example, was technically inspired by a video tape of Rod Laver that he constantly watched.

The symbolic theory, on the other hand, believes visualisation helps players to 'understand' their movements. Achieved by creating a motor programme in the central nervous system, it works best when the task is predominantly cognitive (e.g. tactics). And finally, the psychological skills hypothesis considers visualisation to work through the development of psychological skills such as concentration, stress management, stress inoculation, etc.

11.2. FUNDAMENTALS OF VISUALISATION

WHY IT WORKS?

Several reasons have been offered to explain why visualisation works:

— Organises a plan for performance that enhances mental acuity.
— Integrates all the elements of performance: Physical (feelings, visions), cognitive (thoughts) and emotional (sensations), to more closely approximate the actual demands of match play.
— Assists players understand what they intend to do through rehearsal of shots, tactics and emotional responses.
— Simulates psychological states.

WHAT RESEARCH TELLS US...
Research has clearly demonstrated the many benefits of visualisation: levelling emotions, enhancing confidence, and facilitating technique modification and tactical training (Noel, 1980).

WHAT TO IMAGINE?

PRACTICAL APPLICATION:

Winners seem to have clear pictures and feelings of themselves competing successfully. They see what they want to happen. They see themselves as the winners they are. Losers see what they fear might happen.

What players visualise is largely individual but some of the most commonly 'viewed' examples include:

— Successful execution of stroke or specific point sequences.
— Improvement of mechanical flaws.
— Playing perfect tennis.
— Efficient court movement.
— Powerful body language between points.
— Exuding confidence and positivity between points.
— Dealing with adversity and errors effectively.
— Imagining the future, as players want it to be.
— Imagining a successful on-court return for players that are injured.

HOW TO DO IT?

REMEMBER:

Not all people have the same ability to use imagery. Some are good at visualising images; other sensations or sounds. Players should use their preferred senses to enhance the visualisation experience.

Visualisation can be done **internally** (visualising a movement as it is usually seen by a person, using a realistic visual perspective that simulates what the player experiences) or **externally** (visualising a movement as if watching a video of oneself). Internal visualisation is recommended for use in re-creating tactical or more open situations, while visualising externally is preferrable for honing technical or more controlled and simple tasks (Weinberg and Gould, 1995).

The more technically precise, realistic and vivid the images are, the better. Combining visualisation with physical practice to consolidate one's confidence in performing the visualised task is also very important.

In summary, for visualisation to be used optimally, it should be practiced regularly and correctly, in a quiet, relaxing and appropriate place where all senses can be accessed. As a guide, visualisation training that is progressive and systematic may be introduced as follows:

1. Learn to relax.
2. Divide the movement into sequences.
3. Visualise a static object.
4. Visualise a moving object.
5. Visualise a player moving.
6. Visualisation directed by other person.
7. Visualise with words of the player.
8. Visualise before the match.
9. Visualise during the match.

Note: Upon beginning to visualise each new object or situation, players may benefit from first establishing sensory awareness, before enhancing object/situation vividness, and finally maintaining image control.

WHAT RESEARCH TELLS US...
Some research points to there being no real benefit in using video feedback (video taped modelling, video instructions) in technique learning (Van Wieringen et al., 1989), or with beginners (Emmen et al., 1985) as compared to more traditional modes of instruction (Bouchard and Singer, 1998). Likewise, providing cues to players when serving was more effective than visualisation in reducing unforced errors and anxiety, and improving attention (Taylor, 1992). Audio instruction combined with mental practice was found the most efficient training routine to teach the forehand (Surburg, 1968).

WHEN AND FOR HOW LONG?

Before individualising their routines, players can practice visualising for five minutes pre- and post-training session. Its integration into matches (e.g. visualising the serve, the return or the ideal point, between points and changes of ends) can be pursued shortly thereafter. Players are unlikely to realise benefits immediately, and it may take up to two months of practice before transferrable performance improvements are realised. Similarly, as with many tennis skills, the higher the level of play, the longer the practice required (Girod, 2003).

Finally, visualisation can vary quite significantly in duration. That is, it can be as short as a few seconds (between points), last a matter of ten or more minutes (post-match debriefing or prophesying an event), or up to one hour (pre-match).

WHAT EQUIPMENT IS NEEDED?

Videos, CD's, images, words, photos ... whatever sensory inputs best enhance the mental picture players wish to create. Photographs, mirrors, film, or video replay may also strengthen and improve the accuracy of the mental picture players may conjure.

REMEMBER:

Experts recommend players to:
- Visualise internally most of the time.
- Visualise in blocks of five minutes.
- Imagine difficult situations, errors and solutions.
- Visualise in real-time (i.e. the image lasts the same duration as the actual performance).

PRACTICAL APPLICATION:

Encourage players to create CD's (of music, photos, video clips) to enhance the efficacy of their visualisation experience (Quinn, 2003).

Players are known to use the time during the change-over to visualise what they want to achieve in the next couple of games.

WHAT RESEARCH TELLS US...
Indications are that visualisation practice alone is better than no practice at all, and that visualisation when combined with physical practice is more effective in improving stroke performance than either alone (Atienza et al., 1998; Noel, 1980; Rhea et al., 1997; Wilkinson, 1996).

RITUALS AND COPING BEHAVIOURS 12

12.1. DEFINITION AND IMPORTANCE

Rituals or coping techniques and behaviours, also called routines, are combinations of mental, behavioural, physical, cognitive, and nutritional strategies used to help players achieve their Ideal Performance State (IPS). Like any other skill, routines must be practiced to become automated and best enhance performance. Players use a variety of routines both in training and competition (pre-match, during match, and post-match). For example, they may be sufficiently general so as to relate to sleep, eating, drinking or studying habits, or more specific and concern equipment preparation, training and scheduling, medical and physical check ups, and warming up and cooling down.

Coaches should endeavour to educate players as to the function and therefore importance of routines, while simultaneously helping them to tailor routines to their personalities and playing styles.

REMEMBER

All top players have routines whose timing remain the same throughout a match because they have been planned, perfected and practiced. As compared to inexperienced players, experienced players display more consistency and confidence in their rituals (Whittaker, 1980). Poorly behaved players have also been suggested to less diligently follow between point routines (Jaenes, 1995).

12.2. PRE-MATCH ROUTINES

Covassin and Pero (2004) have demonstrated that players' mental states prior to the start of matches are result-determining. This being the case, the role of routines in assisting players to prepare for competition cannot be understated. Taylor (1996) agrees, and highlights the vital role of pre- match routines in building players' consistency of thought and action, while concurrently increasing their self-confidence and feelings of control.

The best pre-match routines are those that totally prepare players for competition through optimal meal preparation, physical warm-up and stretching, court inspection, and mental preparation. However, rather than being prescriptive, pre-match routines are largely personal so players should develop a repertoire of routines that suit their individual needs.

PRACTICAL APPLICATION:

Players should list what they need to do before a match. Then, by deciding the best time to complete each listed 'item', they can begin to create their own individualised pre-match routine. Having followed the routine for a couple of months, it will soon become second nature and provide players with the best chance to execute their "A" game each and every match.

Coaches may need to provide players with feedback so as to optimise their pre-match routines.

WHAT RESEARCH TELLS US...
Non-verbal winning behaviours have been shown to include: fixing the hair, keeping your head up, putting the racquet behind your head and resting it on your shoulder, as well as walking faster; whereas players exhibiting non-verbal losing behaviours hold their heads down, look around or at the racquet, shake their head, circle in the corner of the court, throw their racquets, and walk slower (Whittaker, 1983).

II. Mental training: Techniques and plans

12.3. IN-MATCH ROUTINES

Between points, in preparing to serve and return serve, players should utilise and benefit from routines. That is, by employing appropriate combinations of cognitive and emotional control strategies, they should assume optimal states of physical and mental readiness. In Table 12.1 we have put forward some examples of routines for specific situations that arise during matchplay.

PRACTICAL APPLICATION:

In his study of concentration skills needed for the return of serve, Prapavessis (1993) concluded that in order to successfully execute a return a player needs to be able to:
- Focus attention on the cognitive, emotional and behavioural processes of the return;
- Discriminate between effective and ineffective service delivery cues and;
- Recognise when distracted and be able to refocus attention on demand.

WHEN	WHAT
BEFORE THE SERVE	- Use a rhythmic and systematic serving ritual. - Go to the spot from where you will serve. Adopt a relaxed stance and try to loosen your muscles. - Take a deep breath and bounce the ball (as many times you think necessary). - Visualise a perfect serve. - Focus on your specific cues for your serve. - Decide the type and placement of serve, and focus on the ball toss and on hitting up. - Balance the racquet and the arm, and then serve.
BEFORE THE RETURN OF SERVE	- Keep focussed and know when to activate or relax depending on the situation by observing your opponent. - Use self-talk if needed (motivational: pump up, or instructional: goal-related). - Decide how and where to return; visualise the desired return. - Take a deep breath and assume a comfortable, ready stance. - Focus on the server and the ball toss.
TIME BETWEEN GAMES	This period should be productive, and see players use any one or combination of drinking water, towelling off, aligning strings, and deep breathing among other commonly used strategies, to maintain game focus. Evaluating, mentally rehearsing and planning tactics should also be completed in this down-time.
TIME BETWEEN POINTS	Loehr (1988) developed a routine called the '16 second cure'. It comprises of a series of short physical and mental exercises within a four-stage response: 1. Physical (as soon as the point ends), 2. Relaxation or activation, 3. Preparation and, 4. Ritual. Slaikeu and Trogolo (1998) also developed the 3R (Release, review and reset) which will be covered in Chapter 13.
AFTER MISSING A SHOT	Rehearse the stroke positively and assertively, and then move on, completing the rest of your standard between point routine. Keep your mind in the now.
FOLLOWING A DISTRACTION	Take time to settle, put the racquet in the non-dominant hand, visually focus on something 'neutral', breathe calmly, plan the point, activate, move into position and finally complete the serve or return of serve routine.
OTHER SITUATIONS	When the opponent intentionally delays the game, stop for a second, take a deep breath, and perform your routine again.

Table 12.1 Suggested routines that can be completed in response to specific situations that may arise during matchplay (adapted from Pérez, 1995; and Ojea and Vicente, 2002).

WHAT RESEARCH TELLS US...
Rhythmic and consistent serving rituals promote successful performance (Southard and Amos, 1996). Preparatory behaviours in the return of serve depend on the receiving skills of the player (Hennemann and Keller, 1983), while between points, winners tend to initiate more contacts (eye contact, distance of interaction, intimacy and smiling) than losers (Heckel, 1993).

12.4. POST-MATCH ROUTINES

As important as pre-match routines are to immediate performance, so too are post-match routines to future training and competition. Standard post-match rehydration, nutrition and physical recovery (active cool-down, hot-cold showers, stretching, massage, etc) strategies are a must.

Activities that help players to relax are largely individual (e.g. reading, watching movies, shopping, …) and they too, should be incorporated into the global post-match routine.

Debriefing or match review of player performance is also central to any comprehensive post-match routine. However, rather than try to undertake the analysis immediately post-match, it may be best to do this when the player is physically and mentally recovered (Davis, 1991; Dunlap and Berne, 1991).

REMEMBER

The need of some players to repeat, recreate or avoid certain situations (e.g. playing in the same shirt, eating the same food and in the same place before each match, not stepping on the lines of the court between points, demanding that the coach sit in the same seat) are not routines. They relate to superstition, and can be performance limiting if a player's dependency on them is fostered over time (Ojea and Vicente, 2002).

12.5. WIDER USE OF ROUTINES

Common to most techniques outlined in Part II, the main goal of routines is to assist players achieve their IPS. However, routines comprise a wide variety of behaviours that can span all facets of life and help individuals deal with any problems, joys, disappointments, and stresses encountered.

Indeed, a lack of effective general routines (sleep patterns, nutrition, time management, and if the player is a student, study skills) can propagate higher stress and thus greater risk of injury (Quinn, 2001b). As the same stressful life event will be experienced differently by each individual, the specificity of players' routines becomes critical. And like the learning of the games' other skills, it is through deliberate practice that players develop effective and specific routines.

PRACTICAL APPLICATION:

The number of inappropriate on-court behaviours may be reduced by providing players feedback on those behaviours, setting goals to eliminate them, and posting them publicly (Galvan and Ward, 1998).

Routines can also be followed to better cope with off-court demands such as match analysis.

II. Mental training: Techniques and plans

COGNITIVE STRATEGIES 13

13.1. TYPES OF COGNITIVE STRATEGIES

Cognitive therapies assume that the changes in certain thought patterns will produce associated changes in behaviours. In a tennis context, we have already outlined several of the more commonly used cognitive strategies such as visualisation and self-talk. A number of other techniques do exist however, and the means through which they can improve a player's mental performance are outlined below.

INTELLECTUAL PREPARATION

Have players use systematic and specifically focussed learning to develop higher cognitive function and better apply it on court (Slder, 1996). Resources such as books, video footage or instructional materials can help players increase their knowledge of the game, while watching opponents' matches, talking to other tennis persons and observing how other players practice can also be useful.

PROBLEM SOLVING

A problem can be considered as an opportunity to learn and improve as well as the difference between the actual situation and that which is desired. To this end, coaches should design game situations and drills that challenge players to solve the 'problems' they are likely to encounter during matchplay. In doing so, coaches may wish to guide players in problem exploration (clarify and place the problem in context), goal-setting, arriving at possible solutions, and selecting, implementing, and evaluating a course of action. Here, coaches need to recognise that players respond to stimuli and learn differently, so the ways in which they interpret and then solve problems are likely to vary.

POSITIVE THINKING

Controlling one's thoughts through positive thinking is a most effective cognitive strategy, and may encourage players to:

— Think positively and confidently even in the face of adversity and failure; identifying 'positives' in each situation.
— Eliminate irrational thought, and replace negative thought with more positive reflections.
— Visualise success.
— Mentally prepare.
— Believe in themselves.
— Formulate and follow a game plan.

PRACTICAL APPLICATION:

Positive thinking, whether it be operative (technical), action-oriented (verbal or non-verbal), or creative, can be fostered by eliminating irrational thinking, being disciplined in the use of routines, and enjoying success.

WHAT RESEARCH TELLS US...
Cognitive and behavioural recovery strategies used by competitive players include mind absorption, rationalisation, identification of 'positive' aspects, use of external and internal controllable attributions, and the development of a plan that involves future successful experiences (Davis, 1991). Dunlap and Berne (1991) found that stress was the most pervasive psychological problem identified among junior elite players.

THOUGHT-STOPPING TECHNIQUES

Thought-stopping techniques can also be very useful in helping players to 'let go' and optimally prepare for each point. The 3 R´s Mental Training System (Slaikeu and Trogolo, 1998), devoid of prescriptive guidelines, is a common thought-stopping tool which encourages players to:

— **Release**: React to the point just finished, dealing with any pent up energy or feelings. Move forward, fresh and ready.
— **STOP**: Between each stage.
— **Review:** Where the match is at through imagery, self-talk, body language, etc.
— **STOP,** and
— **Reset:** Perform an individual routine to get ready for the next point.

SYSTEMATIC DESENSITISATION

PRACTICAL APPLICATION:

The use of metaphors aimed at reducing distractions in the early phase of learning skills has been shown to facilitate skill acquisition and enhance the activity experience (Efran et al., 1994).

Here, events that cause anxiety are recalled in one's imagination prior to a relaxation technique being used to dissipate anxiety. With sufficient repetition, the imagined event eventually loses its anxiety-provoking power. The three steps in self-administered systematic desensitisation are: 1. Relaxation, 2. Constructing an anxiety hierarchy (anxiety producing situation), and 3. Pairing relaxation with the situations described in the anxiety hierarchy (Wolpe, 1958).

COGNITIVE RESTRUCTURING

A group of cognitive techniques that see individuals learn to identify irrational beliefs and develop personal tools to overcome them.

— **Rational emotive behavioural therapy (REBT)** (Ellis, 1955) stimulates emotional growth by teaching people to replace their self-defeating thoughts, feelings and actions with new and more positive ones.
— **Cognitive behaviour therapy (CBT)** (Beck, 1963) focusses on thoughts, assumptions and beliefs. Players may learn to recognise and change faulty or maladaptive thinking patterns to gain control over repetitive thoughts which often feed or trigger anxiety.

Positive thinking is a simple but often under-rated cognitive strategy.

WHAT RESEARCH TELLS US...
For players to gain maximum benefit from cognitive therapies, they need to select their preferred strategy and practice it extensively (Weinberg et al., 1981).

STRESS INOCULATION

Stress inoculation assumes that anxiety can be reduced naturally, by repeatedly and gradually thinking about increasingly stressful situations (Epstein, 1983). Theoretically, players would learn to view the situation more realistically, tempering their fear response. In putting stress inoculation into practice, Meichenbaum (1985) describes three stages:

— **Education phase:** Specific information about what to expect is given to players. For instance, players preparing to compete in a big tournament are better equipped to cope if they know exactly what to expect.
— **Rehearsal phase:** Players practice/visualise/recreate the 'stressful' event in safe surrounds. For example, players who are anxious about playing in front of a large crowd may first want to rehearse at home or at their club.
— **Implementation phase:** Players actually perform in the 'stressful' environment.

PLAYING THE "INNER GAME"

Gallwey (1975) described two games of tennis: the outer game, played against the opponent(s) on the other side of the net, and the inner game, played against the opponent(s) inside a player's head! In general, players that concentrate on the inner game perform better, have more fun and also win. In developing this premise, Gallwey introduces the concepts of Self 1 and Self 2.

— Self 1 is our thinking, judgmental and criticising ego.
— Self 2 is our non-thinking and spontaneous body.

The key to better tennis is derived from 'quietening' Self 1 by using four inter-related 'inner' skills:

— **Letting go of self-judgement:** Ability to observe and not evaluate what is happening.
— **Creating images:** Ability to visualise shots and desired outcomes.
— **Letting it happen:** Ability to put trust in one's body (Self 2) to hit the ball.
— **Concentration:** Most importantly, the ability to calm the mind (Self 1) to focus on the present.

MISTAKE MANAGEMENT TECHNIQUES

Mistakes are part of tennis play and players need to be able to manage them effectively to elicit optimal performances. Common mistake management techniques include:

— **Error parking** (deleting errors from memory).
— **Using keywords** (to reinforce positive behaviour).
— **Simulated practice** (to recreate match pressure).
— **Error assessment** (evaluation of the characteristics of errors).

ASSERTIVENESS TRAINING

Players behave assertively when they know their personal rights and interests on a given issue or in a given situation and then defend them objectively, rationally and fairly. Assertiveness training can help players acquire the necessary related behavioural and cognitive skills such that they can achieve greater control over their daily activities and better manage potential stressors. Players will learn to:

— Differentiate between assertive, non-assertive and aggressive behaviours.
— Eliminate cognitive obstacles.

ROLE MODELLING / PLAYING

This technique consists of role play by players and it can be used on- or off-court. It can assist players to better manage mistakes or solve problems by interpreting specific situations (bad calls, press conference, arguments, doubles play, etc.) and / or another person's point of view (i.e. parents, officials, umpires, agents, media, etc.). The video-recording of role playing sessions allows for player-coach evaluation and can further benefit player learning.

TIME MANAGEMENT

Successful time management is a key cognitive strategy, and can be facilitated by:

- Being aware and clear of your key goals and roles in life and tennis.
- Learning to prioritise on a daily, weekly, and monthly basis to spend time on things that matter.
- Using day, week, month, year planners, mobile phones with email or internet facilities, voicemail, personal digital diaries, etc.
- Limiting procrastination (i.e. to put off doing something).
- Learning to delegate.
- Making 'to do' lists every day, learning to say "no", getting a good night's sleep, communicating your schedule to others, and keeping things in perspective.
- Including time-out in your annual plan.

MIND ABSORPTION

Mind absorption is a process through which a player's mind focusses on one idea or object. It can be achieved using different strategies such as hypnosis, meditation, yoga, sophrology, contemplation, etc. For the mind to become one with the idea / object, high levels of concentration must be reached.

RATIONALISATION

Rationalisation is the explanation or justification of players' actions or feelings such that they are not threatening to them. It is believed to explain a player's true motivation and can be achieved by making behaviour, feeling or thought seem consistent with a given purpose (e.g. increasing performance, reducing stress, etc.).

Rationalisation may be effective in assisting players compete in front of large audiences for the first time.

SKILLS ASSESSMENT AND PLAN DEVELOPMENT

Closely related to goal-setting, this technique can help players to change both thoughts and behaviours by reviewing, assessing, and implementing an action plan for their tennis and life skills. In so doing, they need to consider their personal and career needs and objectives, natural aptitudes, interests, transferable skills, values and personality type, among others.

FOSTERING INDEPENDENCE

Coaches, parents and meaningful adults can help players foster independence on and off the court. Players should progressively assume responsibility for organising practice, warming-up and preparing their own equipment. Ultimately, this should help them to accept responsibility for their tennis development, become more proactive both on and off the court, and increase their commitment and satisfaction (Loehr, 2001).

APPROPRIATE DEFINITION OF SUCCESS

Success should not always equate to winning. Rather, for the most part, it should be internally referenced and related on one's own performance (internal and controllable attributions). Coaches should understand that players likely have their own perspectives of success, and that their role is to shape them in such a way that players are able to continually develop, improve and grow as both sports people and human beings.

NEUROLINGUISTIC PROGRAMMING

Neurolinguistic programming or NLP was developed by Grinder and Bandler in the mid 70's. Where 'Neuro' refers to the neurological basis of our thought and behaviour, and the importance of sensory impressions, 'Linguistic' relates to the importance of words in ordering our thoughts and behaviour. The way in which we choose to organise ideas to get results comprises the 'Programming'.

NLP is a model rather than a theory, which focusses on the process and not the content. It is a branch of cognitive and behavioural psychology and is based on the assumption that behavioural and cognitive excellence can be identified and copied (or modelled). This can be done by (1) communicating with other people and / or (2) changing or managing personal life, thoughts, feelings, and behaviours.

NLP has some fundamental principles such as:

— **Process**: The ability to change the process by which we experience reality is often more valuable than changing the content of our experience of reality.
— **Communication**: The meaning of communication is the response you get.
— **Positiveness**: Positive self-worth is always held constant. People are not their behaviours. Behind every behaviour there is a positive intention.
— **Respect**: An individual's world view should be respected.
— **Solutions**: NLP emphasises solutions rather than analysis of causes. There is a solution to every problem.
— **Hope**: If one human can do something then, potentially, anyone can.
— **Mistakes**: All results and behaviours are achievements, whether they are desired outcomes for a given task /context, or not. Redefine mistakes as feedback, so if what you are doing is not working, do something else.

NLP techniques include 'modelling', 'anchoring', 'changing history', rapport, and reframing. Furthermore, general mental techniques such as relaxation, goal-setting, visualisation and hypnosis are also used in NLP (Girod, 2005).

OTHER BEHAVIOUR MODIFICATION TECHNIQUES

Additional behaviour modification strategies include:

— Direct instruction.
— Reinforcement techniques:
- Social praise.
- Material reinforcers, and tokens.
— Punishment-oriented techniques:
- Verbal reprimand.
- Response cost.
- Time-out.
— Group contingency techniques (i.e."Good Behaviour Game").
— Behavioural contracting.
— Self-instructional training to improve attention and problem-solving.
— Counselling: health, exercise, and nutritional.
— Emotional expression.

ATTENTIONAL CONTROL 14

14.1. INTRODUCTION

Mentally staying in the present tense is the key to being focussed during matchplay. According to Girod (1999) this skill to 'not to worry about the future or the past' requires that players obey the principle of the three unities:

— Unity of person: I am centred on myself (ME).
— Unity of place: I am here (HERE).
— Unity of time: I am in the present tense (NOW).

In tennis, it only takes players to fail to respect one of these three unities for attention to begin to wander and focus to be lost. Otherwise known as a loss of concentration, it is important for players to identify which unity is being compromised, and therefore sanction measures, such as those highlighted below, to address it.

REMEMBER:

The movement/reaction speed of players and the direction of their attention are two variables that coaches can readily observe to gauge the extent to which players are concentrating.

14.2. GUIDELINES TO IMPROVE CONTROL OF ATTENTION

While the most effective strategy to improve concentration is likely to vary from individual to individual and be situation-specific, some general guidelines that can be followed, include:

— Directing players to attend to specific visual, auditory or kinaesthetic relevant cues such as the sight or sound of the ball, one's own breath, grip tension, contact point…
— Plan matches where players will experience varied auditory and/or visual distractions.
— Programme drills that demand high levels of precision (serves to targets) at the end of sessions when players are fatigued.
— Place coloured targets at specific sites on court when drilling (Zanolli et al., 1990).
— The development or refinement of important life skills such as time-management, communication, responsibility and independence through proper goal-setting may be required to improve a player's concentration. This is particularly applicable to players suffering from personal or other problems that may compromise skilled performance.
— Encourage players to control their attention with the use of a refocussing technique called DAD (Step 1: Distract. Players learn to recognise and then interrupt/cut off distractions as quickly as possible through thought-stopping commands (e.g. stop, shut down, freeze). Step 2: Attend. Players learn to attend to breathing patterns to relax and clear their minds. Step 3: Direct. Once re-gained, players learn to direct their attention to the relevant cues (Prapavessis, 1993).
— Schedule practices where players' sight is directly (eye patch) or indirectly (barrier on court) occluded.
— Use tennis-specific concentration techniques (i.e. meditation) (Burke, 1988).

PRACTICAL APPLICATION:

Anticipation training should include training players to attend cues (body alignment, zone of ball contact, ball path or toss, discrete racquet positions, etc.), learn opponents' tendencies (favourite patterns or technical idiosyncrasies that may predict shot location) and ascertain situational probabilities (percentage tennis and pattern play) (Steinberg et al., 1998).

WHAT RESEARCH TELLS US...
The timing ability of players rests upon a mechanism of a higher order than concentration/attention (Vom Hofe and Fery, 1991). The strategy of focussing on the ball leaving the racquet as compared to focussing on the ball coming towards the player has been shown to facilitate learning (Wulf et al., 2000).

II. Mental training: Techniques and plans

- Off-court exercises such as video observation, grid tests or reaction time protocols can also help improve selected components of concentration.
- Contrary to popular belief, Moran (1996) has shown that psychological strategies such as breath control, progressive muscle relaxation, and biofeedback are effective for arousal control but not for attentional control.

REMEMBER:

Encouraging players to direct their attention to the postural or body language cues of their opponents has been shown to facilitate early anticipation (ability to discriminate task relevant cues and predict shot direction) (Buckolz et al., 1988; Jones and Miles, 1978; Smeeton et al., 2005).

As mentioned in Chapter 5, concentration is closely related to anticipation. How effectively players anticipate or 'determine what opponents will most likely do...or not do next' is governed by players' perceptual skills and experience, their knowledge of opponents' strengths and weaknesses, and their ability to calculate situational probabilities (Steinberg et al., 1998). For example, research has unveiled differences in the visual search strategies of players of different playing levels returning serves (Shim et al., 2005). That is, elite players selectively and preferentially use earlier-occurring and proximal body cues from the server (i.e. racquet arm or the server's head prior to impact) while lesser level players are unable to process such information, and thus have less time to co-ordinate appropriate responses (Luis et al., 2003).

Nevertheless, participation in specific on- and off-court training situations where the perceptual / anticipatory abilities of players are challenged has been shown to improve decision-making (predicting shot locations, e.g. serve), response times, and stroke accuracy among players of all levels (Farrow et al., 1998; Haskins, 1965; Scott et al., 1998; Singer et al., 1994; Williams et al., 2002). Readers are referred to Chapters 18 to 22 for examples of similar training drills.

Cues like the location of the ball toss or rotation of the shoulders in the serve may help players to anticipate serve direction or type.

WHAT RESEARCH TELLS US...
In endeavouring to gather information on the intended direction of an opponent's shot, beginner and intermediate players attend to later-occurring, more visible and distal cues (e.g. racquet movement), whereas advanced players hone in on more proximally located movements (e.g. trunk orientation or hip alignment) (Goulet et al., 1988, 1989; Singer et al., 1996; Ward et al., 2002).

14.3. VISUAL TRAINING

Improving attentional control is also closely related to visual training. Research has shown that visual abilities do affect tennis performance and the acquisition of motor skills as well as being amenable to training. Their development may thus well be important.

Tennis players are subject to high visual demands, and their ability to cope with these demands is likely affected by:

- **Visual attention**: Observation of fast movements that occur in tennis.
- **Peripheral vision**: Awareness of motion outside the visual field.
- **Ocular dominance**: Every person has a dominant eye that processes and transmits information to the brain a few milliseconds faster than the other. As a result, it tends to guide the movement and fixations of the other eye (Kluka, 1991).
- **Eye movements**:
    - Saccadic: For rapid scanning.
    - Vestibulo-ocular: Coordinates the eyes with head motion and assists balance.
    - Vergence: Focusses on objects at various distances.
    - Smooth pursuit: Continuously follows moving objects.
- **Visual Accuracy / Discrimination / Acuity**: The ability to visually discern detail in an object. It can be static or dynamic. The factors that affect it are contrast, lighting, motion, time, colour and age, as well as attentional demands.
- **Contrast sensitivity**: The processing or filtering of spatial and temporal information (pertaining to objects and backgrounds) under varying lighting conditions.
- **Stereopsis**: Perception of three-dimensional depth.
- **Other**: Hand-eye co-ordination, reaction time, focussing speed, and spatial location; also are crucial for successful tennis performance.

When observing the trajectory of a tennis ball or the racquet path in a stroke, coaches and players should remember that it is not typically possible to maintain visual focus on objects that are moving fast and in close proximity. Consequently, players should observe one or two critical features of the movement or trajectory rather than trying to track the entire path or movement. For example, the cue 'watch the ball hit your racquet' could adversely affect performance by encouraging exaggerated head motion and less visual attention earlier in the trajectory of the ball. The cue 'use your eyes to lock onto the ball as it is released' might be more appropriate (Knudson and Kukla, 1997).

REMEMBER:

Cues for ball tracking in catching should emphasise focussing attention to as tight an area as possible, minimal or smooth head motion, and attention to specific characteristics of the ball (seams, spin, etc.). Coloured balls or markings on racquets can be used to highlight or focus player's attention on relevant visual cues in catching.

PRACTICAL APPLICATION:

In planning daily training sessions, visual perceptual skill exercises can be seamlessly integrated into typical training drills to improve visual performance (Buckolz et al., 1988).

WHAT RESEARCH TELLS US...
Research with former Wimbledon champions demonstrated that blurring of the dominant rather than the non-dominant eye resulted in improved accuracy when hitting balls to a target. This indicates that input to the binocular system is essential, and that the non-dominant eye plays a significant role in aiming (Griffiths, 2003).

CHARACTERISTICS OF A MENTAL SKILLS TRAINING PROGRAMME

15.1. CONDUCTED BY WHOM?

It is generally agreed that mental skills training (MST) programmes should be planned by qualified sports psychologists (Weinberg and Gould, 1995). This planning will ensure an educational (mental skill development, etc.) and /or a clinical approach (use of psychopathology and crisis intervention techniques), and involve players' coaches to varying extents. In some instances, practitioners may work with players indirectly through the coach; recognising this to be a more fruitful and effective means to elicit performance improvements.

If circumstances prevent players from having access to a sports psychologist, coaches with some training in sport psychology should be able to map out basic MST programmes. Indeed, some coaches already fill this role, especially on-court where MST needs to be integrated in fashions similar to the training undertaken for technical, tactical and physical development.

To effectively develop mental skills, coaches must possess sufficient 'content' knowledge of MST strategies and considerable 'process' knowledge as to their effective implementation and individualisation (Gould et al., 1999a). Coaches need both content and process knowledge as research suggests that there is a clear contradiction between coaches' perceptions as to the need for MST and their actions (Gould et al., 1999b; Moran, 1995a). That is, coaches believe MST to be of significant value and necessary as highlighted in Table 15.1, yet its practice fails to reflect as much. This paradox is visible in both the coaching of club and professional players where some drills may inadvertently challenge a mental skill, but specific and concerted MST is almost a non-entity.

REMEMBER:

Just like nutritionists and physical trainers - other members of players' support staff - sports psychologists can provide a path…ultimately however it remains the player who determines how diligently it's followed.

PRACTICAL APPLICATION:

In evaluating whether or not coaches' perceptions match their actions, Gould et al. (1999a) recommend that coaches ask themselves the following questions: "Do I feel that MST is important? Do I currently prescribe MST? If not, why not? Do I monitor players' MST needs? Do I think mental skills should be practiced as much as physical and technical skills? Do I care to know more about this area?"

COACHES' PERCEPTIONS	%
Relative importance of mental skills to success in junior tennis	89
Players perceived to have trouble with a mental aspect of their games	80
Players with parents who interfere with a mental aspect of their games	60

Table 15.1 Coaches' perceptions of the importance of mental skills (Gould et al., 1999a, 1999b).

For the many coaches that acknowledge there may be some disparity between what they say / think about MST and what they in fact do, *how can we more effectively introduce MST into tennis?* Well… hopefully the ensuing pages provide coaches some answers, but in the meantime, it is well worth considering how physical training has evolved as there are certain parallels that can be drawn to the current state of MST.

In the first half of last century, tennis was regarded as a battle of technical prowess and tactical nouse. Training reflected as much, predominantly consisting of drills to improve these two qualities (rallies, 2 against 1 drills, playing points, practice matches, etc). Physical training was a virtual after-thought with most players being devotees of a 'we are playing to get fit' philosophy. In time, with the advent of sport science, physical training was proven performance-determining.

WHAT RESEARCH TELLS US…
Gould et al. (1999a, 1999b) found that some of the roadblocks or impedences to mental skills training are: a perceived lack of time; a lack of support and interest from coaches, parents and players; myths and misconceptions about mental skills (e.g. being only for top or 'problem' players); a lack of coaches with knowledge and experience in sport psychology; and a paucity of sport psychologists specialised in tennis.

II. Mental training: Techniques and plans

This triggered the integration of planned conditioning into players' overall programmes. Training contents, largely adapted from other sports, included continuous runs and general gym workouts. More recently, this general approach which saw most exercises performed off-court and guided by conditioning experts from other sports, has evolved into a sophisticated, individualised and highly tennis-specific process that sees some players employ tennis conditioning specialists full-time. Much of the conditioning work has been shifted back on-court with competent coaches playing an increasingly prominent role in leading sessions.

With MST in mind, part of this picture should sound familiar!

15.2. IMPLEMENTATION OF MST: WHEN AND HOW?

REMEMBER:
Planned purposeful practice of mental skills is what makes perfect! (Loehr, 1990; Terry, 1994).

Experts agree that coaches dedicate considerable time to improving the strokes and strategies of players and yet spend little time developing the minds of winners. Coaches consistently miss golden opportunities within on-court sessions to develop mental skills, especially in young players. In fact, most coaches tend to be preoccupied with technical development when technical and mental skill development can go hand in hand if coaches are a little more imaginative (Eraña, 2004).

The means through which players can acquire mental skills are very similar to those they use to hone their other tennis skills. So, just as they rehearse elements of their physical, tactical and technical repertoires virtually every day, so too should they train their mental skills. Some examples of common on- and off-court training strategies that can be used to do just that are provided in Table 15.2.

CONTENT	LOCATION	EXAMPLE
Technical	On-court	Basket, rally with the coach, rally between players drills
	Off-court	Biomechanical observation and analysis (video, computer)
Tactical	On-court	Matchplay situations, patterns drills, practice matches
	Off-court	Video analysis of matches, study of match charting results
Physical	On-court	Footwork, medicine ball exercises, ladder drills, circuits, tennis-specific movement patterns, etc.
	Off-court	Gym workouts, long distance runs, etc.
Mental	On-court	Routines, visualisation, mistake management drills, etc.
	Off-court	Relaxation techniques, goal-setting, planning, etc.

Table 15.2 Examples of on-court and off-court exercises for the different skills needed for tennis play.

As happens with other training mediums, the duration of MST will reflect factors such as the competitive calendar, standard of play, personality characteristics and psychological strengths and weaknesses of the player. However, in applying the universal training principles of specificity, individuality, variety and recovery, there is no reason why MST cannot be practiced daily, for at least 15 minutes.

WHAT RESEARCH TELLS US...
When players engage in individualised, systematic, and developmental mental training programmes their performance improves significantly and specific performance problems are reduced (Surburg, 1968; McAleney et al., 1991; Davis, 1991, 1992; DeFrancesco and Burke, 1997; Daw and Burton, 1994; Mamassis and Doganis, 2004).

15.3. HOW TO DO IT? THE IMPORTANCE OF PLANNING TRAINING

In beginning to address the lack of well-developed daily mental skills practice, coaches should understand how players think and respond under pressure. This msut be a priority so as to assist players maintain their ideal performance states at all times (Young, 2000). From here, the drills that comprise MST and that can lead to performance enhancement are generally simple to learn and easy to incorporate into daily training. The challenge for coaches lies in matching each player's needs to appropriate drills or training situations (Butler and Hardy, 1999). Adapted from Gould et al. (1999a), Figure 15.1 proposes a framework of the different ingredients that interact with one another to shape MST.

REMEMBER:

Gould et al. (1999a) reported that coaches spend an average of 66.8 minutes on MST per week: a very small percentage of total training time. A simple way in which coaches can immediately increase their MST emphasis is by providing players with constant 'mental reminders' (e.g. talking positively, projecting good body image, visualising good shots, etc) during practice sessions (Harwood, 2000; Lubbers, 2001).

A	COACH'S GENERAL ORIENTATION/RECEPTIVITY TOWARD MENTAL SKILLS TRAINING		B	PLAYER'S MENTAL SKILL NEEDS	
	- Formal education in sport psychology - Informal experience - Reflection on importance of mental skills for tennis - Desire to help players improve mental skills			Session plan / goals / injuries? Ability of the coach to recognise the player's needs (e.g.): - Increase self-confidence - Arousal regulation. - Improve sportsmanship - Other	
C	MENTAL SKILLS TRAINING CLIMATE				
	Player attributes	Coach-player relationship		Outside factors/obstacles	
	- Gender - Skills - Culture	- Awareness/ability to read players - Communication skills - Trust		- Parental views of mental skills - Time constraints	
D	COACH MENTAL SKILLS TRAINING KNOWLEDGE				
	Content			Process	
E	MENTAL SKILLS TRAINING PROGRAMME				
	Exercises	Drills		Activities	Feedback
F	PLAYER MENTAL SKILLS DEVELOPMENT				

Figure 15.1 Framework for coaching mental skills in tennis (adapted from Gould et al., 1999a; 1999b).

Here, integrated training can provide coaches with a user-friendly, effective and time-efficient means of incorporating MST into their players' training programmes. Introduced briefly in point 15.1, this type of training has been used by coaches — unknowingly — for decades, and is a crucial link between practice and actual game play (Higger, 2002). By integrating or combining training goals (e.g. physical - technical, mental - tactical), players are exposed to game-like situations and challenged to become more aware of the relationships between the game's different skills. Using the game situation of the serve as an example, Table 15.3 illustrates how easy it is to arrive at different technical, tactical, physical and mental training objectives within this broader theme. Table 15.4 goes one step further and highlights how these objectives could be integrated into a training session on the serve.

PRACTICAL APPLICATION:

Mental skills cannot be treated casually or turned on and off at will. They need to be integrated and practiced regularly, both on and off-court, just like technique, tactics, and physical skills (Lubbers, 2001).

GAME SITUATION / TRAINING GOAL	SERVE
TECHNICAL WORK	Enhance coordination between the lower and upper bodies
PHYSICAL WORK	Improve lower body power (to assist leg drive)
TACTICAL WORK	Work on consistency of the first serve
MENTAL WORK	Focus on a specific cue (e.g. knee bend) (concentration) Expect to serve a great first serve (positive thinking)

Table 15.3 Examples of integrated training goals for the serve.

I. Mental training: Techniques and plans

GAME SITUATION / TRAINING GOAL		SERVE
TIME	CONTENTS	DRILLS
9.00 - 9.05	Introduction	Session plan / goals / injuries?
9.05 - 9.15	General Warm-up	**Physical:** Dynamic warm-up exercises for the whole body. **Technical:** Rally starting with mini-tennis gradually moving back. **Mental:** Focus on feeling positive and exhibiting high energy levels.
9.15 - 9.30	Specific Serve Warm-up and Assessment	**Physical:** Specific dynamic warm-up exercises for the serve (e.g. swing throughs, ball throws, tuck jumps, …) **Technical:** Gradually build serve speed, and hit a set number of first serves in. **Tactical:** Direct first serves to both service boxes depending on the position of the receiver. **Mental:** Focus on smoothness of movement. **Video assessment:** Evaluate serve motion and associated performance criteria through video analysis.
9.30-10.00	Physical / Technical work	Lower-, upper- and whole-body plyometric drills that simulate entire serve movement or its components. Serving drills that incorporate training aids to encourage more leg drive (resistance bands, …) and linking upper and lower body motion (hitting smashes,…).
10.00-10.05	Rest	Hydrate, re-fuel and review performance.
10.05-10.35	Mental / Tactical work	Serving drills to targets - while setting goals and using self-talk. - counting the number of targets hits or consecutive serves in.
10.35-10.50	Game play	Serving competitions against one-self or against others.
10.50-11.00	Cool down / Closing	Fun drill. Cool down exercises. Session close, review and debrief.

Table 15.4 Contents for a specific, two hour integrated training session with competitive players.

REMEMBER:

The development and maintenance of a love for the game can transcend all levels of tennis and perhaps stands out as one of the most important ingredients of success. A player's love of tennis must be consistently nurtured within the framework of mental training (Bloom, 1985; Gibbons, 1998; Saviano, 1999).

Rather than reverting to very general verbal instruction or feedback (e.g. 'Watch the ball!' or 'Come on, control your temper!', or 'Just relax!') in the faint hope that players will improve, coaches need to begin to integrate MST more comprehensively into training sessions and develop their own means of practically, systematically evaluating and improving mental skills (Dorsky, 1996; Lubbers, 2001, 2003). Continuing to rely on former modes of instruction would be privy to coaches telling players to 'Hit their backhands with more topspin!', 'Make your opponents move!' or 'Serve with more power!' without practicing the topspin backhand, consolidating patterns of play or performing any form of plyometric exercise for the serve!

Mental skills specific to the serve, such as positive thinking, can be emphasised and developed in typical training drills with relative ease.

Tennis Psychology

GUIDELINES TO INTEGRATE MST INTO PLAYER TRAINING

The following guidelines will likely assist coaches achieve the aforementioned objective of better assimilating MST into player training (Bloom, 1985; Gibbons, 1998; Harwood, 2000; Jaenes, 2001; Lubbers, 2001; Saviano, 1999; Taylor, 1996; Terry, 1994):

Needs analysis / background information

— Know yourself as a coach and your players as people. This provides a starting point for both coach and player in the quest to learn, develop and strive for excellence.
— Understand the mental challenges of tennis, and the factors that are likely to shape MST (e.g. coaching philosophy, player's personality and competitive experience, training plan,...).
— With appropriate player input (player needs), develop a psychological profile of your players and identify behaviours/skills in need of improvement.
— Recognise the need to improve a certain psychological skill and identify the behaviour needed to do so.

Goal-setting

— According to the player's profile, set goals to create player ownership and independence, while simultaneously motivating players to achieve.

Practice / implementation

— The goals should help guide both training and competition planning. Schedule purposeful mental skills practices daily as well as group practices several times per week so players understand the link between quality training (with intention and purpose) and peak performance.
— Practice the needed behaviours.
— Foster a love for the game in your players.
— Integrate a mental component into the warm-up, where players spend time relaxing, re-focussing and energising.
— Do not discount the potential value in direct intervention on behalf of a sport psychologist.
— Simulate matchplay situations in which players are expected to win. Put players 'on the line' to help them adapt and better respond to the stresses of competing.
— Teach body awareness (e.g. level of muscular tension and relaxation) and its relationships to performance (e.g. skill errors...).
— Promote self-awareness whereby players learn to evaluate how they think about their tennis and begin to entertain only constructive and focussed thoughts.
— If required, schedule individual counselling sessions to prevent potential or recurring problems.
— Progress the practice of mental skills from training or simulated game scenarios, to actual competitive matchplay (Figure 15.2).

General mental skill development	Tennis specific mental skill development	Individualised performance routines
Introduce / Explain Learned or achieved in a neutral setting	Trained through practice	Use before, during and after matches Maintained throughout the season Constant evaluation of mental skills

Figure 15.2 Progressive steps in a mental skills training plan (adapted from Duda, 2001a).

Evaluation and feedback

PRACTICAL APPLICATION:
Computerised or video-driven mental skills training programmes can complement more traditional mental training practices (Heller, 2001; Martens-Scholz, 2003; Taylor, 1996).

— Effectiveness of mental training is evaluated using objective data (e.g. performance tests / measures of competence) and competition results as well as player, coach and psychologist reports.
— Seek player input regarding their mental performance.
— Fine-tune or amend the programme regularly (new player profile / goals) to elicit maximum performance improvements.

15.4. THE WAY FORWARD

REMEMBER:
Players aspiring to high performance tennis need to become competent mental competitors. To do so, the onus is on coaches to assist these players learn and foster the mental skills required to meet the psychological demands of the game.

With communication of the benefits and design of MST improving through more applied sports psychology research, individualised, systematic, and specific MST plans are gradually becoming the player development norm. Indeed, they should cover all mental aspects of performance, and be developed progressively; as with the plans created for the refinement of the game's other skills.

PHASES OF A MENTAL SKILLS TRAINING PROGRAMME 16

This chapter introduces the phases of a periodised MST programme (Figure 16.1). It then elaborates on what comprises each phase and what players and coaches can expect to realise as part of the entire process.

In an effort to blend the empirical work of sports psychologists with the findings of related research, Balaguer (1998) proposed that mental training could be grouped into four phases: assessment and goal-setting, training, application and evaluation. These phases, in turn, can correspond to specific phases of a player's periodised annual plan. In paralleling the model of technical analysis (preparation - evaluation - analysis - intervention - re-evaluation) proposed by Knudson and Morrison (2002), this phasic form of MST would also be on-going.

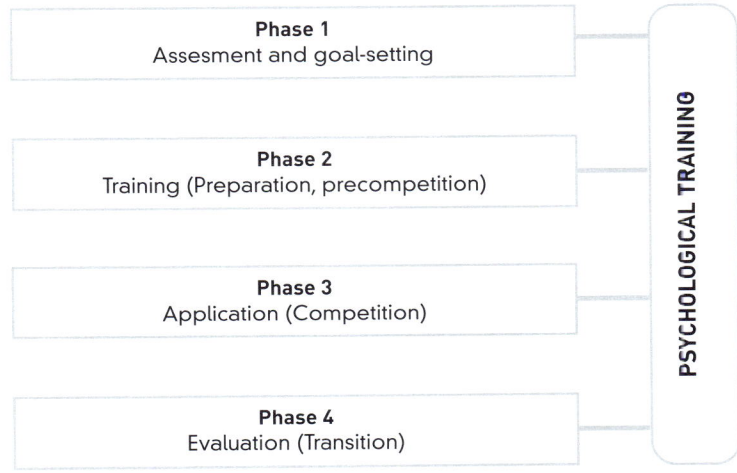

Figure 16.1
Phases of a mental skills training plan (adapted from Balaguer, 1998).

As part of her Mental Skills Training programme, Anatasia Myskina would assess (phase 1), train (phase 2), apply (phase 3) and then re-evaluate (phase 4) her mental skills set.

II. Mental training: Techniques and plans

The objectives of mental training are likely to vary in terms of content and priority according to the phase of the player's periodised training and competition plan. For example, Table 16.1 highlights common goals that relate to overall player performance as well as more specific mental training objectives during the different phases of a periodised training and competition plan.

PERIOD/PHASE	GENERAL OBJECTIVES	MENTAL TRAINING OBJECTIVES
GENERAL PREPARATION	Develop basic technical skills and general fitness.	- Evaluate and assess mental skills (psychological profile). - Learn basic mental skills in quiet, controlled setting. - Develop satisfactory learning and training (motivational) environment.
SPECIFIC PREPARATION	Perfect technique and basic tactics, develop tennis-specific fitness.	- Adapt and refine mental skills in practice situations. - Use mental skills to help attain training objectives.
PRE-COMPETITIVE	Make training competition specific. Raise intensity.	- Develop and practice a pre-competition plan. - Consolidate basic mental skills.
TAPERING	Regenerate in preparation for main competition.	- Use mental skills to aid regeneration and reduce stress.
COMPETITIVE	Maximise competitive performance.	- Evaluate and refine the pre-competition plan. - Mentally prepare for specific opponents and competitions. - Use mental skills for stress management.
TRANSITION	Get active rest. Maintain training gains.	- Perform recreational activities to prevent mental staleness and maintain fitness. - Evaluate the mental skills training programme.

Table 16.1 The general performance and more specific mental training objectives common to the different phases of periodised training and competition plans.

16.1. PHASE 1 - ASSESSMENT AND GOAL-SETTING

The nuances of each player's development dictate that coaches must individualise MST programmes. Much like when formulating the physical, technical or tactical progression of players, doing this requires that a player's mental skill set (e.g. strengths and weaknesses) first be assessed (Lubbers, 2001).

REMEMBER:
Players need to be made aware that the assessment of psychological skills can help to direct training to areas of specific need. The information gained about the players must remain strictly confidential.

The analysis and evaluation of a player's mental skills helps to determine perceived strengths and weaknesses, identify long-term goals, design training plans, maximise player motivation and adherence to the training plan, clarify the player's and coach's vision (and highlight any differences) of the key determinants of elite performance, establish areas where players might resist change, monitor any changes (progress) over time, and build better coach-player communication. Coaches should stress that there are no right or wrong answers involved in the process but that honest appraisal will facilitate more productive outcomes.

ASSESSMENTS

So, while technical, tactical and physical performance can be directly observed, how can coaches assess the mental side of a player's game when they cannot readily observe what is going on in that player's mind?

Phase 1 of a MST programme should encompass a general assessment of the game and the player, as well as another more specific player assessment. Both forms of general assessment can be achieved through the selective use of questionnaires or inventories (see Table 16.2), interviews, game observation, match statistics and player performance profiles. The specific assessment should comprise of behavioural observation of players in training and competition, charting of 'psychological momentum' and specific psychological skills questionnaires and interviews to allow coaches an insight into player commitment and disposition, family dynamics, attitude to study, relationships with significant others, and the presence of any external pressures.

Some of the most commonly used specific-psychological skills questionnaires are highlighted below, while the appendix contains examples of mental skills' interviews and a basic psychological momentum charting tool that coaches can use with their players.

INVENTORY	PSYCHOLOGICAL SKILLS MEASURED	COMMENTS
Psychological Performance Inventory. Loehr (1986)	- Self-confidence, negative energy, attention control, visual and imagery control, motivational level, positive energy, and attitude control.	- For players. Used in applied settings. - Poorly researched, not widely used.
Psychological Skills Inventory for Sport. Mahoney et al. (1987)	- Anxiety, control, concentration, confidence, mental preparation, motivation and team emphasis.	- Most popular tool for assessment. - Characterised by some statistical limitations.
Athletic Copying Skills Inventory. Smith et al. (1995)	- Coping with adversity, peaking under pressure, goal-setting/mental preparation, concentration, freedom of worry, confidence and achievement motivation, and coachability.	- Stronger psychometric background. - Does not include certain mental skills and techniques (i.e. visualisation, self-talk, relaxation).
Test of Performance Strategies. Thomas et al. (1999).	- In competition/training: Self-talk, emotional control, automacy, goal-setting, imagery, activation, and relaxation. - In competiton: Negative thinking. - In training: Attentional control.	- Well suited to assess psychological skills training. - More research required to validate this tool within different populations.
Performance Assessment for Tennis. Rees et al. (2000)	- Loss of composure, feeling flat, determination, worry, and flow.	- Discriminates between winners and losers. - Does not cover only psychological skills.

Table 16.2
General psychological skills inventories.

— **Self-confidence:** Sport Confidence State (SSCI) and Trait (TSCI) (Vealey, 1986).
— **Self-efficacy:** Self-efficacy (Bandura, 1977).
— **Motivation (goal-setting / goal perspective) and motivational climate:** TEOSQ (Duda and Nicholls, 1989), PMCSQ-2 (Walling et al., 1993).
— **Anxiety:** CSAI-2 (Martens et al., 1990), STAI (Spielberger, 1966).
— **Attention:** Test of Attentional and Interpersonal Style (TAIS, Nideffer, 1976), Tennis Test of Attentional and Interpersonal Style (Van Schoyck and Grasha, 1981).
— **Mood States:** Profile of Mood States (POMS; McNair et al., 1971).

PERFORMANCE PROFILING

Performance profiling is one of the most thorough means of assessing players' psychological skills as well as their technical, tactical, and physical competence (Butler and Hardy, 1992). From a MST perspective, an example of the step-by-step process that should be followed in implementing performance profiling is highlighted below.

— **Step 1:** With players who understand the importance of MST or after introducing its significance to those that do not, the coach can present players with the following question: 'In your opinion what are the key mental qualities of world class tennis players?'
— **Step 2:** Players can take 5-10 minutes to list the qualities they feel to be important. In a typical session, 15-20 key psychological factors are identified.

REMEMBER:

Coaches and tennis psychologists should observe both practice and matches to gain a comprehensive insight into the mental performances of players. This is often referred to as practice/match psychological charting.

— **Step 3:** Upon completing the list, players then evaluate the importance, from 0 (not at all important) to 10 (extremely important), of these factors for a world class tennis player (I).

— **Step 4:** Next, players use the same 0-10 scale to self-rate themselves (Subject Self-Assessment or SSA) in relation to an ideal state of 10 (Ideal Self-Assessment or ISA). A simple calculation is then carried out, taking into account both the importance ascribed to the construct and the subject's self-assessment in relation to the ideal. This is known as the 'discrepancy score'. Higher discrepancies indicate areas that may need to be addressed through training or other intervention. Table 16.3 provides a hypothetical example of the calculation of discrepancy scores for part of a tennis player's profile (Butler and Hardy, 1992).

— **Step 5:** Once completed, the results in their tabulated, easy-to-read form facilitate the ease with which they are processed therefore streamlining the dialogue between coach and player. For example, the player profiled in Table 16.3 would appear to need to work on becoming more confident on court. Consequently, discussion could take place regarding the selection of appropriate interventions such as self-talk or a routine that appropriately would suit the player's personality and game.

SKILL	IDEAL (I)	IDEAL SELF ASSESSMENT (ISA)	SUBJECT SELF ASSESSMENT (SSA)	(ISSA-SSA)	DISCREPANCY = (ISSA-SSA) X (I)
Motivation	8	10	7	3	24
Emotional control	9	10	8	2	18
Self-confidence	10	10	6	4	40
Concentration	10	10	9	1	10
Commitment	9	10	8	2	18

Table 16.3 An example of a player's performance profile.

Player involvement is key to the effectiveness of any assessment procedure. Where some assessments may require psychologists to make evaluations independent of player input, for the most part, we encourage players to be actively involved in the decision-making processes (Butler and Hardy, 1992). With vision /goals agreed, player adherence to the MST is also likely to improve.

To complement the player-led performance profile, coaches may nonetheless wish to carry out their own assessment of players to ascertain the congruity of their perceptions and those of their players. Alternatively, players can compare their current status in relation to the agreed constructs with a previous best standard rather than an ideal. If the performer has regressed as a result of an injury, this may provide more realistic and motivating short-term feedback.

Rather than relying on verbal feedback or instruction to communicate and then discuss the results with players, most coaches and psychologists prefer to present the information visually. This tends to be more practical and easily understood by players. Figures 16.2-16.4 reveal three ways in which practitioners commonly portray information gleaned from psychological assessments. The first graphic illustrates some incongruity between coach and player appraisal of the player's mental skills. In such circumstances, video analysis of the player's performance both during practices and matches can be a good way to resolve differences and produce agreement on how to proceed. Figures 16.3 and 16.4 show how different targets can become easy-to-interpret mental profiling tools (where 10 = Excellent and 0 = Poor).

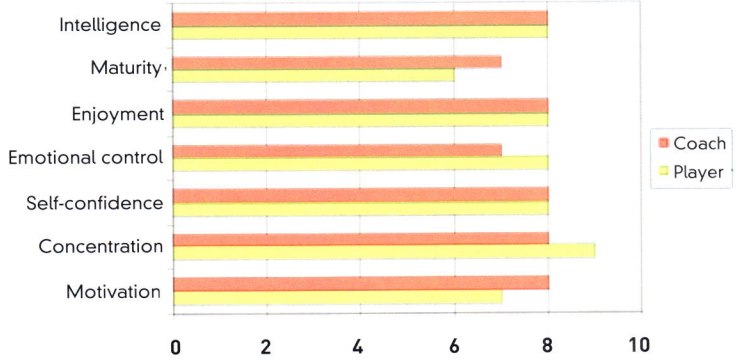

Figure 16.2 Coach and player assessments of the player's mental skills.

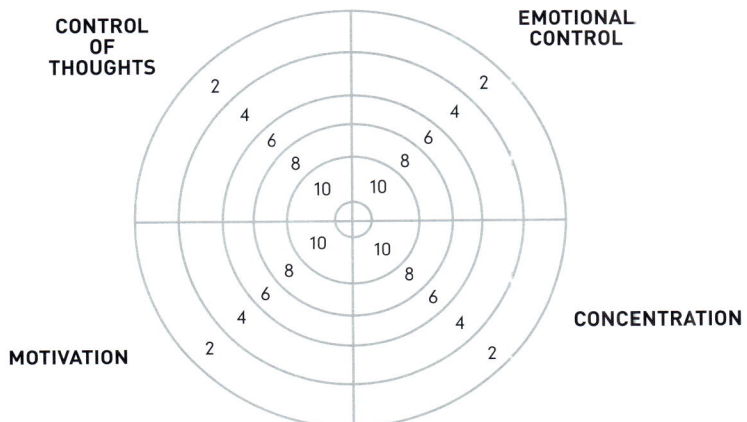

Figure 16.3 A target designed to assess a player's general mental performance.

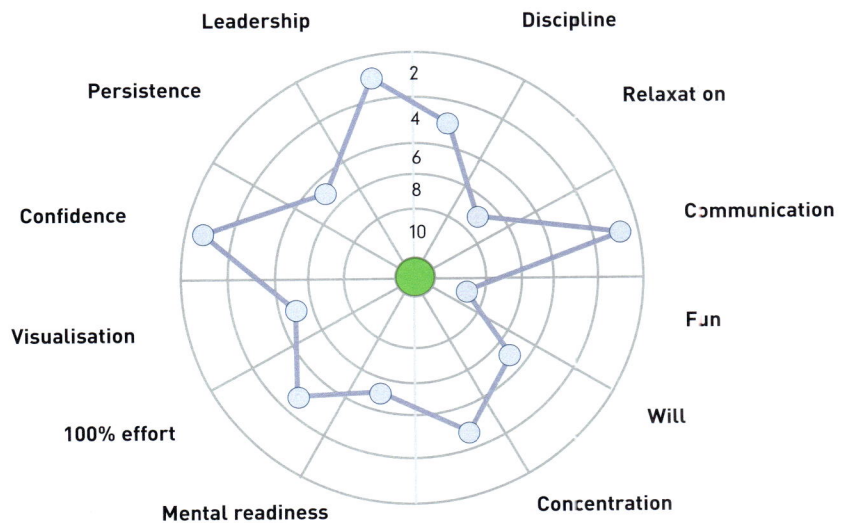

REMEMBER:

As result of the integrated nature of performance, coaches should take great care when evaluating players' mental capacities and planning interventions (Lubbers, 2001). That is, emotional problems during matchplay can just as readily be caused by physical deficiencies as mental ones (Loehr, 2001). For example, a lack of physical recovery in the form of sleep, rest, poor nutrition or hydration can completely derail a player's ability to summon the right emotions at the right time. So too, can poor fitness undermine both mental focus and biomechanical efficiency.

Figure 16.4. Target-based assessment of a player's specific mental performance.

II. Mental training: Techniques and plans

16.2. PHASE 2 - TRAINING: PREPARATION AND PRE-COMPETITION

GOAL-SETTING

Having completed the players' psychological assessments and identified their 'mental' strengths and weaknesses, it's time to set goals. Using the procedures outlined in Chapter 7, specific individual goals need to be formulated. If the players train in a group environment, the coach is well-advised to also set some common group goals so that sessions can be tailored to suit group as well as individual MST needs (see Table 16.4).

WHOLE GROUP	SMALL GROUP	INDIVIDUAL PLAYER
Learning of basic psychological techniques (on- and off-court) - Relaxation - Concentration - Visualisation, etc.	Routines between points (on-court) - Physical response - Relaxation - Preparation - Rituals	Specific mental skill development (on- and off-court) - Concentration - Self-confidence - Relaxation - Positive attitude

Table 16.4 Differentiation of group and individual mental training goals within a group lesson (adapted from Balaguer, 1998).

FREQUENCY OF MENTAL SKILLS ASSESSMENT

The mental skills assessment can also be used to monitor progress, and pending the selection of effective training interventions, discrepancy scores should reduce over time. Reassessment should take place every few months and relate to the same constructs identified in the initial profiling process. If clear progress is observed, this can be a strong motivating force, while if it is not, indications are that training may need to be altered.

PREPARATION PHASE

PRACTICAL APPLICATION:

The preparatory training phase is an excellent time to introduce different mental training initiatives. For example, yoga - perhaps more revered for its physical benefits in tennis circles - can facilitate a player's ability to relax, focus and use breath to manage stress (Singh, 2003). Indeed, professional players such as Maria Sharapova are proponents of the spiritual and psychological benefits of yoga (Australian Tennis, 2005).

During the preparation phase of the training plan, the main goal of MST is to 'lay the foundation' of basic mental skills (motivation, concentration, emotional control, self-confidence, etc.) that will be needed throughout the year, season or cycle.

Once the goals of the MST have been identified in Phase 1 (based on the evaluation and assessment of mental skills and the psychological profile of the player), the onus is on the coach to ensure training environments are motivating and conducive to learning. Providing players with the necessary templates (e.g. drills, matchplay situations,...) through which these goals can be achieved is also expected of the coach.

As with the physical, tactical and technical training performed in this phase, MST will be characterised by high repetition and be demanding and motivating. On-court psychological drills can be performed both during specific parts of training sessions or be combined with other training goals in the shape of integrated training drills. Off-court psychological work should also represent a portion of daily training programmes and be specific to individual player's goals.

Recommendations are that this phase of psychological training last for at least 2 months, with three to five specific mental-skill sessions of 15 to 30 minutes performed each week (Balaguer, 1998).

PRE-COMPETITION PHASE

During the pre-competitive phase of training, the main goal of MST is to develop increasingly specific pre-competition plans and match routines.

The function of pre-competition plans is to best prepare players to compete. Indeed, many players will already employ basic pre-competition plans prior to reaching this phase. However, they are unlikely to be sufficiently individualised to maintain their IPS and should be reviewed by player and coach. In doing so, factors that player and coach should see feature in the pre-competition plans are outlined in bullet point form below, while Tables 16.5 and 16.6 provide some guidelines to assist players establish a key part of any individualised pre-competition plan: preparatory routines.

— Familiarisation with or knowledge of the opponent and environment.
— Recognition of the situations that trigger stressful mental and / or physical responses pre-match.
— Coping mechanisms to optimise arousal levels.
— Appropriate for use during time between matches.
— Depending on the individual, they may encompass strategies to optimise sleep, breakfast, equipment preparation, travel to the competition site, physical and technical warm-up, tactical review of the match plan, psychological warm-up, etc.

REMEMBER:

Developing group atmosphere, team harmony, and using an effective communication style with the players (fostering a positive motivational climate) will help to overcome the mental and physical stress of the hard but challenging and motivating work performed during the preparation and pre-competition phases.

PREPARATION THE NIGHT BEFORE	PREPARATION ON THE DAY (MORNING)
- Ensure racquets and clothes are ready. - Re-hydrate and eat a well-balanced meal, high in carbohydrate. - Confirm travel to competition site. - Allow time for visualisation. - Plan a good night's sleep; going to sleep at a regular time may help.	- Set a specific time to eat a winning pre-match meal. - Conduct a warm-up routine and some light stretching. - Visualise how you want to compete and complete an on-court warm-up. - Understand that players with preparation routines enter the court with a slight edge, enhancing one's confidence and performance.

Table 16.5
Guidelines for routines the night before and on match day.

ROUTINES ON ARRIVAL	IN THE LEAD UP TO MATCH TIME
- Arrive at the club in enough, but not too much time. - Familiarise yourself with the court (and conditions). - Relax (e.g. listen to music).	- Whatever gives you that winning feeling, do it! Take your time and go onto court to have fun, knowing you have done all the hard work. - Individualise time spent relaxing (e.g. listening to music), reviewing your game plan, and nutritionally (eat and drink to win), physically (light activity to get the feet moving), and psychologically (quiet time) preparing. - Be prepared to perform this routine more than once in the event of uncertain start times. - Dress to win. Wear what makes you feel great.

Table 16.6
Guidelines for routines on arrival and in the lead up to match time.

Once player and coach have agreed upon an individualised pre-competition plan, like any other skill, it needs to be practiced. Here, specificity is important. The coach needs to be able to set up practice matches and point play situations that 'stir' the emotions that players are likely to experience prior to a tournament match.

16.3. PHASE 3 - APPLICATION: COMPETITION PHASE

REMEMBER:
In the lead up to a tournament or competition it may be necessary to acclimatise. This may mean travelling to a hot climate to prepare or training under different conditions to better prepare. For example, several top Australian players have been noted to perform 'hot yoga' in 38°C heat prior to competing. The mental benefits of this far outway the physiological benefits.

The competition phase should see MST consolidate individualised, between point and between game routines (thoughts, feelings and behaviours) such that IPSs are more readily achieved. As alluded to in Chapter 12, the 16 second cure by Loehr (1988) and the 3 R system by Slaikeu and Trogolo (1998) are among the most common strategies used to optimise 'down-time' between points. Readers should refer to Chapters 17 to 22 for examples of on-court drills that can be used to hone players' use of matchplay routines.

Mental skills training (e.g. visualisation) should continue throughout this period. This is not to say that the sudden introduction or learning of new mental skills is desirable: it is not and should, where possible, be avoided. Coaches and players should however, set aside time within daily and / or weekly schedules to fine-tune the mental skills that have been developed throughout the preceding preparatory and pre-competition phases.

16.4. PHASE 4 - EVALUATION AND FEEDBACK: TRANSITION PHASE

REMEMBER:
Continuous evaluation of MST is necessary to optimise its effectiveness. Player feedback should be encouraged, and if revisions are required they should be integrated seamlessly.

Following the rigours of the competitive season, the transition phase provides players the opportunity to 'switch off' and mentally 'recharge their batteries'. Rest, fun, time away from the sport and cross training are commonly used strategies to help players re-establish mental and physical equilibrium. When appropriate, this period can also be used by coaches and players to reflect on the success of the MST conducted in the recently completed season, and therefore begin to identify areas of improvement for future campaigns.

At the end of the tennis year, players can look forward to reflecting on their performances and begin to plan for future success.

PART III.
ON- AND OFF-COURT PSYCHOLOGICAL DRILLS AND ACTIVITIES

"I used to throw my racquet like you can't probably imagine. It was like helicopters flying all over. I was getting kicked out of practice at age sixteen non-stop. Now I have learned to relax on the court." *Roger Federer*

GETTING STARTED 17

Inadvertently whether coaches recognise it or not, players will be required to access their psychological skills as part of their technical, tactical and physical work. It follows that while most coaches have little trouble prescribing specific technical, tactical or physical drills, it is rare to see coaches utilising on-court drills specifically designed to improve the psychological skills of their players. Consequently, the purpose of Part III is to provide examples of on-court drills that can assist coaches do precisely that.

All tennis drills need to have goals. In fact, they may have a primary goal as well as additional or related secondary goals. These goals should relate to drill contents (technical, tactical, physical or psychological) and consider at which stage of the learning process players find themselves (e.g. learning - something new for the player, stabilisation - grooving the skill, and improvement - correcting the skill). Coaches also need to be cognisant of the fact that drill emphasis (technical, tactical, physical or psychological), and therefore goals, can shift quite significantly by altering just one element of a drill. An appreciation of this is key to the design of MST that actually trains mental skills!

17.1. PSYCHOLOGY OF THE FIVE GAME SITUATIONS

The on-court development of mental skills can be achieved per mental skill, or per game situation (i.e. serve, return of serve, baseline game, approaching and playing at the net, and passing the net player). We have decided to adopt the latter approach in the belief that it better reflects the integrated demands the game as well as providing coaches with more familiar templates for on-court work with high performance players.

Planning MST in this fashion requires that coaches understand the mental intricacies of and psychological skills needed for each game situation (Table 17.1).

REMEMBER:

The basis of drilling is the correct repetition of strokes (technique), movements (physical condition), patterns (tactics)...or behaviours (psychology) such that optimal responses become automated during match play.

Players like David Ferrer specifically train the mental skills needed to compete successfully at the net.

REMEMBER:

The tactical performance of players can give the coach valuable information not only on the technical and physical strengths and weaknesses of the player but also on the mental skills they need to apply and improve in the different game situations (Sledr, 1996).

MENTAL SKILLS AND TECHNIQUES MOST NEEDED	GAME SITUATION		
	SERVE	RETURN	BASELINE GAME, APPROACHING, PLAYING THE NET AND AGAINST THE NET PLAYER
Goal-setting (planning what to do)	First serve in, wide, body, T serve, serve and use best shot, serve and volley, etc.	Play the serve back, make the server volley, return to the weak side, attack the return, etc.	Attack, keep the ball in, play deep, open the court, play to the centre, etc.
Concentration (focussing on the task)	Bouncing the ball, centering vision on the target, etc.	Watching for cues or information from the server that might indicate serve direction and/or type.	Changing the focus from the opponent hitting or moving, to ball flight, and to the player hitting the ball.
Emotional control (remaining calm and alert)	Breathing; relaxing or activating through physical adjustments.	As for serve.	Breathing.
Control of thoughts, self-confidence, and/or positive thinking (maintaining control, confidence and positivity)	Self-talk: 'Go for it!'	Self-talk: 'Be aggressive!'	Self-talk: 'Work the point!!'
Anticipation (determining an opponent's intention)	Depending on variables such as serve direction and an opponent's court position anticipate the type of return.	Cue detection of the opponent that may indicate serve direction and/or type.	A product of the point situation and tactical tendencies or technical limitations of the opponent.
Visualisation (foresee shot intention)	Serve type and placement, and subsequent movement.	The speed and location of the response.	See/visualise the shots you want to play and then their placement.

Table 17.1 Psychological skills most needed in the 5 game situations.

Once established, and the players' psychological strengths and weaknesses identified, the design of realistic drills similar to those presented in the chapters to follow becomes second nature.

Table 17.2 is included to provide an overall vision of the best way to improve the different psychological skills.

PRACTICAL APPLICATION:

Correct and purposeful practice makes perfect. Drills are the basic elements that define the structure of all tennis practices. Mental training drills on-court are a must if psychological skills are to be improved. Coaches can decide how they can work these skills: Within each game situation (serve and return, baseline game, approaching and net game, and passing the net player) or per mental skill (motivation, concentration, emotional control, self-confidence). Each skill has some techniques or strategies that best develop these attributes (Table 17.2).

PSYCHOLOGICAL SKILL	BEST WAY TO IMPROVE
Motivation	Motivation can be improved through goal-setting and training diaries, fun and optimal challenge drills or drills that demand 100% effort from the player, creating the adequate motivational climate with varied and enjoyable practices, ensuring that players win more matches than they loose, setting competitive drills against other players or against themselves, etc.
Emotional control	Emotional control can be developed using activation or relaxation techniques (breathing control, bio-feedback, music, yoga, meditation, centering, PMR, autogenic training, humour, etc.), visualisation, behaviour modification techniques (stress inoculation, systematic desensitisation, cognitive restructuring), and routines.
Concentration	Concentration may be improved through focussing drills using visual cues (targets, coloured balls) or auditory distractions (music, noise, etc.), consistency and endurance drills, routines before and after the point and during change overs, goal-setting, visualisation, etc.
Self-confidence	There are numerous ways to increase self-confidence: Using self-talk, self-evaluation, powerful verbal and non-verbal communication, drills in which the strengths of the player are worked on, providing positive and realistic feedback, setting competition drills against other players or themselves, cognitive strategies (thought stopping, positive thinking, problem solving, cognitive restructuring, mistake management, assertive training, role modelling / playing, time management, rationalisation, etc.).

Table 17.2 Best way to improve different psychological skills.

Tennis Psychology

17.2. PSYCHOLOGY OF GAMESTYLES

Throughout this process it is also beneficial for coaches to be mindful of the obvious relationship between psychology and game styles. On the one hand, court surface aside, the gamestyles adopted by players influences the psychological demands of competition, and therefore the mental skills that need to be trained. On the other hand, players are typically considered to define the 'way they play' based on their physical, technical, tactical... and mental characteristics. Indeed, most coaches, players and sport psychologists agree that personality plays a large role in defining game styles.

In general, the mental challenges presented to players using the three most common game styles include:

— **Aggressive baseliner:** With sufficient time (relative to other playing styles) for stroke production, concentration lapses or 'paralysis by analysis' may proliferate. More decisions (by virtue of the fact thay they are likely to hit more shots) may need to be made, and mental 'endurance' is a must.

— **Serve and volleyer:** Reduced time for stroke production can exaggerate motivational and emotional responses to affect concentration and decision-making.

— **All court players** are challenged psychologically by a combination of the above as well as by the need to remain focussed and motivated when competing, so as to avoid boredom and lapses in concentration.

> **PRACTICAL APPLICATION:**
>
> There are techniques or strategies such as goal-setting, visualisation, breathing, NLP, etc., that can be used for more than one mental skill. The individual characteristics of the player and the specific goal of each drill will determine which strategy is most appropriate.

17.3. PSYCHOLOGICAL WARM-UP

WARMING-UP MENTALLY!

There are many benefits to physically warming-up before a match. Indeed, research has quantified some of the physical advantages thought to be realised through conducting appropriate, dynamic activity pre-performance (Kokkonen et al., 1998). Empirical reports also proliferate to document the associated, positive psychological benefits of physical warm-ups. Few concerted attempts however, are made by players to follow specific, psychological warm-ups on- or off-court.

While the routines outlined in Chapter 12 may combine to represent the mental warm-ups to be performed off-court, additional emphasis must be placed on ensuring the integration of specific mental preparatory techniques on-court. A relatively simple process; it can even be achieved by shifting emphasis to the psychological skills inherent in the activities already performed in technical or physical warm-ups (see Tables 17.3 and 17.4; Castellani, 2001, Girod, 2005; Samulski, 2004). Although coaches may have to initially direct players to attend to specific psychological skills at various stages of the warm-up, players will in time, individualise their approach.

Table 17.3
An example of a combined physical and mental on-court warm-up.

PHYSICAL WARM-UP	MENTAL WARM-UP
Gentle jogging	Motivation: Happy to run, ready for action.
Mobility drills	Emotional control: Breathing, etc.
Dynamic stretching	Focussing: Awareness of body response and environmental conditions.
Final activity	Control of thoughts: Being positive.

Table 17.4
An example of a combined technical and mental on-court warm-up.

TECHNICAL WARM-UP	MENTAL WARM-UP
Mini-tennis.	Motivation: Having success.
Gentle hitting from the baseline.	Emotional control: Relaxing the muscles, etc.
Using the whole court.	Focussing: Concentration on impact point.
Playing some points.	Control of thoughts: Use of rituals and routines.

SERVE AND RETURN OF SERVE — 18

18.1. MOTIVATION THROUGH GOAL-SETTING

1. SET THE SCENE

Before commencing the point, Player A tells the coach where he is going to direct his serve. Player B, the receiver, informs the coach where he is going to return the serve.

- **Scoring:** The winner of the point receives 1 point (or goal!) while either player that successfully serves or returns as intended is awarded 2 points. By awarding points in this way, coaches place more emphasis on goal achievement (or the performance) while avoiding simultaneous and complete devaluation of the outcome.
o **Integrated training concept - tactical:** Players are also required to tell the coach why they intend to serve or return in that fashion. If the coach considers their justifications to be tactically sound on "x" number of occasions in a row, they receive a bonus point. The coach should take note of any tactical concepts to positively reinforce or for revision.

2. BUILDING

Before serving, Player A tells the coach where he is going to direct his serve and how he intends to play his second shot. Player B provides the coach with the same information with respect to his return and second shot.

- **Scoring:** As for 'Set the scene' but players may be awarded 2 points for the correct implementation of each part of their point plan: direction of serve or return and use of shot 2.
> **Variation:** As for 'Set the scene'.

3. YOU AGAINST YOU

Four 1x1m flat targets are placed in the corners of the service boxes. Players assume their ready positions on the baseline ready to serve.

- **Scoring:** Players play a set against themselves where depending on their level of play, (consecutively) directing "x" number of "x" serves into the target areas = a game won. For example, advanced players may decide that in order to win a game they need to hit 2 first serves into each target area in a row. If they miss any serve in the series, they lose the game (Cascales, 2001).
> **Variation:** Mix first serves with second serves. Adapt target areas and number of serves to different playing standards. Present receivers with flat targets on-court, so they too are challenged to hit "x" number of successful returns to win a game, while failure to do so would result in a game lost.
> **Variation:** Using serve only, two players play a set against each other.
o **Integrated training concept - technical or physical:** The drill may be tailored to simultaneously develop technical skill (e.g. back leg drive in the kick serve) or designed to challenge certain physical qualities (e.g. power endurance) fundamental to successful serving.

4. PATTERNING

Player A serves a given pattern (3-2-1; 2-1-3; etc: 3 wide, 2 body, 1 T). The receiver returns similarly (3-2-1: 3 down the line, 2 centre, 1 cross court). Coaches can place cones on the court for extra motivation.

- **Scoring:** Every time players successfully execute the pattern (e.g. the three serves or three returns) they earn 1 game. Players play a 'set', alternating roles every 6 serves / returns.
- **Integrated training concept - tactical:** Incorporate pre-planned second shots for both the server and receiver (e.g. in a similar direction-specific 3-2-1 format or according to the type of ball received, the player is presented with a series of shot choices).

5. STOP AND GO

A serving contest between two players that sees players aim to hit five consecutive flat serves in.

- **Scoring:** Players earn a 'game' only if all five serves are in, and each one is progressively 'harder/faster' (as indicated by location of 2nd bounce). If a serve is missed or not hit harder, players alternate. First to 6 games wins.
- **Integrated training concept - tactical or technical:** Rather than having to hit serves with more power, players can also be challenged to hit serves with more slice or kick, or follow pattern variations.

18.2. EMOTIONAL CONTROL

1. LEVELLING / AWARENESS

Players play points using serve and return only. Upon committing an error or not taking advantage of an opportunity to win the point, players indicate to the coach how they feel and which emotional control strategy they are going to use (e.g. relaxation: adjusting the strings, or activation: bouncing on the spot) while readying themselves for the next point. The coach charts what strategies are used and discusses their effectiveness with the players.

- **Variation:** Players play a best of three 'tie-break' match with only serve and return they self-rate (out of 10) their use of emotional control strategies after each tie-break. If performed within a group, other players can act as buddy coaches and observe or 'mate-rate' the emotional control strategies employed. These ratings are then ultimately compared to the evaluations by the coach.

2. COMPOSED REACTION

Players play a set, hitting first serves only. Points end following the (un / successful) return. To receive, players have to assume a position one metre inside the baseline. Prior to starting, both players agree to actions or behaviours that represent a loss or mis-direction of emotional control.

- **Scoring:** The server can win a point by hitting an ace or forcing the receiver into error on return, while the receiver can win points by successfully returning the ball into court (or a target area). Coaches can award point penalties to either player observed to lose emotional control.

3. SERVE TO THE BEAT

Players hit 10 first serves while wearing heart rate monitors. Before assuming their ready positions for each serve, they must take time to establish optimal levels of arousal. In doing so, they should take note of their heart rate response and set a desirable range (e.g. 100-120 beats per minute).

o **Integrated training concept - tactical:** During subsequent set play, players will monitor their heart rates and only serve when their heart rates are within the target range that has been set. The coach monitors how players adapt their routines or employ emotional control strategies in response to the biofeedback provided.

4. BREATHING

Players play serve and return points, adopting different breathing patterns depending on whether they need to energise (through short and intense breath) or relax (via slower and deeper breath) between serves, returns or points.

5. TENSING

Players hit serves and returns, with varying amounts of looseness and tightness in the hands, arms, trunk, legs, etc. Self-analysis should lead players to establishing an optimal level of muscle tension to generate maximum power without losing control (Loehr, 1990).

18.3. CONFIDENCE THROUGH VISUALISATION AND POSITIVE THINKING

1. NOW YOU SEE IT, NOW YOU DON'T

Players direct their (first or second) serves and returns to strategically placed flat markers. After seven serves and returns, the coach then removes the markers and asks the players to visualise them, continuing to serve and return as if they were still there.

Players can be challenged to visualise successful strokes through the strategic placement and removal of flat markers or cones.

- **Scoring:** One point is earned for successfully hitting the markers positioned on the court, while players are awarded two points for successfully directing their serves or returns to the target areas (as ascertained by the coach) in the markers' physical absence. Players play first to 11 before alternating serving and receiving roles.
- **Integrated training concept - tactical:** The same process is followed, however, the receiver would have different returning options depending on the type of serve.

2. SIMULATION

With the agreement of the coach, players identify a professional player whose serve or style they would most like to possess. On court, a collection of video clips or sequential pictures are shown of the professional player serving and the coach encourages his players to focus on the serve accordingly. Players, with a clear mental picture of how they would like to serve or what they need to do, then practice five sets of five serves. Between sets, the coach and players discuss any pertinent feedback.

> **Variation:** Perform the same process with the return of serve.

3. SERVE CLIP

Players A and B serve. Before each serve, they try to visualise the execution of the perfect serve. After each serve, the players indicate which aspects of their serve they feel could be further improved so as to then more specifically direct their visualisation.

> **Variation:** The process is recorded and players then watch and evaluate the effectiveness of the strategies they put in place.

4. THE CRUNCH

Player A serves only second serves to the deuce and then advantage courts with one ball in his hand. He plays a match against himself with a serve in, counting as a point won, and a serve missed, a point lost. Two consecutive serves missed, counts as a game lost. The receiver also plays a match against himself with a return in earning him the point, and a return missed costing him a point. Again, two consecutive return errors would see the player lose the game.

> **Variation:** Target areas and goals (e.g. "x" number of balls missed = game lost; first serves only) are adapted to the playing standard of the drill's players.
> **Variation:** Players only use one ball and have to walk to either end of the court following each serve to retrieve the ball and ready themselves to hit their next second serve. The time between serves should be used to visualise a successful serve.

5. BE POSITIVE

Players hit three sets of 20 serves and returns. The sole instruction from the coach is that prior to serving and returning the players must use some positive self-talk (e.g. 'Go for it!!'). The coach observes what phrases are used and the group discuss the outcomes afterward.

> **Variation:** Players are encouraged to expand their positive thinking to encompass technical ('toss in front'), tactical ('attack it'), and physical ('drive up') components of performance. These more specific statements, which impact on subsequent performance, are then discussed.
> **Variation:** Players should first verbalise their positive self-talk to the coach, before repeating it internally.

18.4. CONCENTRATION AND ANTICIPATION

1. HONING

Player A serves ten points and before each point he utilises a different concentration strategy (e.g. focussing on an object: strings, court, ball; 'switch-on/switch-off'; etc). Player B prior to returning each ball performs the same psychological drill.

- **Scoring:** Players play first to 21, with points awarded to the winner of the point as well as to either player that successfully integrates a concentration strategy fives times in succession. As players play points, the coach also reserves the right to call 'let' following a good serve or return. This may upset their concentration and increase their emotional response and then forces players to refocus quickly.
> **Variation:** Players A and B have partners (i.e. players acting as buddy coaches) who observe the different concentration strategies they use. After every five points, if the buddy coach has correctly observed the strategies employed (as determined by consultation with his partner and the coach), his team is awarded a bonus point. Players alternate roles every ten points.

2. BULLSEYE

Three circles are drawn in each service box to encourage players to narrow their concentration to a particular point on court. The use of cue words and visualisation strategies may also assist players here.

- **Scoring:** Player A nominates a circle at which to direct his serve; if successful it is 15-0, if he misses: 0-15. Player B then repeats the process with the game's score being adjusted accordingly. Players play a set, alternating serves to the deuce and ad sides.
> **Variation:** Use first and second serves. Adjust circle diameter to the standard of the players.
o **Integrated training concept - tactical or technical:** Coupling this drill with specific circle placement can also train certain tactical or technical characteristics of the serve.

3. THE MARKSMAN

Balls are marked 1, 2 or 3. Player A hits second serves, alternating service boxes as he would in matchplay. In returning the serves, Player B endeavours to 'see' the number on the ball as early as possible and call out the direction of his return (1 = down the middle, 2 = wide, 3 = into the body) prior to his racquet-ball impact.

- **Scoring:** Player B counts how many serves he needs to face in order to correctly 'locate' five returns. Players then swap roles. The player requiring the least number of serves to correctly locate the five returns earns one point. Play first to five points.
> **Variation:** Use first serves. Adjust the receiver's court position to accommodate more or less challenge.

4. WHAT ARE YOU LOOKING AT?

Players play a four game set. Prior to serving, Player A tells the coach what cues he will use (where he will focus) in order to determine serve type and direction. For example, is the decision based on whether or not the receiver is stronger or more consistent off one side, or is it through attention paid to the player's grip or court position? Likewise, Player B indicates which cues he has picked up in trying to anticipate serve direction.

- > **Variation:** Players play up to 21, rotating serve every six points. The receiver needs to indicate type of serve (flat, topspin or slice) before the server contacts the ball, or its direction ('wide, middle or body') before the ball crosses the net. If a player wins the point, he earns one point. However, correct or incorrect anticipation of serve type and/or direction results in players earning or losing an extra point respectively.
- o **Integrated training concept - tactical:** Ask the servers to expand upon why they decided to serve in that fashion.

5. WHERE IS IT GOING?

Players play points with just the serve and the return. The coach, who is located behind Player A, indicates to Player B the direction to which he should serve. In returning the serve, Player A has to call out serve direction just before Player B impacts the ball.

- ◆ **Scoring:** Players face 30 serves and have the option to nominate serve direction or say 'no'. Correct anticipation sees players earn 5 points, while incorrectly nominating serve direction results in players losing three points. Players that are unsure of serve direction and that therefore say 'no' will have 1 point deducted from their score. Scores are tallied after both players have received 30 serves.
- > **Variation:** Prior to the return being played, the server must move to the side to which he believes the return will be played. A scoring system similar to that outlined for the receiver can be applied.
- > **Variation:** According to a serving pattern elaborated by Player B and the coach, Player B hits 10 serves to the deuce and then ad side. Player A tries to identify the pattern, including type and location of serve.

6. COLOURED BALLS

Player A serves red and yellow balls that Player B returns. Red balls should be returned cross court, whereas yellow balls should be directed down-the-line.

- ◆ **Scoring:** Players play a set with serve and return only, with the receiver earning a free first point in their service games if he is able to direct all returns according to colour in the preceding return game. Only one mis-directed service return is allowed per game; further 'errors' result in the immediate loss of the point.
- > **Variation:** The colour-coded returns can be altered to block or hit, forehand or backhand, etc.
- o **Integrated training concept - tactical:** Players are given the option to decide to play two returns of their choice (e.g. returns that do not have to be played according to colour) per service game.

What are you looking at? Between points, players can indicate to coaches which cues they are attending to help anticipate their opponents' shots.

7. CHAMELEON

Players practice returning to targets against a backdrop (e.g. back fence that is painted many different colours or has images projected against it) that disrupts the visual processing of the server's ball toss.

> **Variation:** Cover the net with something opaque.
> o **Integrated training concept - tactical:** Players play a set comprising of points not lasting longer than four shots. If any point extends beyond the serve, return and next two shots, it is replayed.

8. LISTEN ... CAREFULLY!

Player A randomly alternates 20 flat, slice and topspin serves. Player B, who is facing the back fence behind Player A, should listen to the contact and call out the type of serve that has been hit (flat, slice and topspin).

- **Scoring:** One point is awarded for every correct response. The player with the most points after listening to 20 serves, wins.

9. BLIND SERVE

Players serve with eye shades that limit the amount that they can see. This emphasises the need for them to concentrate on particular aspects of the serve, most notably the location of the ball toss.

18.5. ACHIEVING THE IDEAL PERFORMANCE STATE THROUGH ROUTINES

1. GET COMFORTABLE WHEN SERVING

Players play points with only serve and return, alternating serve every two points. They should perform their individual routines before serving (e.g. 'I adjust my arousal level in recovering from the last point. With a clear purpose in mind, I decide where and how I want to serve. I then step up to the baseline, take a deep breath, visualise the serve and bounce the ball as many times as necessary to heighten my focus, release the tension and let the motion occur as if I was on automatic pilot'...).

- **Scoring:** First to ten. The coach awards bonus points related to the consistency of the players' routines: if the players used the same 'effective' routine in all ten points they receive ten points; in nine of the ten points they receive nine bonus points.
> **Variation:** Receivers can be awarded a bonus point for effectively - but not unfairly - disrupting the server's routine.
> **Variation:** Players and coach discuss how to adapt the routine (i.e how many times they should bounce the ball) depending on the situation and the players' mental state. Players then experiment with the discussed variations of their routines and rehearse as appropriate.

2. GET COMFORTABLE WHEN RECEIVING

As above but now players focus on consolidating the routines they use when returning and consider:

— **Visual:** 'I observe cues from the server (ball toss, racquet path, body movement, etc.) that may indicate serve direction/ type or intention post-impact, and will help me to decide where I want to return (direction, depth, height, etc.) and how to do it (type of shot, effect, etc.)'.
— **Kinesthetic:** 'I take my ready position, adapting it as needed, and keeping the feet active'.
— **Motivational:** 'I say to myself cue words to pump up or remember my goals to execute'.
— **Instructional:** 'I set a tactical goal - where (direction, depth, etc.) and how (effect, etc.) to return'.

3. CHECKING ROUTINES

Prior to starting a best of five serve and return 'tie-break match', players write down and give the coach their individual, serve and return of serve routines.

- **Scoring:** Normal tie-break scoring is followed. The players however, agree that the coach has the authority to 1. distribute point penalties if either player fails to follow their routine, and/or 2. award either player a bonus point if they successfully perform their routines five times in succession. The coach takes note of any missing elements or areas to improve in the players' routines and discusses them with the players afterwards.
> **Variation:** If performed in groups of four ask two players to assume the roles of coach (e.g. observe one of the player's routines). Alternate players' roles after each tie-break.

18.6. MENTALLY DEALING WITH EXHAUSTION

1. END IS IN SIGHT

Player A needs to serve a given number of first serves 'in' at the end of the training session. The player may wish to indicate how many serves he will need to hit to achieve his goal.

2. THE MINEFIELD

The coach, standing on the service line, serves 75 balls in quick succession, one after another, to a player in the baseline ready position. The player, who must split step between each serve, endeavours to make as many returns as possible.

> **Variation:** The coach or a player serves from the baseline and the receiver returns from one metre behind his service line.

3. GOING FOR 20

Players A and B are serving at the same time to different service boxes. First player to hit 20 consecutive serves 'in' wins. When players miss a serve, they return to 0.

BASELINE GAME 19

19.1. MOTIVATION, COMMITMENT, 100% EFFORT, FIGHTING SPIRIT THROUGH GOAL-SETTING

1. KEEP GOING

Players A, B and C rally from the baseline. Player A, positioned on the baseline on one side of the net, plays crosscourt shots that should land inside the singles court, while Players B and C, on the other side of the net, play down-the-line to the doubles' alleys.

o **Integrated training concept - physical:** drill repetition and duration can be varied to elicit a specific metabolic training effect (Cascales, 2001). The intensity of work can also be manipulated by changing shot direction (e.g. Player A plays down-the-line …) and the number of players involved in the exercise.

2. GO FOR IT!

Depending on the players' level of conditioning, the coach can feed anywhere between 5-25 balls to distant parts of the court before presenting the players with easy balls to kill… if they can!!

> **Variation:** A 2:1 drill with two players at the net, volleying, and one player on the baseline, moving and hitting, can provide a similar training stimulus.

o **Integrated training concept - physical:** As for "Keep going" drill above.

3. EVERY BALL

Players rally from the baseline for a set time. Consistency is the overriding goal, and the idiom 'do not waste a shot' is applied, so players rally with only one ball. Every time they commit an error, they should run to pick up the ball to resume rallying. Players need to give 100%, and any lapse in mental or physical effort should see coaches bring it to the attention of the players, and if necessary, schedule rest periods until players feel they are again ready to work at 100% (Harwood, 2000).

4. SAY IT, DO IT!

With the players on the baseline, the coach feeds fl court balls from the basket. Instead of 'Let's play 5 good forehands' or 'I will feed you forehands until the basket is empty', players are presented with: '"How many balls do you need to play 5 very good forehands…or to hit the target?' Players should indicate how many balls they think they will need before starting the drill.

o **Integrated training concept - tactical or physical:** Strategic target placement or the incorporation of decision-making can introduce a tactical element to the drill, while challenging players to play the forehands 'on the run' or under physical pressure could provide some physical training stimulus.

5. THE MAGICIAN / COMMENTATOR

Players play points out of the hand (first to 11) but before each point, they take turns in providing a commentary of what is going happen.

6. PERCENTAGE PLAY

The player and coach agree that the player needs to improve his ratio of winners to unforced errors. Currently at 1:3, the player wants to set a goal of 1:1. The coach might suggest that a ratio of 1:2 would be more realistic and that it could be changed if the player reached this goal (by a specific date). To supplement the statistics realised from tournament play and help players to continually monitor their progress, they can periodically practice hitting 20 groundstrokes in simulated matchplay conditions and record their winner:errror ratio.

19.2. EMOTIONAL CONTROL, HANDLING ADVERSITY / PRESSURE

1. CHANGING GEARS

Players rally from the baseline at different speeds. One is very slow and ten is very fast. Players should try to vary speeds without losing control or making mistakes.

> **Variation:** As above but players, imagining they are cars, start hitting at 10 km/hr, and then without missing a ball, increase rally speed to 15 and then 20 km/hr. They continue to progressively increase rally speed until an error is forced.
o **Integrated training concept - technical and tactical:** Target areas can be set (e.g. between the baseline and service line, in the doubles alleys, …) to help players to consolidate the relationship between form (technique, or more specifically variation in racquet speed) and function (tactics, e.g. opening the court).

Learning to 'change gears' is central to proficient tactical play, and equally effective in facilitating arousal control.

2. MUSCLE MAN

To help players establish an 'optimal level of muscle tension', the coach calls out a number from 1 to 10 every 5-10 seconds during baseline rallies. One would see players relax and become very loose, while upon hearing ten players would tighten up maximally. Players adjust their level of muscle tension according to the number called out.

> **Variation:** Rather than calling out numbers, the coach can ask players to play each stroke with a different spin or, at a different speed while attending their individual levels of muscle tension. This enables them to associate muscle tension with different strokes and situations.

3. TAKE IT EASY

Prior to starting a 5 set groundstroke sparring match, Players A and B provide the coach (in writing) the emotional control techniques (e.g. breathing, body relaxation …) they plan to use when anxious after committing an unforced error, or after failing to take advantage of an opportunity to win the point, etc.

- **Scoring:** Players introduce the ball with hand feeds and play 5 sets of 'first to 11 points' from the baseline. The players agree that the coach has the authority to 1. distribute point penalties if either player fails to follow their emotional control technique, and/or 2. award either player a bonus point if they successfully perform their techniques five times in succession. The coach takes note of any missing elements or areas to improve in the players' techniques and discusses them with the players afterwards.
> **Variation:** Players play a 'groundstroke only' set with each game starting from a different score. An example of a 'four score sequence' that could be repeated throughout a set is: Game 1 - 0-0, Game 2 - 0-15, Game 3 - 0-30, Game 4 - 0-40. The same bonus point scoring guidelines as those outlined above are followed.
> **Variation:** If performed in groups of four, ask two players to assume the roles of coach (e.g. observe one of the player's techniques). Alternate player roles after each set.

4. MASTERING ANXIETY... PHYSICALLY

Players play a set using groundstrokes only. When they recognise that they are starting to get nervous, they should employ a physical strategy to control their anxiety:

— Relaxing the muscles of the arms, neck and hands by developing and then releasing the muscle tension.
— Understanding bodily signals: A 'rapid heart beat' can be a sign of readiness not a sign of tension.
— Smiling when feeling tension coming on.
— 'Shaking out' the muscles of the hands, shoulders and neck.
— Creating a strong mental and physical image.
— Slowing down: Taking more time between points.
— Removing the racquet from the dominant hand or exaggerating footwork.
— Going through rituals looking confident, calm and in control.

Coach and players discuss afterwards.

5. MASTERING ANXIETY... PSYCHOLOGICALLY

Players play a set using groundstrokes only. When they recognise that they are starting to get nervous, they should use a psychological strategy to master their anxiety:

— Realising that being nervous is a sign that they care, and treat the situation as a naturally-occurring reaction to wanting to perform well.
— Remembering that the opponent may be experiencing similar sensations.
— Focussing on one point at a time and on doing the best they can.
— Thinking positively.
— Having fun.
— Using humour to break tension.
— Playing more aggressive high percentage tennis.
— Playing to win instead of not to lose.
— Leaving mistakes behind.
— Establishing a good game plan and sticking to it.
— Playing every point as though it were the most important one.

Coach and players discuss afterwards.

6. BREATHING

When rallying or during point play, coaches should encourage players to coordinate breathing in with backswing or preparatory stroke movements and breathing out with the forwardswing and impact. To become familiar with what is required, players may initially benefit from exaggerating the depth of their breathing.

> **Variation:** Before starting the baseline rally, players adopt different breathing patterns depending on whether they need to energise (through short and intense breath) or relax (via slower and deeper breath).

7. TENSING

Players play from the baseline, manipulating their muscle tension (e.g. varying amounts of looseness and tightness in the hands, arms, trunk, legs, etc.) while executing their groundstrokes. Self-analysis should lead players to establishing an optimal level of muscle tension to generate maximum power without losing control (Loehr, 1990).

19.3. CONFIDENCE / BODY IMAGE / LANGUAGE

1. SHOW AND TELL

Players play first to 15 from the baseline. They, along with the coach, agree to a number of characteristics or behaviours that represent positivity in one's body language. At the coach's discretion, bonus points are rewarded to players observed to be demonstrating one or more of these behaviours. The coach and players discuss the performance afterwards.

> **Tactical variation:** As above, but Player A receives the instruction that for him to win the point when more than 4 shots have been played, he must play a drop shot. Player B is free to play without any constraints. Players swap roles.

2. GIMME THAT ONE!

The coach, having asked players what their best groundstrokes are, feeds high half court balls to the players so that they are able to further increase their confidence in that shot.

- > **Variation:** The coach feeds easy balls to the groundstroke that players have less confidence in ('weakness'), with a view to building their confidence in that stroke
- o **Integrated training concept - physical or tactical:** Provide a specific metabolic training stimulus by manipulating work:rest ratios and the number of balls played in any one set. The type/location of the fed balls can also be considered in establishing target positions to groove shot selection.

3. JUST WORDS

Players play a groundstroke only tie-break. The coach provides no instruction other than that players should compete to win. The coach does however observe the self-talk used by the player. If he observes the player using any form of negative self-talk, he intervenes and asks the player to repeat it. He then asks the player 1. How he would feel if the coach said that to him? 2. What he thinks the coach should say in that circumstance?, and finally 3. To reprogramme and repeat the phrase in a positive manner.

4. MEMORISING

Players are required to document and describe all of the 'significant' successes (e.g. decisions, shots, …) that they experience during baseline point rallies and/or points. After a set time has elapsed, players discuss these events with their coach.

19.4. CONCENTRATION AND ANTICIPATION

1. TWO FOR YOU

Players, positioned at the baseline, rally with two balls at the same time.

- > **Variation:** Still using two balls, players play first to 11 from the baseline. A point is lost by failing to keep a ball in play or making an error. Players have to alternate calling out the score before each point.

2. CROSSFIRE

The coach feeds balls with hand or racquet very quickly to Player A, positioned at the baseline, who executes forehands and/or backhands.

- > **Variation:** Can be used to challenge the same psychological skill in other game situations.
- o **Integrated training concept - tactical or technical:** Through considered target placement, players can be encouraged to simultaneously improve a specific technical skill or repeat a tactical pattern.

3. PLAY IT AGAIN SAM

Players rally, hitting each ball in a different way. The coach can either call out the type of shot (e.g. angle crosscourt!) or a different shot (effect and/or direction) can be played in response to the ball received (e.g. reply to a heavily topspin forehand with a backhand slice).

4. BOUNCE AND HIT

Players play points from the baseline and have to say 'bounce' when the ball bounces in the opponent's court and 'hit' when the opponent hits the ball. Likewise, when the ball lands in their half of the court they have to say 'bounce' and 'hit' when they hit the ball. Throughout, points are awarded to the winner of the rally as well as to the player/s who say 'bounce' and 'hit' at the appropriate times.

> **Variation:** Players play with an eye shade (occluding the vision of one or both eyes) or ear plugs.
> **Variation:** Players are instructed to coordinate their split step with their opponent's hitting of the ball.
> **Variation:** Players concentrate on breathing out at contact, saying a long 'yesss'.

5. COLOURFUL TENNIS

The coach feeds balls of different colours from the basket. Red balls are to be hit down-the-line and yellow balls crosscourt.

o **Integrated training concept - tactical:** The different coloured balls can be fed to simulate and trigger the appropriate stroke response in specific matchplay situations.

6. FILLING THE MENTAL SPACE!

While rallying, players focus their attention on the ball in play. They let the moving ball fill their entire mental space. Letting any interfering thoughts go, they keep focussing on the ball and on it only (Girod, 1999).

> **Variation:** As above but attention is now wholly directed to the sound of the ball (e.g. bounces, contact with the racquet ...). Players should let themselves be taken up by this rhythm.
> **Variation:** As above but players focus on their breathing. They should breathe in with their nose when their opponent hits the ball, and breathe out when they hit the ball.
> **Variation:** During point play, the players are instructed to mentally repeat words such as 'step in', 'attack', and '100%' prior to hitting or moving to the ball. Again, these words should fill the players' entire mental space.

7. HIT TO LOCATION

Players A and B rally from the baseline, each hitting six shots to strategically placed targets. Following some repetition, the coach removes the targets and asks players to visualise their positions in continuing to rally to the set pattern. Coach and players discuss afterwards.

o **Integrated training concept - tactical:** Adjustments made to the targets' positions as well as to the number of balls hit can increase the drill's tactical specificity so that players can train patterns of play central to their game plans or that can be used against specific opponents.

8. 30 PLUS

Players hand feed to commence point play from the baseline. Intent (e.g. cooperative or attacking) should be determined by the coach but for high performance players it should be aggresive (e.g. players should try to win the point).

- **Scoring:** Both players start on 0. The player that wins the point, retains the number of balls he hit as his score. The player that loses the point returns to zero. Players build their scores by winning consecutive points (e.g. if Player A wins three points in a row hitting 10, 5 and 3 shots respectively, his score would be 18. If he were to lose the next point, he would return to 0, and Player B's score would reflect the number of balls he hit to win the point). The winner is the first player to hit '30' consecutive shots without losing a point.
> **Variation:** Adjust the number of consecutive shots players are required to hit in accordance with drill intent and the players' standard of play. Players' scores can also increase based on the shots played by both players as opposed to just the player who wins the point.
> **Variation:** First to 100 balls over the net in a row. Every time one player misses the ball, the number of balls hit over the net is also awarded to the other player.
o **Integrated training concept - technical or tactical:** As a technical or tactical training aid, target areas may be set with players required to rally within these areas. To encourage tactical variation in stroke play, players rally but no two consecutive shots can be hit with the same spin and/or direction.

9. GRAND SLAM

Within a training session, players plan to 'play' all four Grand Slams with no serving and only playing from the baseline.

- **Scoring:** Each Grand Slam comprises a five set match, with each set being the first to 21 points. Players hand feed to start each point and the first player to win 3 points in a row in any set, automatically wins that set.

The appropriateness of the goals and scoring systems used in all on-court MST drills is key to their effectiveness.

III. On- and off-court psychological drills and activities

10. UMPIRE

Players play points from the baseline with no serve. Before each point, players have to alternately announce the score.

11. JUST... IN OR OUT?

Two players rally between the service line and baseline. Another two players are standing at either end of the court in line with the baselines. A competition of correct calls can be established where the players watching have to call the balls - in or out - that bounce on the other side of the net.

- **Scoring:** Each correct call is awarded 1 point, while an incorrect call results in players losing 2 points. Players play first to 30, before rotating roles.

12. HEAR THE BOUNCE

Players listen to the sound of the ball bounce while rallying from the baseline for five minutes. Before continuing to rally for a further 5 minutes, players place earplugs in their ears. Afterwards, the coach and players discuss what the coach has observed and what the players felt.

13. TENNIS BALLET

Players simulate the movements involved during point play using only groundstrokes. They focus on the position of their bodies, their balance, how they accelerate and decelerate, and their movement during the backswing, forward swing, and follow-through, thus working on their proprioceptive and kinaesthetic control.

> **Variation:** Acrobatic and gymnastic movements can also be incorporated selectively so as to further challenge kinaesthetic awareness (Sledr, 2001).

14. CONCENTRATION TRIGGERS

Players rally from the baseline. When the point has finished, they should try to find an 'action' that triggers concentration (e.g. crossing the baseline, saying a cue word, switching on - switching off, etc.). Having rallied in this fashion for five to ten minutes, the coach and the players evaluate what the coach observed and the players experienced.

15. FOCUS ON THE SCORE

Players play points from the baseline. The scoring system is as follows:

- The first point played counts as 1 point.
- The second and third points played count as 2 points each.
- The fourth and fifth points played count as 3 points each.
- The sixth and seventh points played count as 4 points each.
- The eighth and ninth points played count as 5 points each.
- The tenth point played counts as 6 points.

Players play 2 sets of 10 points. The same player serves throughout the set.

20. PLAYING AT THE NET AND PASSING THE NET PLAYER

20.1. MOTIVATION THROUGH GOAL-SETTING

1. HOW MANY DO YOU NEED?

Coach feeds from the basket to players at the net. Players are asked 'How many balls do you need to play 5 very good forehand volleys...or to hit the target?' Players should indicate how many volleys they will need before starting the drill.

o **Integrated training concept - tactical, technical or physical:** Placement of targets can be altered to simultaneously develop specific technical or tactical skills, while alternating smashes and volleys may also challenge the anaerobic abilities of the players.

2. VOLLEY GOALS

Players volley 12 randomly fed balls. The coach asks the players to self-rate their performance on each volley after each shot. Their self-ratings are then compared to those made by the coach, and any discrepancies discussed.

20.2. EMOTIONAL CONTROL

1. SINGLES HOT SEAT!

Two on one drill in which the two baseline players have the opportunity to play hard shots to the body of the player at the net. This player has to demonstrate quick reaction as well as effective mistake management and coping stategies so as to best deal with the situation.

2. SOFT-HARD HANDS

Player A is at the net and Player B is at the baseline. Player B mixes up passing shots and lobs. Where possible, Player A should play winning smashes or winning drop volleys, demonstrating sound 'feel' and emotional control.

3. MISTAKE MANAGEMENT

The coach feeds easy volleys and smashes to the players, who should put them away. A successful volley or smash earns players 1 point, while an error (or shot that the coach is able to retrieve) earns the coach a point. The first (player or coach) to accumulate 11 points wins. Throughout, players should demonstrate that they are able to accept mistakes, learn from them and ready themselves for the next point.

4. KILL THAT SMASH!

The coach feeds 'x' number of lobs to players at the net. As fatigue begins to set in, they have to continue to commit to go after the smash and recover their court position.

> **Variation:** Use a combinations of low volleys and smashes, drop-shots and smashes, mid-court short balls and volleys, etc.

> **Variation:** 2 against 1 drill. Player A smashes to the deuce side to Player B, who plays a lob back to A. Player A then smashes to the ad side to Player C, who also lobs back to A. Following this third lob, the point is played out.

20.3. CONFIDENCE

1. WHET THE APPETITE

The coach feeds five easy lobs for players to smash. A competition related to precision and/or consistency can be established between the players.

2. YES!

The coach feeds balls to players at the net. They should volley, saying 'yes' after each good volley they play.

> **Variation:** Players can rally one up, one back or in volleying exchanges.

3. WHEN?

The coach feeds balls to players at the net, who set themselves the goal of only playing 'good' (as ascertained by the players themselves) volleys. When they execute accordingly, the coach provides the players with positive reinforcement, while if the volley did not meet the necessary criteria to be considered 'good', the coach immediately feeds the players another volley.

Players need confidence at the net to consistently 'close' out points during matchplay.

20.4. CONCENTRATION AND ANTICIPATION

1. WHICH WAY?

Player A, positioned on the baseline, receives a short ball fed by the coach. He plays an approach shot to one of the corners of the court and tries to anticipate Player B's passing shot, indicating to the coach where he is focussing (e.g. Player B's court position, grip...) in order to anticipate the pass. The coach takes note of the cues the player attends and whether or not he successfully anticipates the pass. Afterwards the coach and players discuss the results.

2. WHERE IS IT?

Coach hand feeds balls to the players, who positioned at the centre mark in the baseline have to sprint forward and play the ball back after the first (or second) bounce. There is a shade over the net to prevent the players from watching the hand of the coach.

> **Variation:** Player A alternately hits deep, short and angled volleys. Player B is on the baseline readying himself to play the ball back to Player A. The net is covered by a shade resulting in Player B being unable to see what shot is being played by Player A.

3. GETTING A FEEL FOR EQUIPMENT

Players A and B volley back and forth to one and other using balls of different weight, size, colour, and material.

> **Variation:** Players use the same ball but experiment with racquets of different composition and size (Sledr, 2001).

4. WHERE ARE YOU?

Players start from their respective baselines. Player A puts the ball in play with a firm stroke, placing Player B, the opponent, on the defensive. Seeing this, Player A comes to the net. The objective for Player B is to conceal his shot and pass Player A at the net. Player A, on the other hand, endeavours to anticipate Player B's pass and then volley a winner. The point should be played out if neither player hits or volleys a winner (Steinberg et al., 1998).

— **Player A (volleyer):** Being at the correct spot and hitting a volley winner = 2 points. Being at correct spot and putting the volley in court = 1 point.
— **Player B (baseliner):** Hitting a first passing shot winner = 2 points. Winning the point with the second passing shot = 1 point.

5. THE SHOOT-OUT!

Standing at the net, the player faces away from the coach who is at the other end of the court. Then, upon hearing a noise (e.g. coach's racquet-ball contact), the player turns, reacts to the ball fed by the coach and tries to volley it back.

6. THE SURPRISE

Player A is at the net and Player B at the baseline. Players rally cooperatively and the coach randomly and intermittently feeds an extra ball to Player A, who has to play it back to a target while continuing to rally the other ball with Player B.

o   **Integrated training concept - physical:** To develop agility, Player A may volley between 2-6 balls and at any time the coach can feed a deep lob which Player A has to smash/chase down as quickly as possible. To challenge Player A's coordinative abilities and footwork, all fed balls could be played as half volleys.

7. FOCUS ON THE TASK!!

Player A is volleying and Player B is trying to pass him using pre-determined patterns. The coach asks Player A to focus on several task-relevant cues (e.g. the ball, the opponent's swing, position, footwork, etc) to best anticipate the different types of passing shots (Young, 2000).

8. WATCH THE BALL!!

Players participate in fast volley exchanges. The eyes will do a lot of subconscious work without the players realising it (Harwood and Dent, 2003).

>   **Variation:** Player A serves to Player B, who is located at the service line, and has to hit half-volley returns.

'The Focus on the task' is an excellent drill for challenging the net and passing player's concentration skills.

MATCH PLAY SITUATIONS 21

21.1. MOTIVATION THROUGH GOAL-SETTING AND 100% EFFORT

1. THE COUNTDOWN

Players play points. Player A starts serving and has seven shots (including the serve; two serves = two shots) to win the first point. If successful, he then has six shots to win the second point. If he loses the point, Player B serves and has seven shots to win the point, and so on.

- **Scoring:** The winner is the first player to win seven points (e.g. with 7, 6, 5, 4, 3, 2 and 1 shot/s).
- **Variation:** Advanced players must win all seven points in a row.

2. TELL ME

Players play a best of five 'tie-break' match. Prior to each point, players must tell their partners (standing at the back of the court) their point plan.

- **Scoring:** One point is awarded for playing the point to plan, and another if the point is won.
- **Variation:** Rather than tie-breaks, a practice match is played and players have to tell their partners their tactical plans for each game during the changeovers. If the partners, in consultation with the coach, assess that the players do follow their plans, they are awarded a bonus point in the subsequent game.

3. MAKE TENNIS FUN!

During training sessions when the coach feels it appropriate, players are given the opportunity to select subsequent drills or drill goals.

4. ROLE MODEL

Before commencing a practice match, players are asked by the coach to identify their favourite role models for both the way they play and their behaviours on- and off-court. The coach awards players one bonus point for every two games that they can accurately portray/imitate their role model's behaviour and/or style of play.

5. MY GOAL FOR TODAY

Before starting the practice session, the coach asks the players to set a goal (and sub-goals if necessary) for the session. In doing so, the coach should emphasise that there is no one ideal goal for all players, but rather it should reflect the player's vision and be meaningful to the individual (Young, 2000).

6. GRINDING IT OUT

Players play points. The coach asks the players to give themselves a mark out of 10 for how hard they are working, and then asks the player why they are at "x" out of 10 and not a higher number.

7. RUNNING THE WHOLE COURT

Players play a singles match in which the receiver plays in the doubles court and the server in the singles court.

8. WHAT IF SCENARIOS

Matchplay is scheduled whereby different scenarios (e.g. bad calls, breakage of strings, windy conditions, partisan crowd, poor court, worn balls, playing in the rain) test players' coping mechanisms and mental toughness.

9. THE PUNISHER

Players perform a 20-minute high-intensity interval training session prior to playing a best of 5 'tie-break' match. During the match, the coach assesses the 'fight' of both players when fatigued (Gould et al., 2001).

21.2. EMOTIONAL CONTROL

1. UNDER THE PUMP

Players play a set with their service games alternately starting at 40-15 and 15-40.

> **Variation:** Only second serves are allowed (or no volleys or groundstrokes are allowed).
> **Variation:** Players play a five set match with one of the players starting from 4-1 down in each set. It can be the same player throughout the entire match or roles can be reversed from set to set.

Coaches often appraise a player's ability to maintain composure by implementing different point scoring systems during practice matches.

2. PRESSURE PERSONIFIED

Players play 'first to 11' sets alternating serve every 4 points.

- ◆ **Scoring:** A point won is worth 1 point, however, Player A's mistakes are penalised with Player B gaining two points. Player B's mistakes are not penalised. Roles are reversed each set.
- > **Variation:** Player A can only win points at the net.
- o **Integrated training concept - physical, technical or tactical:** As above but Player A is only allowed to play with one groundstroke.

3. VOLLEYBALL TENNIS

Players play first to 20.

- ◆ **Scoring:** Players can only win points when serving. Players must win a point off their opponent's serve to earn the right to serve.

4. BE POSITIVE

Players play first to 15 from the baseline. They, along with the coach, agree to a number of examples of positive self-talk and body language that can be used to help players refocus or manage mistakes.

- ◆ **Scoring:** A point won is worth one point. At the coach's discretion, he awards bonus points to players upon his observation of one or more of the positive behaviours. The coach and players discuss afterwards.
- > **Variation:** As above but players experiment with different emotional control strategies (e.g. deep breathing, count to 10, …) to facilitate mistake management. The coach and players discuss afterwards.

5. THINK, THINK, THINK!

Players alternate serves every two points and play five sets of 'first to 7' points. After each set, the coach asks the players to reflect on the set through:

— Similar past situations / experiences that have been positive.
— Recognition of positive, negative or uncharacteristic play brought about by a particular situation.

6. STROKE GONE AWOL

Players play points but Player A has to serve underarm, artificially recreating a match play situation where part of a player's game is not functioning as desired.

7. HEAD TO HEAD

Players play points against each other but are constantly looking to collect bonus points from their opponent by identifying chinks in their mental armour. Players agree as to what these weaknesses might be.

- ◆ **Scoring:** A point won is worth one point, and any player to show a weakness would see his opponent receive a bonus point. This may be in the form of poor body language, or negative self-talk indicating frustration, worry and/or self doubt.

> **Variation:** Players play a practice match under a more stringent code of conduct. Agreed upon penalties apply and are enforced by the coach.

8. FREEBIES

Players play a set during which each player is able to 'take' a total of four free points at any time.

9. READY, SET, GO!

Players play points. Players are only allowed to start the next point when they are emotionally ready (e.g. much like a pilot does before take-off: 'fuel', 'check', etc., so should a player: 'Confidence - check, energy level - check', etc). The coach intermittently asks players to tell him what their self-talk was prior to starting the point.

10. TIME-OUT

Players play a three set match. They are allowed a total of four, three minute time-outs that can be taken at any time during the match. Retrospectively, the players and coach discuss the timing of the interludes.

11. SCORING THE RALLY

Players play points with serve. The winner of the point is rewarded with a score that equates to the number of balls he hit during that point (e.g. 3). If he wins the next point he adds the number of balls he hit (e.g. 4) to his score from the previous point (e.g. 3 + 4 = 7). However, if he loses the point his score returns to 0 and his opponent's score becomes the number of shots his opponent hit during the point. Players play first to 10 or 15.

12. CONVERTING OPPORTUNITIES

Players play points, alternating serve after each point. Both players start on zero, and if they win a point courtesy of a winner, they earn one point. A point lost as a result of an unforced error sees players lose one point. First player to reach to +5 wins.

21.3. CONFIDENCE

1. THE SWAP

Players play points. Players have an equal number of small pieces of paper in each pocket. For each time they talk to themselves positively they place a piece of paper from the 'negative pocket' to the 'positive pocket'. For every time they talk to themselves negatively they take a piece of paper from the positive pocket and move it to the negative pocket. The goal is to have a pre-determined number of pieces of paper in the 'positive pocket' (Lubbers, 2001).

2. MANTRA

Players play points. The players have to decide upon a positive phrase to say to themselves within the first three seconds of the point finishing and then attempt to repeat that phrase for as long as they feel necessary.

3. REINFORCING

Players inform their coach of their best shot (e.g. inside-out forehand) or tactical play (e.g. serve and volley). They play a best of five 'tie-break' match and are rewarded with double points for every time they are able to use that shot or tactic to win the point.

4. WELL PLAYED!

Players play a set but the coach can intervene and award the point to either player following good play on their behalf. This means that the point does not have to necessarily end with an unforced error: a common scenario with young developing players.

5. BODY IMAGE RULE

The coach establishes certain 'body language' rules for the session (e.g. walking tall, shoulders back, racquet head up), particularly between points and after mistakes. He asks players to ask themselves: If I had confidence in myself, how would I feel? What would my attitude be like? How would I walk? The trick for players asking themselves these questions is to reproduce, during practice and matchplay, what they identify to characterise confidence in stance (head up, eyes looking straight ahead, shoulders back and broad, straight position, walking tall), gesture (confident steps, sure movements), respiratory rhythm and amplitude, as well as muscle tone. A point system is developed to reward those who follow the rules (Harwood, 2000).

> **Variation:** As above but rather than rules relating to body language, the coach creates certain 'positive self-talk' rules for the session.

21.4. CONCENTRATION

1. THE COMMENTARY

Players play points. After each point, players take turns in providing a retrospective commentary of the point to the coach.

> **Variation:** Players talk to the ball, telling it where they are going to hit.

2. INTERNALISING

Players play a set with the sole instruction from the coach (at any one time) being for them to focus their attention on:

— The ball in play.
— The sound of the ball when it bounces and when racquet-ball contact is made.

— Their breathing.
— Repeating words such as 'step in', 'attack', or '100%' prior to hitting each shot.

The coach and players discuss the results afterwards.

3. DISTRACTIONS

Schedule matchplay at clubs next to train stations or construction sites, during fading light, particularly windy afternoons, etc.

o **Integrated training concept - tactical:** In windy conditions for example, some learning regarding how to play against and with the wind should take place.

4. FLICK THE SWITCH

Players play the best of three tie-breaks. The coach encourages the players to practice the 'switch-on/switch-off technique' between points. That is, after each point, players divert their attention from the pressure of the situation and put their minds at ease ('switch-off') before re-focussing ('switch-on') to play the next point.

> **Variation:** Players use the volume control technique: they adjust the intensity of their concentration (i.e. reducing its volume) between points so that they are relaxed but aware of the situation. When beginning the next point, players then increase the 'volume' of their concentration.
> **Variation:** As above but the coach encourages the players to use triggers to heighten concentration: stepping over an imaginary line on-court, saying 'let's go', towelling down, adjusting shirt sleeves, etc.

5. SHORT VIDEO CLIP

Between points, players should let a motionless or moving virtual image pop up on their mental screens. The image can be a specific tactical plan, positive image of themselves or **a written** word such as: 'CALM', '100%', 'COME ON', etc. Players are encouraged to focus on this image as part of their between point routine (Girod, 1999).

Players can learn techniques to improve their concentration through drills like 'Flick the switch' and 'Short video clip'.

Tennis Psychology

21.5. MENTAL PREPARATION THROUGH ROUTINES

1. MAKING A HABIT OF IT

Players prepare to play three to five tie-breaks. Each tie-break is to be considered a new match and players will have ten minutes before each to prepare psychologically, physically, tactically, technically. The coach should observe the processes the players go through and the group should discuss the coaches' observations afterward.

> **Variation:** The coach also takes note of the consistency and effectiveness of the routines that the players use between points and during the change-overs.
> **Variation:** Players play the best of five 'three game' sets. They are instructed to go for a toilet break once during the match. The coach observes the routine of the 'waiting' player.

2. RITUAL MAKER

Prior to playing a set, players tell their coach the type of between point and between game rituals they are going to employ (e.g. Stage 1: Physical response immediately after the point ends. Stage 2: Relaxation response. Stage 3: Preparation response. Stage 4: Readying response). The coach observes and documents any instances where these rituals are not employed and the player is accordingly penalised point/s in the following game. Afterwards, the players and coach discuss the effectiveness of the players' routines and how they fit each individual's personality, etc.

> **Variation:** As above bu players are instructed to devise and use individual versions of the 3R's technique (Release, review, and reset) to enhance their thought and behaviour control (Slaikeu and Trogolo, 1998).
> **Variation:** As above but 'match day' competition is simulated with scoreboards, officials, and an audience. Players should use pre-match strategies and routines: goals, positive self-talk, arousal control, warm-ups, etc. Retrospectively, players - along with the coach - evaluate how they responded to and prepared for the circumstances (Dent, 2002).

3. BETWEEN GAMES

Players play a practice match. They should change sides and sit down during the change-overs and use one of, or preferably a combination of the following routines: drink, towel off, review the game plan and plan performance goals for the next game, etc. The Code of Conduct is applied. The coach and players discuss the effectiveness of the players' change-over routines post match.

> **Variation:** As above but 'changeovers' are introduced after each game.

4. LOOK AT ME!

Players play points. Player A outlines three characteristics of his routine that are readily observable. The coach and/or Player B reserve the right to deduct a point from Player A if they observe him to fail to complete his routine.

5. READY, SET

At any time during point play or simulated matchplay, the coach can call out 'routine', whereby players have 20 seconds to perform their between point routines (Harwood, 2000). The coach does not have to wait for the point to end but rather can call out 'routine' mid-rally.

6. 'AUTOMATIC PILOT'

Players play a practice match in which the coach asks them to minimise their logical, analytical thinking. They should try to play on 'automatic pilot' and suspend all critical self-talk (Loehr, 1990). The coach and players discuss possible benefits of this technique afterward.

21.6. FOSTERING POSITIVE MOMENTUM

1. THREE IN A ROW... STARTS THE FLOW

Players play a set. Any player to win 3 points in a row, wins the game.

2. WAR / LAR

Players compete, awarding points according to an assessment of their performance rather than the point's outcome. They can play some points in which the winner assesses the rally (WAR) and others in which the loser assesses the rally (LAR) (Dent, 2002).

> **Variation:** The coach can also assess the rally (CAR).

3. PSYCHOLOGICAL CLIPPING

Players play points and the coach specifies a psychological skill that will be subject to player self-evaluation. Each player has ten paper clips in his right pocket and each time he believes that he has successfully engaged the specified skill, he moves one clip to his left pocket. After 'x' time or 'x' number of games, the coach and players get together to discuss what has transpired (Lubbers, 2000).

4. SELF-COACHING

Players play a set. Three times during the set, the players must approach the coach to explain their behaviours and decisions. Coaches should take note of their rationale so as to discuss it and provide feedback following the set.

5. IPS CHECK!

Prior to commencing point play against each other, players have to rate their state of readiness (1 = ideal performance state, to 5 = poor). They are encourged to engage strategies to help them to maintain or move closer to their Ideal Performance State (IPS) throughout the session.

OTHER SITUATIONS 22

22.1. PSYCHOLOGY OF DOUBLES

1. COMMUNICATING BETWEEN POINTS

Players commence point play and should communicate between each point to establish that which they endeavour to do or to implement in the subsequent point. The coach and players review the effectiveness and appropriateness of the players' communication after 20 points.

2. COMMUNICATING DURING THE CHANGE-OVERS

Players play a set and should communicate between change-overs in order to agree that which they endeavour to do or to implement in the following game. A buddy coach (i.e. additional player) is used to review each team's communication between games. The coach, buddy coach, and all players discuss what was observed and said every seven games.

3. ALL TO ONE!

Players play a set but one team is instructed to play all shots to one player of the opposition team. Players change roles after four games. Post-set, the coach and players discuss the psychological challenges this situation presented.

4. ROLE PLAYING

A set is completed with each team assuming doubles formations that they do not normally employ (e.g. serve and stay back, both back, ...). Upon completion of the set, the players discuss with the coach how they coped with any frustration posed by this role playing exercise.

Positive communication between points is one of the cornerstones of successful and enjoyable doubles play.

III. On- and off-court psychological drills and activities

22.2. SPORTSMANSHIP

1. THE CODE

Players play a practice set under the code of conduct.

> **Variation:** The coach organises a mini-tournament during practice sessions in which all players should, at least, umpire one match. The code of conduct needs to be enforced (see ITF Tournament Regulations).

2. MY SPORTSMANSHIP GOAL FOR TODAY

Before starting the practice session, the coach asks the players to set a goal relating to sportsmanship for the session (fair play, respect the opponent, the equipment, etc). Again, there will be no one ideal sportsmanship goal for all players but rather it will reflect each player's vision of gameplay and personality (Young, 2000).

22.3. ENVIRONMENT AND OTHER INFLUENCES

1. PARTISAN CROWD

Players play a match in a noisy place or on a court which is surrounded by moving (human or vehicle) traffic.

> **Variation:** Players play a match with music they do not like playing over loudspeakers.

2. TORNADO!

During a very windy day, the coach asks players to perform a control drill, such as serving to targets, or rallying in the doubles alley. Players need to understand that matches are also played under these conditions.

3. NEW BALLS?

The coach asks the players to play points using tennis balls which are in poor condition.

4. BORROW A RACQUET

The coach asks the players to play points using their opponent's racquet.

5. PLAY NOW...NO WARM-UP

The coach asks players to play points with a very short (less than 2 minutes) on-court warm-up or no warm-up at all. Players should be observed to use specific routines or strategies to deal with this challenge (e.g. shadow strokes to 'warm-up' between points, implement plans to groove strokes while playing, etc.).

22.4. SITUATIONAL DISTRESS / BREAKS IN PLAY

1. QUESTIONING CALLS

The coach asks players to play points in which they are given the 'green light' to question calls. The player whose call is being questioned needs to use specific routines to deal with the situation (e.g. dealing assertively with the situation, using self-talk, taking time to calm and then re-focus on the game plan, etc.)

2. OPPONENT BREAKS PLAY

The coach asks players to play points in which they can break play (e.g. toilet break, injury time out). Again, specific routines (e.g. keeping the mind on the match, visualising the next point, focusing on neutral things, taking time to breathe slowly and re-focus on the game plan, using a routine to get ready, etc.) should be followed to help players continue to perform well after the interruption.

3. DELAY

The coach asks players to play points. The coach can break play and plan a delay during the match. Players should use specific routines to deal with these situations (e.g. having a plan, conserving energy, using the time to review their performance, setting a plan for when play resumes, etc.).

4. SINGLES - DOUBLES

Four players rally down the line as if playing a singles match on half court. After a given number of shots, the coach calls out: "doubles!" and the four players should play out the point in a doubles format.

OFF-COURT MENTAL SKILLS PRACTICE

23

Armed with an inventory of on-court mental training drills, it is now time to expand upon how the more traditional practice of off-court MST can be best integrated into player training. It may be pouring with rain or perhaps it is impossible to get a court or find good practice partners, however, that does not mean players cannot work on their games... these opportunities represent the perfect time for players to hone their mental skills, even in the comfort of their lounge rooms! The purpose of this Chapter is therefore to highlight some practical off-court mental training activities that players can perform to consolidate the good mental habits they should be simultaneously aspiring to develop on-court.

As with the mental work performed on-court, MST can be tailored to meet different training objectives off-court as well. That is to say that the same mental skills outlined in Part II as integral to tennis play - motivation, concentration, emotional control and confidence - can also be improved with specific off-court initiatives. Similarly, player independence, maturity, responsibility, social skills, sportsmanship, supportive player-parent relationships and coach-player compatibility; all of which have been identified as important in a player's mental development can be effectively trained off-court. To this end, mental training off-court should be viewed in much the same light as fitness training in the gym, tactical analysis pre-match or video-assisted evaluation of a player's technique; all of which are performed off-court but potentially are no less important than their on-court 'brothers'.

23.1. MOTIVATION

1. MENTAL PERFORMANCE PROFILE

Players like to model themselves on the game's best players, all of whom possess some common psychological characteristics. The coach asks the players to list the mental skills that are most important for successful tennis performance. After some discussion between the players and the coach, players are asked to rate their proficiency in each of the mental skills listed. Players attribute a score out of ten to each skill with ten being outstanding, five average and one poor. The players and coach then discuss the results in a group and/or individually, and players should be able to pinpoint three mental components of their games to improve (Gould et al., 2001).

2. PLAN FOR SUCCESS

One of the very first sessions in establishing a MST plan needs to be devoted to goal-setting. In using the previous mental performance profile as their starting point, players should set mental goals that are challenging yet realistic. As part of the process, they should identify the steps that need to be taken to ultimately possess outstanding mental skills. Throughout, the coach should collaborate with and guide the players.

o **Integrated training:** This process should be repeated for technical, tactical, and physical areas of the players' games. Subsequent goals should have a target date and be regularly reviewed (Quinn, 2004).

3. SET GOALS FOR EVERY PRACTICE AND MATCH

Players are asked to fill in a simple goal-setting card for every practice session they plan and every match they play. In general, they should relate to the specific goals of their MST plans. After the practice or match, players should record if the goals were achieved and review potential reasons why or why not with the coach (Gould et al., 2001).

> **Variation:** When it comes to developing tennis skills, and more importantly in this context, psychological skills, there is simply no substitute for hard work and self-discipline (Quinn, 2001a). So after each practice or match, ask players to rate their intensity, commitment and self-discipline.

4. MAKE A SUCCESS POSTER

Coaches can ask players to make a treasure map or poster of exactly how they want to play, what they want to achieve, and how they want to look. They can go through old tennis magazines and find pictures of their favourite players that reflect just that. Reinforcing messages that their coach constantly tells them and good quotes to keep them focussed and goal-oriented may also be added. When complete, it should be displayed in a prominent place so that the players see exactly what they want to achieve each and every day (Quinn, 2004; Sosa, 2005).

> **Variation:** To players unfamiliar with the concept, the coach explains what it is to be a tough competitor. Players are then asked to come up with several characteristics that epitomise tough competitors and put forward names of tennis professionals considered to be exactly that. Following some player and coach discussion of what has been suggested, the group assesses how these characteristics can be best fostered in training sessions (Gould et al., 2001).

5. BECOME A DJ

Players can compile (in CD or mp3 form) about five of their favourite songs that stimulate confidence and enjoyment or stir emotions similar to those they experience when playing their best tennis. Once compiled, players should listen to them several times a week - on their way to tennis, in the car, on planes - and visualise playing outstanding tennis whilst listening to the music. Players should become so familiar with the music that whenever they listen to it or play one of the songs in their heads, their ideal performance state is triggered (Quinn, 2004).

Listening to music that stimulates confidence or stirs emotions can help to trigger players' IPSs.

6. PLAYER DIARIES

The coach can ask the players to keep a daily log of their practice, training regime, match results, physical condition, nutrition, etc. This will help them maintain motivation and focus. The coach may provide players with a diary template or players may prefer to create their own.

7. SURROUND YOURSELF WITH SUCCESSFUL PEOPLE

The coach explains to the players the importance of surrounding themselves with encouraging and supportive people because success breeds success and successful people leave clues. They are not merely lucky and may lead by example. They have a strategy and specific things they do on an ongoing basis to create the environment of success in their lives. Players are asked to identify people they want to become like and to find ways to look at life in a more positive way and to mix with people who think that way (Quinn, 2001a).

8. VIDEO ANALYSIS

The matches of players are analysed alongside those of top professionals so that they can develop a better appreciation of what the game demands. Special attention is paid to any noted differences between the mental performance of the players and the professionals.

> **Variation:** Players watch video tapes of top players, observing their between point and between game routines with a view to enhancing the rituals they use during matchplay. Players may also take notes on what they perceive their role models to be doing mentally and then discuss this among themselves or with their coach.

9. PERSONAL MOTIVATION

Players are asked to write down three reasons why they play tennis as well as provide an insight into the type and timing of the words and images they conjure up to motivate themselves (Gould et al., 2001). While principally used to assist coaches understand what drives their players, any implications for performance should be discussed.

10. PROBLEM SOLVE

The coach introduces players to problem solving as a mental training tool. Players then describe the characteristics of a problem previously encountered (e.g. playing badly against better players) before being encouraged to re-define it through goal-setting. As part of this, players should search for possible solutions and rank them, prior to establishing a plan for action, implementing the action and completing a post-action evaluation.

23.2. EMOTIONAL CONTROL

1. YOGA

Players attend a yoga class where they are introduced to and perform some basic asanas such as the Tree pose, Chakki chal, Taar asan, Trikon Asan, Bhujang and the Natraj pose (Singh, 2003).

> **Variation:** Players perform conventional dynamic flexibility exercises but shift focus from the physical nature of the exercise to controlling their breathing rate and rhythm.

2. PROGRESSIVE MUSCLE RELAXATION

Players practice progressive muscle relaxation (PMR) using a CD to guide them through the procedure. Players start practicing the basic and more comprehensive procedure off-court, before graduating to using an abbreviated on-court version that sees players relax without having to fully contract each muscle group. PMR should initially be practiced for 10-15 minutes every day before players are comfortable with its use and can perform it at their discretion.

> **Variation:** Autogenic training (see Chapter 10) is introduced and practiced in a similar, graduated fashion.

3. MEDITATION: "ONE POINTING"

Players sit comfortably in quiet surrounds and focus on one object (e.g. the seams of the tennis ball). They endeavour to hold their focus for as long as possible. Repeating one word over and over, focusing on your breath and certain body postures can also be used to enhance this meditation experience.

4. SELF-HYPNOSIS

Self-hypnosis is induced by players. By listening to relaxation tapes, using visualisation, meditation or a relaxation technique, players experience a moderate level of relaxation but maintain a certain level of conscious awareness to optimise arousal and offer creative suggestions for better performance.

5. SYSTEMATIC DESENSITISATION

The psychologist explains the role of systematic desensitisation to the players by outlining that it is a means through which they can overcome their fears. The procedure can be self-administered or administered by a psychologist and takes approximately 30 minutes. Players go through the following steps: relaxation (use a known technique), rank in descending order 10 situations where they have experienced anxiety, and finally pair specific relaxations with the situations of ranked anxiety.

6. CENTERING

Players practice breath control: slowly inhaling through their noses and filling their stomachs (not chests) with air. In so doing, they should think of a point behind their navels and say 'centre'. Next, they should exhale slowly through their mouth and consciously relax their bodies' muscles. As they exhale, they should say 'relax' and let their bodies do just that. Repeat the centering technique for five minutes or until players have a good feel for it. After some discussion regarding the appropriateness of its use, the players go on court to play a tie-break and perform the centering technique when they feel appropriate (e.g. before returning serve, after errors ...) (Gould et al., 2001).

7. COMBINING BREATHING TECHNIQUES

The coach outlines the importance of using different breathing techniques according to the demands of the situation. Players are asked to practice two types of breathing: relaxing breath (combining long inhalations with short pauses and long exhalations to the count of ten), and energising breathing (performing short and intense inhalations along with immediate and brisk exhalations) (Girod, 2004).

8. STRESS INOCULATION

Players recreate problems or challenging situations that they may face in matchplay (e.g. playing on a windy day or in front of a big crowd, rain delays, disputed line calls …). As part of the role play, players practice the coping strategies they would use to deal with the situations effectively.

23.3. CONFIDENCE

1. BECOME AN ACTOR

The coach explains to the players that they can use their body language in many ways: to help rid themselves of negative emotions like fear and discouragement; to intimidate their opponents and show them what a fighter they are; as well as to demonstrate their confidence and composure. However, all of this requires rehearsal and practice. The coach asks the players to practice at home in front of the mirror, walking tall around the house, pumping their fists. Their script is to exude confidence, positive energy, calmness, fight, and determination. Players are asked to picture the type of player they want to be and begin acting like that player (Quinn, 2004).

2. CATCH YOUR THOUGHTS

The coach explains to the players that the conversations they have with themselves (self-talk) are crucial for shaping attitudes and beliefs. He emphasises that what they focus on is often what they get, and that for self-talk to be of benefit they should learn to control it at all times, not just on the court. The coach asks the players to catch their thoughts using questions such as: Do you think like a winner? Are you positive all the time? Do you doubt yourself? What do you think of your tennis? Do you control your self-talk so it is only filled with positive statements? Do you challenge yourself to greatness? Do you compliment yourself regularly and acknowledge what you are doing daily? Do you speak to yourself like you mean it, full of energy and vibrancy? Do you speak with confidence to create it on and off the court? Players are asked to write down the positive and negative thoughts they have and when they have them. Coaches ask players to counter each negative thought with a really positive one and write them down (Quinn, 2004).

> **Variation:** With players aware of the significance of positive self-talk, they write down positive phrases that are emotive (e.g.'Great', 'Excellent shot') or task-related (e.g.'Bend your knees!', 'Contact early!') for use in different match situations (e.g. first serve, return or serve, after losing the first set, end of change-overs, match point). These phrases will then serve as the player's self-talk vocabulary.

> **Variation:** Players perform a self-interview (i.e. avoiding any potential embarrassment associated with face-to-face interviews), voice-recording their answers to questions like "When does self-doubt occur?, How do I recover from mistakes?, Am I afraid to hit certain shots?, Do I really expect to play well?, How do I react to adversity?, Does my confidence change throughout a match?, When am I overconfident?, Do I enjoy tough, tight matches?" Players give the voice recording to their coaches, and implications for performance are then discussed.

3. DO NOT PHONE HOME - PHONE YOU!

Players are asked to make movies or take pictures with their phones in order to facilitate their pre-match preparation. Players should take photos of exactly what they want to look like on the court - intense, aggressive, calm, focussed - whatever the look, they should photograph or video it and then watch themselves performing in this fashion. Players should create those perfect images in their mind first and then create them on-court (Quinn, 2004).

4. SWO ANALYSIS

Players need to view tennis matches as challenges; not threats. To encourage this, players can perform a SWO (not SWOT!) analysis, documenting their strengths, weaknesses and opportunities, prior to an upcoming match or tournament. Players and the coach discuss the results of the SWO analyses.

> **Variation:** Players who periodically experience self-doubt prior to matches they perceive as tough, may benefit from matching themselves against their opponents, skill for skill.

5. ASSESSING YOUR PHYSICAL FITNESS

The coach explains to the players that in order to feel confident on the court, they should be in the best physical condition possible because fitness is key to player confidence. Conditioned tennis players go into matches knowing they will not fade in the fifth set. Further, as conditioning may be the difference between winning and losing, the coach asks the players to rate their level of physical fitness per component and to determine when and how they will improve them (Quinn, 2001a).

6. ACKNOWLEDGE YOURSELF

Players are asked by the coach to acknowledge the great things they are doing. This can be achieved by:

— Constructing and regularly updating a confidence list with their achievements, strengths and aspirations.
— Creating a success file of their personal triumphs: For example, they can collate letters of praise, awards, videos of great matches, or articles on people they admire.
— Coming up with a signal or gesture they can repeat every time they play a great point.
— Asking powerful questions at the end of each day, for example, "What did I learn today? What did I do really well today?"

7. THE VOCAB SHIFT

Transformation of vocabulary can have a powerful effect on self-confidence and an individual's emotional state. Players should trial the impact that these 'vocab shifts' can have on their entire outlook: instead of 'I failed', say 'I learned something'; rather than 'I am fine', use 'I am fantastic!'... (Quinn, 2001a).

8. ASSERTIVENESS TRAINING

Players should be assertive - not aggressive - in defending what they believe to be 'right'. They are asked to imagine themselves in specific situations where their rights are being compromised (e.g. bad calls, team selection, opponent's behaviours or aggressiveness, etc) and then to develop appropriate and assertive responses. Along with the coach, they discuss how effective these responses may be in the proposed situations.

9. SELF-ESTEEM: AVOID COMPARISONS

The coach outlines to the players that they need to avoid comparing themselves to others. They need to look at the bigger, longer term picture. A list of medium-term goals with dates of accomplishment should be encouraged to help players continue to focus on their performance rather than the outcome (Quinn, 2001a).

10. COGNITIVE RESTRUCTURING (ATTITUDE ADJUSTMENT)

The coach highlights the importance of identifying, analysing and modifying negative thoughts. Players are then asked to think of how these thoughts influence their performance with a view to identifying positive and more rational thoughts to counter them. Afterwards, the players and coach review the process.

23.4. CONCENTRATION

1. NOW

Players are provided information to explain the importance of playing in the 'now', and thus not think about past mistakes or future success. They are then asked to write down the strategies they can use to do so (e.g. meditation, yoga or deep breathing), before self-evaluating (out of 10) how effectively they are employed.

2. CONCENTRATION - MEDITATION EXERCISES

Girod (1999) suggests that coaches ask players to perform one of the following concentration exercises, progressively increasing its duration:

- "**Take a tennis ball**. Place it in front of you. Stare at this motionless ball. Focus your attention on it. Let it take up the whole of your mental space. Close your eyes. Visualise your 'mental screen' and see that same tennis ball. Focus on this virtual image".
- "**Take a metronome**. Start the metronome. Focus your attention on its regular beats. Let the rhythm take up your entire mental space. Should any thoughts come to your mind, let them go past just like a passing cloud".
- "**Choose a word (or sentence), preferably a positive one**. Repeat it to yourself. Go over it in your mental space as if you were playing the same record over and over again".
- "**Be attentive to your breathing**. Feel the air coming in (counting to 4) and out (counting to 4) of your lungs. Let your breathing fill you. Each time you breathe in, you amplify the level of your concentration. Each time you breathe out, you chase away the thoughts that could interfere. Breathe in through your nose, and breathe out through your mouth".

3. EATING OR WALKING MEDITATION

The coach introduces the players to a meditation exercise in which they have to focus their total attention on the process of eating or walking. If their attention shifts, the players need to refocus immediately. Loehr (1990) suggests that this can be practised several times a day.

4. SHIFTING ATTENTION

Players assume a comfortable sitting position, close their eyes and try to relax. They start by focussing on what they can hear (first isolating one sound from another and then experiencing all of them at once), before attending to their sometic sensations (again, in isolation and then collectively). Players then repeat the process, turning their attention to their thoughts and emotions. Finally, in opening their eyes, players focus on one object in front of them and then as many as possible (Gauron, 1984).

> **Variation:** Players hold an object in their hands and focus on it. They retain this focus as they place the object down. The duration for which their focus can be maintained is recorded. Once they can do so for several minutes, they should repeat the exercise with some distractions present (Gauron, 1984).

5. THE GRID DRILL

Players are presented with a block grid containing two digit numbers from 00 to 99. Their goal is to sequentially identify all numbers in as short a period of time as possible (Gauron, 1984).

6. PLAY ON CUE (WORDS)

The coach asks the players to do shadow strokes in the gym or in a room, preferably in front of a mirror or a window where they can check their form. For each stroke, players should select a cue word. The coach can help them choose the best word for each particular stroke. For example, it could be 'early', 'low', 'dynamic' or 'feet'. Players practice playing the strokes and saying the cue words. The coach explains to them that this is a useful way of focussing or re-focussing when concentration is broken during a match as well as an ideal exercise for a rainy day or during warm-ups (Quinn, 2004).

Player burnout may be averted by interpreting the information in players' training diaries.

Tennis Psychology

23.5. VISUALISATION / IMAGERY

1. BASIC VISUALISATION

The coach explains to the players the importance of using visualisation both on- and off-court. The strategy employed should be specific to each player, and may be best performed at different times (e.g. the night before the match, the morning of the match, during the match…). Players can visualise something as basic as a static ball or successfully executing a stroke; alternatively they may be directed to visualise more specific situations or experiences such as:

— Playing well and overcoming pressure situations (e.g. down a break).
— Playing a match according to plan, being tough and giving 100%.
— Performing their pre-match routines, moving around the court and maintaining positive body language.
— Reviewing their best performances.
— **Note**: *Players should always visualise in colour, with as much detail and as many senses as possible. The speed at which events are visualised should be the same as that at which they occur during matchplay.*

2. DREAMING

The coach asks the players to try to visualise and experience the future as they want it to be. The exercise can start with the coach asking the following questions: "Imagine what it would be like to win Wimbledon. Would you be excited? Elated? Overjoyed? Relieved? Thrilled?" The coach should let the players know that whatever their personal reaction, they should be able to feel it in their stomachs and make that feeling a part of them. Ultimately, players should understand that visualisation is like creating the scenes of their own movie! (Quinn, 2001a).

23.6. SELF-AWARENESS

1. SELF-CHECK

Players are explained the importance of monitoring their daily stress levels so as to avoid overtraining and physical or mental burn-out (Loehr, 1990). Players should keep a daily log of physiological parameters such as their bodyweight and morning resting heart rate.

2. VIDEO ANALYSIS

The coach explains to the players the importance of using video analysis not only to analyse their technique or tactics but also to study their mental performance. Players are asked to review videos of their best performances and take notes of the psychological characteristics that facilitated and encouraged their success. The players and coach discuss the findings and explore possible ways of eliciting these performances more often.

3. USING HEART RATE MONITORS

The coach explains to the players the link between their physiological and mental states. Players are introduced to the use of a heart rate monitor as a tool to facilitate the self-monitoring of their physiological responses to certain situations.

4. DEVELOPING A ROUTINE BETWEEN POINTS

Players are asked to document their preferred between point routines when winning easy and ahead, after a bad mistake, after a disputed line call, after some gamesmanship from their opponent, etc. Together with the coach, the players discuss each routine and why they feel it works for them.

23.7. MENTAL RECOVERY TECHNIQUES

1. RRR TIME - BE BALANCED

The coach explains to the players that resting is the easiest part of training and yet the part that most players neglect! Players should be familiar with the need to rest, recover and relax between practice and matches. Recovery however, does not just happen. The coach asks the players to write down the components of their recovery plan (e.g. routines between matches, massage, relaxation, meditation and sleep), which are then reviewed in light of the fact that no matter what the sport or field of endeavour, a rested mind and body ensures better performance (Quinn, 2001a).

2. TIME-OUT! REWARD YOURSELF - HAVE FUN

When players are giving it their all in practice and training, it is especially important to plan time-out and have fun away from the court. The coach should also be aware that it is necessary to reward achievements and to celebrate and enjoy accomplishments along the way. The coach asks the players to make a list of all the things they like to do with their free time and then schedules at least one each week as part of their training and competition programmes (Quinn, 2001a).

3. NAP TO REFRESH

The coach explains to the players the potential value of using a nap to refresh and regenerate. It should not be interpreted as a sign of laziness. Performed for the right reasons, a nap can be useful in reducing fatigue and increasing alertness. The ideal nap time for most people is about eight hours after waking and eight hours before night-time sleep: when a person's body temperature reaches its low point, around 2.00 - 3.00pm. It may not be necessary to sleep during a nap: merely lying down and resting could be as restorative as napping. A nap should be under an hour: longer won't increase the benefits and is more likely to result in the intense grogginess known as 'sleep inertia'. Players should not be discouraged to take naps, especially during heavy training weeks, but their effect on each individual should be monitored closely (ITF, 1994).

4. PERIODISE FOR SUCCESS

The players and coach put together a training and competition plan in which they respect basic principles such as practising for shorts periods of time with high intensity; not playing too many tournaments in a row; ensuring the correct rest and recovery during and between sessions, matches and tournaments; adapting the schedule to challenge the players appropriately; and the setting of realistic goals (Loehr, 1990).

23.8. DOUBLES AND GROUP DYNAMICS

1. TEAM UNIFORM

The coach ensures that all players in the team are given and wear the team uniforms both on- and off-court. This creates a sense of belonging to the group (Loehr, 1990). Specific uniform rules are set to clarify when and how the uniforms should be worn.

2. ASSISTANT COACH

The coach encourages players to expand their match analysis skills and game knowledge. During team ties in which several matches are played at the same time on different courts, the coach assigns one or two players of the team to 'analyse' the match(es) he cannot.

3. DAY OFF!

The coach organises a tennis-free day for all members of the group. The activities to choose from should be appropriate to the age and interests of the group: barbeque, movies, shopping, camping, watching a football match, etc.

4. PLAYER INDEPENDENCE

When travelling or during practice sessions, players can be given specific responsibilities (e.g. booking practice courts, finding practice partners, taking racquets to the stringer, scouting future opponents, etc.) to foster their independence.

5. CHOOSING A DOUBLES PARTNER

To facilitate team selection, the coach asks the players to complete a form that outlines how they perceive their ideal doubles partner (including personality, style of play, etc).

> **Variation:** Players document the type of feedback they like to hear from their partner following a mistake, in pressure situations, when winning easy, when losing playing badly, etc. Preferences can be discussed individually or between doubles partners and the coach (Weinberg, 2002).

6. COMMUNICATION LOGBOOK FOR DOUBLES

Players are asked to keep a logbook of everything they say and think during doubles practices and matches. Players are encouraged to use the logbook as a forum to ask and answer questions regarding their doubles performance (Weinberg, 2002). If agreed, the contents can be discussed in a group or between player and coach.

7. VISUALISING FOR DOUBLES

Players are asked to visualise themselves in doubles situations in which they communicate successfully with their partners (Weinberg, 2002).

23.9. BEFORE THE MATCH

1. READY, SET, ROUTINE FOR THE DAY BEFORE

The importance and benefits of pre-match routines - provide rhythm, increase familiarity, build consistency of thought, heighten concentration, minimise distractions and negative thoughts, increase feelings of control and self-confidence, reduce uncertainty, etc - are discussed with players. However, pre-match routines encompass more than just what players do immediately prior to matches, and the coach asks the players to formalise that which they plan to do the day before an important match. The plans should account for:

— Activities undertaken.
— Equipment and clothes preparation.
— Familiarisation with likely opponent/s.
— Sleep: how much is needed and what helps them have a good sleep.
— Travel to the tournament site.
— Assessment of court and environmental conditions: surface, spectators, weather, etc.
— Eating and drinking strategies.
— Booking of practice courts.

2. PRE-MATCH VISUALISATION THE NIGHT BEFORE

The coach introduces the players to the importance of pre-match visualisation. They understand that it can help prepare them to 'play in the zone' and be completed the night before the match. Players share with others their experiences in visualising the night before the match. Players can discuss how and what to visualise.

3. FOLLOW A ROUTINE FOR THE DAY OF THE MATCH

The coach asks the players to document what they should do on match day. The subsequent routine should prepare them for their emotional, mental and physical peak for the match. While there is no single pre-match routine that players should follow, it may include physical and mental warm-ups specifically tailored to their needs. Preparation should also involve a specific time to eat, a winning pre-match meal, some form of visualisation and an on-court warm-up.

4. FAIL TO PLAN, PLAN TO FAIL

The coach helps players to understand that they should enter each match with a game plan that includes match-specific performance goals. The coach then asks the players to formulate a plan A and plan B for an upcoming match. Together, the players and coach discuss the plans and goals that, if achieved, would help players to execute their plans (Quinn, 2001a).

5. ROUTINE BETWEEN MATCHES

The coach asks the players to detail their between match routine. Often, players will not have formalised or even thought of what they do between matches, so this can be a particularly interesting exercise.

23.10. AFTER THE MATCH

1. FOLLOW A POST-MATCH ROUTINE

The coach explains to the players the importance of having a post-match routine. However, with no ideal post-match routine to follow it becomes important for players to develop their own, individualised process that optimises their physical and psychological recovery, while allowing for subsequent match analysis. The player is usually too emotional to evaluate the match until at least one hour after it finishes. The post-match routine needs to be trialled in practice and may include showering and specific physical, psychological and nutritional recovery strategies (e.g. massage, relaxation, stretching, re-hydration, a meal). Players are asked to develop two examples of post-match routines to be trialled in practice.

Rehydration is a fundamental part of any post-match routine.

2. MATCH REVIEW

The coach and players should review match performance in light of the goals set beforehand. The coach should stress the importance of not linking winning with success and losing with failure, but to try to focus on performance. Players should endeavour to leave any review having learned at least one thing or identified one area of their games to continue to improve. Coaches can prompt players to critique their performances with questions like "What would you do differently if you played that match again?"

3. POST-MATCH VISUALISATION

After the match, the coach asks the players to re-create specific situations that arose in the recently-completed match. This exercise can serve to facilitate learning and future decision-making (and therefore performance). The different situations and players' reactions are then discussed with the coach.

4. A BLACK BOOK!

Following the post-match review, players should be encouraged by the coach to keep a log or diary of the match (e.g. including results, performance, feelings ...) for future reference. In doing so, they should also try to objectively critique the psychological performance of their opponents.

23.11. PARENTS

1. CLARIFYING THE ROLES

The coach should organise to meet with parents to clarify and agree to each person's role within their child's 'tennis support team'. Parents are asked to highlight their expectations of the coach, and how they see themselves fitting in. The coach does similarly, and following some discussion, an agreement is hopefully reached. If possible the coach should provide the parents with some practical information outlining the typical phases of a player's development. Any tips on how to create a positive performance environment at home may also be appreciated by the parents (Loehr and Kahn, 1989).

2. GOAL-SETTING

Parents are asked by the coach to document the life and tennis goals they have for their children. Afterwards, the parents and coach discuss any implications these goals may have on their children's personal and/or tennis development.

3. PARENT PROFILING

Parents are asked by the coach to complete a parent profile that sees them evaluate their strengths and weaknesses, and rate themselves on the appropriateness of their responses in pressure situations. Afterwards, they discuss their profile with the coach (Loehr and Kahn, 1989). See an example in the Appendix.

4. KNOWING THE RULES

The coach asks the parents to become familiar with the rules of tennis, the code of conduct, and the tournament regulations for the age category of their children. If clarification is required, parents are encouraged to consult the coach. Specific meetings dealing with these issues should be organised when the need arises (Loehr and Kahn, 1989).

5. MATCH CHARTING

Parents that are particularly enthusiastic about their child's tennis development or get particularly nervous while watching their children play may benefit from being asked by the coach to chart a specific feature of the match. The results may then be discussed by the coach and player afterwards.

6. EVALUATING HOW THE CHILD DEALS WITH STRESS

The coach asks the parents to observe and document the different strategies their child uses to deal with stress. They are then discussed collectively (i.e. child, parents and coach) with a view to improving the effectiveness of the child's stress management techniques (Loehr and Kahn, 1989).

7. PARENT / PLAYER SCENARIOS

The coach presents different scenarios to parents such as: their child not wanting them to attend their matches, poor behaviour of their child, or alternatively their child no longer wishing to attend school, or continue to play competitively. The parents and coach then discuss possible, appropriate responses or alternative solutions (Loehr and Kahn, 1989).

PART IV.
OTHER IMPORTANT ISSUES

"I'm not afraid of anyone, but sometimes I'm afraid of myself. The mental part is very important." *Justin Henin*

PSYCHOLOGY OF MATCH PLAY: FOSTERING POSITIVE MOMENTUM

24

Why do your players sometimes lose when they had such a fastastic lead? Why are some sets won easily and then the player loses the next set? Why are other matches so unpredictable with so many twists and turns? The answer to all these questions lies in 'momentum' and its flow. Results are not always a reflection of the tactical, technical and physical skills of the player.

24.1. INTRODUCTION TO MOMENTUM IN TENNIS

Momentum as related to stroke production can be defined as mass x velocity. Both of these constituents are vector quantities and therefore possess a magnitude and a direction. In sports psychology, the word momentum is used to describe the 'flow' of tennis matches where it too has a direction (positive or negative, for player A or player B) and a magnitude. In fact, Tables 24.1 and 24.2 include the characteristics and the stages of momentum, each defined by variation in direction and magnitude. With much of contemporary sports psychology directed toward assisting players achieve peak performance, research has revealed parallels between performance and 'psychological momentum' (Weinberg, 2002).

During all close tennis matches there will inevitably be periods where one player holds the edge or advantage over the other, and vice versa. Most players, coaches and even spectators can empirically attest to momentum's existence, highlighting matches where they have observed players experience 'hot' or 'cold streaks'. Surprising as it may sound, some experienced players do fail to recognise and capitalise on the flow of matches (Kriese, 1985).

While great players have the ability to weather the storm when the balance is against them and to take maximum advantage when the flow of the match is in their favour, lesser players may let those same opportunities pass by. Certainly there are countless examples of players winning important rallies on slow clay courts, destroying their opponents' confidence in the process, and then going on to serve a double fault on the very next point. Momentum is lost, the mental initiative thrown away, and the grind starts over again! Here, coaches must be sufficiently skilled to intervene and assist players in learning to control momentum.

REMEMBER:

Momentum can be defined as the feeling a player has during a match when things go for or against him. Spectators often relate it to score but as all players know the score does not always reflect the flow of a match (Higham, 2000; Weinberg, 1988). Nevertheless, if not told differently, most players perceive momentum as a force beyond their control. However, experience has shown that it can be controlled and that controlling it is a vital skill for all players.

The game's best players capitalise on positive momentum, rarely letting it go to waste.

IV. Other important issues

PRACTICAL APPLICATION:

The brains of players work like computers and, ultimately, they will do what players tell them to do. Players have to work with their coach to improve their technique, but also work with themselves to improve their confidence and mental consistency.

STRATEGY	POSITIVE MOMENTUM - WITH THE PLAYER	NEGATIVE MOMENTUM - AGAINST THE PLAYER
Definition	- State affecting performance in a positive direction where almost everything seems to 'go right' for the player(s).	- State of mind affecting performance in a negative direction where virtually everything seems to 'go wrong' for the player(s).
Cause (trigger)	- Over the course of a game or two, a player may serve two aces in a row, make a good passing shot, break a serve, and intercept a couple of passing shots from the opponent.	- A player may commit a double fault, get a warning, miss two easy shots, or get a bad call.
Characteristics	- Increased motivation, expectations of success, highly energised feelings, and bursts in performance.	- It involves negative expectations, a lackadaisical attitude, low energy, and fluctuating confidence.
How it manifests (effect)	- Player is on a roll or looks unstoppable. - Player feels in control. - Ball and court seem big. - Lucky things seem to happen. - Player moves to the ball easily. - Player is relaxed and focussed. - Strokes feel smooth and effortless. - Player does not worry about the score or losing.	- Player begins to miss shots they would otherwise expect to make. - 'Bad luck' and negative feelings and expectations are localised to one end of the court. - Nothing seems to be working. - Ball and court seem too small. - Unlucky things seem to happen. - Players' legs feel heavy. - Players feel unsettled. - Opponent controls play. - Small things get on players' nerves.
When to use it	- In the early stages of matches to create an expectation of success and enhance performance.	- Never!

Table 24.1 Characteristics of momentum (Higham, 1994, 2000; Kriese, 1986; Lawrence, 1995; Love, 1985).

STAGES OF MOMENTUM	TIPS FOR THE PLAYER - WHAT TO DO
Totally with the player	- Know how you got there. - Fight: determination is not only needed when behind. - Win the first point. - Watch for a change in tactics. - Step up a gear.
With the player	- Focus to ensure that potential turning points against you are merely blips. - Fight: never get complacent. - It is not what is going wrong that matters, it is your reaction to it. - Learn to deal with gamesmanship - choose the right battlefield. - Keep the match moving - especially when you are in the lead. - Keep choking in perspective - be a tennis expert.
Neutral	- Do not wait, take the initiative. - Be ready to 'jump out of the blocks' from the first point.
Against the player	- Show fighting spirit. - Do not rush. - Be positive; especially with your body language. - Keep an eye on your opponent. - Spot potential turning points quickly. - Review your tactics. - Try to win 'big points' or 'long rallies'. - Identify patterns of play. - Never use gamesmanship.
Totally against the player	- Do not lose hope. - Take your time and play one point at a time. - Do not allow small or insignificant issues / distractions get on your nerves.

Table 24.2 Stages of momentum, and what to do during each stage (Higham, 1994, 2000; Kriese, 1986; Lawrence, 1995; Love, 1985).

Tennis Psychology

24.2. GUIDELINES TO CONTROL MOMENTUM

Shifts or swings in momentum are often linked to a particular point or event (a turning point) so it becomes important for players to have strategies in place to capitalise on a positive shift in their direction, and minimise any damage created by a swing in the direction of their opponents. The speed with which these shifts occur can vary from gradual to sudden, and factors such as current playing form, personality traits, performance expectations, crowd behaviour and an opponent's disposition can all contribute to the swinging, starting or breaking of momentum. 'Starters' can be early success, positive expectations, playing consistently and crowd behaviours, while 'breakers' include a lack of confidence, inconsistent play and committing errors (Schönborn, 1993). Table 24.3 outlines some guidelines for players when endeavouring to use or swing momentum to their advantage.

REMEMBER:

Whether or not the player feels in control of the situation, appears to be decisive in controlling momentum during match play.

PHASE	GUIDELINES
Practice, practice, practice	- It is extremely important that players get into the mind set of 'practice as you would play the game'. This is often overlooked by players and coaches. - Performance can be facilitated and lackadaisal attitudes avoided by goal-setting, maintaining an appropriate perspective and helping players to focus on the things under their control. - Set high expectations and demand high intensity in practice sessions.

Pre-match mental warm-up	- Involve a visualisation and self-talk regimen with affirmations: 'Poise', 'confidence', and 'control'.
	- If visualising potential momentum shifts, envisage yourself making any necessary adjustments to capitalise on or minimise the shift.
	- Maintain a sameness each time you prepare to go out on to the court.
	- Employ an individual ranking system of opponents and prepare to 'do the hunting or to be hunted':
	    > Considerably weaker opponent.
	    > Slightly weaker opponent.
	    > Slightly stronger opponent.
	    > Considerably stronger opponent.
	- Engage in familiarity exercises such as looking around the court, visually getting in touch with the environment, walking the court, 'feeling' the surface and make sure you are comfortable in the setting before you start to play.

During the match: display a 'go for it' attitude	- If behind, never give up.
	- Maintain a positive attitude.
	- Focus on potential turning points:
	    > At the start of a set.
	    > At the end of a set.
	    > Match point down.
	- A new set is a new start.
	- Have hope - things can always turn around.
	- A service break is only effective if players can hold their own serve.
	- Rain, string breakages, and bad calls can have a big effect on the flow of the match, so be ready to make sure the effect is to your advantage.
	- Do not relax if you get in front!
	- Utilise positive self-talk: 'I expect to play well...' 'I will correct mistakes...' 'I am confident and focussed...' to maintain your focus and control your emotions.
	- Keep your focus on the present.
	- Renew your efforts quickly after a setback.
	- Learn to control your energy - find another gear when it matters.
	- Set your own energy levels - do not copy your opponents.
	- Keep your body language positive.
	- Keep a look out for the negative signs from your opponent but beware of any gamesmanship.

Table 24.3 Suggestions on how players can develop and / or foster positive momentum.

WHAT RESEARCH TELLS US...
While study of the effect of momentum on tennis performance has been inconclusive, it has yielded the following findings:
- Match results support the cognitive illusion explanation of psychological momentum in tennis (Silva et al.,1988).
- Players define momentum as a combination of performance (controlling the situation, being successful) and psychological (increased emotion, confidence) events (Richardson et al.,1988).
- Players perceive momentum to start and end as a result of good play by one player or bad play by the other (Burke et al.,1997).
- Home advantage (Nevill et al.,1997), court dependence (Barrell and Trippe, 1975), gender, and disparate levels of play (Ransom and Weinberg, 1985; Weinberg and Jackson, 1989; Weinberg et al., 1981) have been shown to have a negligible effect on performance.
- Male and female professional players are equally likely to come from behind to win matches, but male juniors mount significantly more come-from-behind victories than their female counterparts (Weinberg and Jackson, 1989).

IV. Other important issues

PSYCHOLOGICAL ASPECTS AT CERTAIN STAGES OF THE PLAYER'S CAREER

25

Psychology is at the core of human growth and development. Indeed, developmental psychology has described the mental characteristics of humans as they mature from child to adult. Applied tennis research has tried to identify the psychological skills that need to be fostered as part of this development process. Largely based on past observations of elite players, the characteristics of these players at different ages often provide templates for future player development.

In this Chapter, specific considerations of which coaches and significant others need to be aware to best develop their players, first as happy and self-confident human beings, then as healthy athletes and, if possible as champions, are highlighted. We also describe the developmental stages (as related to age) that players pass through and provide some broad guidelines for best understanding and interacting with players during each stage.

PRACTICAL APPLICATION:

If we are to consider player development to occur in stages, it becomes important to respect the value of each stage and not sacrifice the practice of its psychological skills in an effort to accelerate player learning and / or progression.

25.1. PSYCHOLOGICAL AND DEVELOPMENTAL CONSIDERATIONS FOR TENNIS PLAYERS

According to Woods (2001), several principles with which coaches should be familiar when working with children and adolescents are:

— Children should not be treated as miniature adults.
— Physical characteristics influence social development and both may influence mental or emotional development.
— Stages of growth and development are gender and age-related, but not determined by chronological age.
— Children progress through the stages at their own rate of development.
— Significant adults have a crucial impact on children as role models.

PLAYERS AGED 10 AND UNDER

In this development stage fun is crucial and practice is rehearsal. Children of this age learn quickly yet concrete verbal instruction is insufficient and demonstrations are key.

Children need to physically practice mental skills in training. As part of this, mental effort will need to be high to account for poor concentration (i.e. attention is short and haphazard in nature) and to take maximum advantage of the potential, accelerated development of mental and technical skills at these ages. Those players who develop a deep love for the sport and are not pushed into serious and heavy competitive environments too early, lay the best foundation upon which to build athletic excellence later in their careers (Saviano, 1999).

According to Van Aken (2004), if an enjoyable task-oriented environment is fostered, mental skills that can be learned by young children include: motivation, basic concentration skills, elementary relaxation techniques, the basics of visualisation, emotional control in adversity, the use of rituals, and familiarity with an optimal arousal level. To do so, Sledr (2001) emphasises the need to tailor learning to the individual as much as possible by using simple, high activity games with few rules. Other skills such as good behaviour and sportsmanship should also be introduced at these ages.

REMEMBER:

Mental skills are important for all players, regardless of level or stage of development. For younger players, however, establishing a base of mental fundamentals related to daily practice and competitive skills is of utmost importance and will serve as a springboard for their continued growth as healthy competitors (Lubbers, 2001).

WHAT RESEARCH TELLS US...
According to coaches, the mental skills most needed by players aged under 10 are in order of importance: enjoyment / fun, focus / concentration, emotional control, honesty / integrity, self-confidence and motivation / passion (Gould et al., 1999a).

> **REMEMBER:**
> From a performance standpoint, the goal of psychological development is to increase one's enjoyment and satisfaction when playing tennis as well as to improve the basic and specific mental qualities challenged during match play.

In their quest to understand their environment, children at this stage are inquisitive and continuously ask questions. By setting up situations that require them to explore and problem-solve, children can be helped to develop their intellectual skills accordingly (Woods, 2001). Discipline at this stage should also be established by setting limits, establishing rules, and bestowing punishments or rewards for behaviour.

Throughout, children are learning to deal with the early stages of social and group relationships by generally enjoying the company of playmates of the same gender and participating in inclusive and rewarding activities (Harwood, 2000). Similarly, their emotional loyalty to their role models - parents, elder siblings and even coach - is pronounced... so be outstanding!

THE 11 - 14 AGE GROUP

Player of this age can be characterised as 'on the cusp'. Mentally, there will be moments of enlightenment where the integration of concrete ideas and abstract thought will lead to heightened problem-solving abilities. They enjoy collecting, classifying, combining and operating with things, as well as often appearing to possess endless energy, enthusiasm, and a vast capacity to learn (Woods, 2001). Emotionally, there will be some confusion as the quest and search for independence begins. Socially, the peer group has taken centre stage (Lubbers, 2001).

> **REMEMBER:**
> Players' social interactions are influenced by family values, socioeconomic status, and opportunities for them to act independently (Woods, 2001).

From a motivational standpoint, players of this age are likely to transition from participation driven by external demands/motivators to the desire to compete and improve independent of others. As part of this, training and competition plays a crucial game development role and players further learn to apply fundamental psychological skills such as emotional control, positive thinking and attentional control, mainly through the use of routines. If this transition does not occur, players usually leave the sport to assert themselves elsewhere.

Socialisation is key in this stage as players begin to respect rules and gain the recognition of significant others. Similarly, as the players' self-concepts are being formed, it is important to allow them to have positive learning experiences that help them enjoy a sense of accomplishment and competence.

THE 14 - 16 AGE GROUP

Psychological skills assume even greater importance among players of this age (Lubbers, 2001), particularly with puberty affecting all players differently. From a cognitive standpoint, players begin to adopt more formal thought and logical operations. Moral reasoning also progresses from just following the rules to understanding acceptable behaviour.

Social development during this stage is strongly affected by the culture of group, thus affecting the individual player's self-identity. Emotions are at all times high as the personality conflict experienced by the adolescent causes a continuous shift of moods, behaviours and attitudes. Consequently, self-development, which is one of the bases of success in life, sport and tennis, becomes increasingly important and should be encouraged. A process, not unlike many others, that demands players first identify where they are at, before putting in place a plan to get to where they want! In effect, players will begin to follow the procedures outlined in Chapter 16 as part of a periodised mental skills training (MST) programme, such that fresh meaning is brought to their lives and reinvigorated purpose to their training.

> **WHAT RESEARCH TELLS US...**
> Coaches believe that concentration, enjoyment / fun, motivation, goal-setting, practice intensity, and self-confidence are the skills most needed by tennis players aged between 11-14 (Gould et al., 1999a).

THE 16 - 18 AGE GROUP AND PROFESSIONAL TENNIS

Intellectually, players of this age are capable of showing mature reasoning processes and assimilating facts systematically. Indeed, typically their thought processes are more advanced than their social skills and emotional development (Woods, 2001).

Social development still sees these groups as the most influential social circle, but with the individual progressing to independence and responsibility. Certainly, their desire to find their place in life and society is accompanied by fundamental life choices and decisions (professional tennis vs. studies and / or play tennis or give up) which are discussed in greater detail on page 179.

As players play increasing amounts of professional tennis, the above mentioned responsibility and independence are at a premium as they will be required to travel on their own, organise individual practices, enter tournaments, deal with agents, the media and fans, and even hire a coach. In these circumstances, where players are required to operate optimally both off and on the court, motivation and emotional control (i.e. ability to cope with stress) can be severely tested. It is here where players are likely to really appreciate the need for specific pre-, during and post-match routines (Woods, 2001).

REMEMBER:

As compared to boys, girls tend to mature earlier, and are more likely to enter professional tennis or quit the game at younger ages.

PUTTING IT ALL TOGETHER

Tables 25.1 to 25.5 highlight the psychological skills that players should look to improve as they develop (Bloom, 1985; Crespo and Miley, 1998; Forti, 1992; Gibbons, 1998; Harwood, 2000; LTA, 2003; Lubbers and Gould, 2003; Woods, 2001; USTA, 1994). While the Tables' contents are by no means prescriptive, if models like this are to be used, principles such as overload and specificity that also apply to the improvement of other skills (i.e. physical, technical…) need to be followed along with an understanding that individual players will move through the stages at different rates.

In general terms, they provide an excellent overview of the mental ingredients that need to be considered along the normal development pathway. Some of the listed psychological skills take on added significance as players mature, and have been more comprehensively discussed in previous chapters.

All players develop at different rates, so coaches need to possess sufficiently flexible teaching strategies to accommodate for this variance.

IV. Other important issues

	BEGINNER / 10 YEARS AND UNDER
Main psychological characteristics	— Want instant gratification / Anxious for immediate pleasure. — Possess poor capacity to concentrate but great imagination. — Egocentric: Only want to play and experience things individually, and be the centre of attention. — Limited social interaction: Initially oriented toward adults. — Great disposition to learn, to gather information, to be useful and to do things well. — Think intuitively and pre-operationally and then with concrete operations. — Slowly begin to accept external rules. Persistent and obstinate. — Lose interest with lack of variety in activities or incompatible stimuli. — Need constant praise, achievement and success. — Start comparing with others, and have a tendency to thrive on rivalry (competition). — Learn through repetition and experience. — Progressive development of self-identity / concept.
Primary emphasis of the stage	— Having fun.
Level of external pressure (parents, coach, etc.)	— Non-existent.
Effort / love of the game	— Emphasise 100% effort and love of the game (at all times). — Promote personal best. — Follow the 'chase every ball' philosophy.
Preferred modes of communication	— Affective and visual. — Limited attention span: action oriented.
Goal-setting principles	— Goals should be simple and largely immediate (drill, training session and match), fostering enjoyment, game play and learning.
Core mental skills	— Acquisition of mental fundamentals: motivation, self-confidence, self-esteem, positive feel, act and react, etc. — Coach to avoid problems that create self-doubt and anxiety. — Winning / losing: positive attitude to winning, losing and skill development.
Media skills	— Not applicable.
Sportsmanship / personal conduct	— Knowledge of rules, fairness and etiquette. — Simple scoring. — Respect for and ability to work with others.

Competition	— Success should be experienced in the following formats:
	   - Self-competition.
	   - Cooperation / free play.
	   - Multiple sports.
	   - Team events.

Rewards from others	— All participants receive the same reward.
Coach's role / key aspects to emphasise	— Positive reinforcement (praise, encouragement) / instruction as role model. — Create varied and fun practices that ensure immediate success. — Focus on the player and the performance, not results / outcomes.

	INTERMEDIATE / 11-14 YEARS OLD
Main psychological characteristics	— Can establish medium and long term goals. — Improved rationality and move toward abstract thinking. — Display greater enthusiasm toward participation in activities. — More tolerant and possess a more established sense of humour. — Socially oriented toward peer interaction, cooperation and approval. — Less accepting of what adults tell them. — Interested in assuming more active roles in their training and practice to improve their skills and gradually accep more responsibility. — Greater understanding of what is required in committing to tennis.
Primary emphasis of the stage	— Learning and performing well.
Level of external pressure (parents, coach, etc.)	— Virtually non-existent.
Effort / love of the game	— Emphasise 100% effort and love of the game at all times.
Preferred modes of communication	— Verbal and concrete.
Goal-setting principles	— Informal with mostly short-term goals (3-6 months), interspersed with more intermediate (6 months - 1 year) goals, and longer-term (career). — Establish specific, measurable, agreed, realistic, timed, evaluated, recorded, and self-determined goals (SMARTERS). — Fosters leisure and enjoyment in learning new things.
Core mental skills	— Mental preparation strategies: rituals for serve / return, match preparation, etc. — Develop self-confidence / self-esteem: walking powerfully self-talk. — Basic concentration skills: focussing. — Introduction to basic stress / mistake management strategies: straighten strings, 3R's (Rehearse, review, reset) and / or others. — Learn to practice with intensity. — Learn to tolerate frustration, win or lose. — Winning / losing: put winning and losing into a healthy perspective.
Media skills	— Not applicable. — For exceptional players refer to media skills for 14-16 y o. players.
Sportsmanship / personal conduct	— Realise the importance of honesty and integrity on-court. — Develop sense of responsibility/ independence. — Good behaviour both on- and off-court.
Competition	— Encourage players to love the battle. — Make use of optimal challenge. — 2:1 win:loss ratio. — League matches.
Rewards from others	— Players should learn and begin to understand the purpose of rewards.
Coach´s role / key aspects to emphasise	— Use cooperative games and drills to practice with purpose / intensity. — Create a task oriented motivational climate / learning environment. — Use open and two-way communication. — Use mental training in on-court tennis practices.

	ADVANCED / 14-16 YEARS OLD
Main psychological characteristics	— Social orientation toward individualising themselves. — Focus more on establishing their own identities. — More questioning and analysing: Complex extractions and concepts. — Abstract and critical thinking. — Can be obstinate, indifferent, but also idealistic and committed. — Have to deal with the conflict between emotion and thought. — Occasional crisis of identity in search of a stable self-image.
Primary emphasis of the stage	— Performing and winning.
Level of external pressure (parents, coach, etc.)	— Moderate.
Effort / love of the game	— Emphasise 100% effort and love of the game at all times.
Preferred modes of communication	— Rational and concrete.
Goal-setting principles	— Goals will be primarily intermediate but a combination of performance (technical, tactical, physical, mental, etc.) and outcome goals (ranking and titles). — Reinforce intrinsic motivation. — Formalise a written plan. — Foster some independence in goal-setting.
Core mental skills	— Recognise the individual's ideal performance state (IPS). — Make use of specific breathing techniques. — Understand mistakes are part of learning. — Learn concentration skills, strategies to enhance self-confidence, and arousal control techniques on- and off-court. — Combine tennis with some academic activities wherever possible. — Learn from mistakes, and to react / solve difficult situations. — Winning / losing: develop balanced attributional patterns for wins and losses, and differentiate between effort and ability.
Media skills	— Be prepared to give post-match speeches, showing gratitude, being humble in victory and gracious in defeat, etc. — Speak positively about opponents. — Be aware of posture and make eye contact with fans and on-court personnel.
Sportsmanship / personal conduct	— Encourage self-management and responsibility. — Players are 100% responsible for their actions. — Congratulate and thank fellow players and deserved tournament staff.
Competition	— Develop competitive spirit. — Learn to assess momentum during matches and in the season. — Develop a game plan and analyse results.
Rewards from others	— Rewards provided for winners, runner-ups, as well as individual attitudes and effort.
Coach´s role / key aspects to emphasise	— Create an optimal competitive / decision making environment. — Ensure players travel with coaches to competitions. — Mental training both on- and off-court is part of the regular training programme.

	ASPIRING PROFESSIONAL / 16-18 YEARS OLD
Main psychological characteristics	— Responsible for their goals. — More controlled personality. — Centered and focussed on the 'big decision' of becoming a 'pro'. — Start to develop stable, clear and deep relationships with others. — Show interest in their surroundings. — Think more about the future. — Less sensitive to external stimuli. — Increased importance of self-direction, self-actualisation and self-expression.
Primary emphasis of the stage	— Winning.
Level of external pressure (parents, coach, etc.)	— High.
Effort / love of the game	— Emphasise 100% effort and love of the game at all times.
Preferred modes of communication	— Abstract.
Goal-setting principles	— SMARTERS goals continue to relate to performance and outcome. — Should illustrate high levels of intrinsic motivation: Showing intensity in practice, attentiveness and dedication to physical training, and evidence of independence as a player and person. — Find ways of continually being challenged and motivated because performance gains will come at a slower pace.
Core mental skills	— Use imagery and breathing as well as other arousal control techniques. — Concentrate / focus on-court. — Use advanced emotional control strategies both on- and off-court. — Fully develop awareness and control of individual IPS. — Automate effective mental skill response on-court. — Winning / losing: learn from wins as well as from losses.
Media skills	— Present a friendly demeanour to reporters. — Speak to and look at the interviewer. — Reveal personality during the interview.
Sportsmanship / personal conduct	— Appreciate what the game has given you and be willing to give back to the game (to youngsters). — Foster self-reliance, independence and responsibility in training and matchplay.
Competition	— Keep competition in perspective. — Demonstrate attributes of a 'tough' competitor.
Rewards from others	— Winners, runner-ups. — Individual attitudes and effort.
Coach´s role / key aspects to emphasise	— Use complex and integrated training. — Practices should demand strong work ethics of the players. — Provide training and competition opportunities to foster independence, social interaction, decision-making, planning, goal-setting and responsibility. — Be available to offer guidance and direction.

	PROFESSIONAL / 18 +
Main psychological characteristics	— Fully responsible for their goals. — Committed to their tennis careers. — Less critical and impulsive. — More analytical. — Know how to learn from experience. — Balanced personalities. — Periods of self-doubt almost surpassed. — Self-identity still being shaped but almost complete.
Primary emphasis of the stage	— Winning.
Level of external pressure (parents, coach, etc.)	— Maximum.
Effort / love of the game	— Emphasise 100% effort and love of the game at all times.
Preferred modes of communication	— Existential.
Goal-setting principles	— Comprehensive, personal and largely self-managed goal-setting programme. — Critically evaluate goals and performance.
Core mental skills	— Use imagery to rehearse motor skills and/or tactics. — Use of emotional control strategies both on- and off-court. — Use of a variety of concentration skills in preparation and during competition / training. — All strategies should be tailored to the players' individual needs and characteristics. — Maintain ambition and persistence under pressure and adversity.
Media skills	— Questions of a personal nature do not have to be answered. — Nothing is 'off the record'. — Understand the importance of personal appearance; make visible the sponsors' logos.
Sportsmanship / personal conduct	— Develop self-regulation skills (learn to take decisions with conviction and manage an increasingly complex physical and social environment). — Increasingly able to deal with injuries and their consequences.
Competition	— Develop interests away from tennis (friends, free time, hobbies, etc.) to ensure a balanced life. — Winning / losing: Prioritise performance and outcome goals.
Rewards from others	— Enjoy the wins but learn from them as well as the losses.
Coach´s role / key aspects to emphasise	— Coaches are virtually enlisted as advisors to players.

25.2. THE BIG DECISION: "I WANT TO BE A PROFESSIONAL TENNIS PLAYER"

Inevitably, for junior players, there comes a time when they begin to contemplate where tennis fits as part of their lives. What it means to them; how much time they are willing to commit to the cause - if indeed there is a cause - are quandaries that these players entertain. That this period coincides with a time where important decisions must be made regarding the player's chosen competitive or recreational tennis pathway, and other developmental issues common to adolescence, makes decision-making an unenviable task.

Career opportunities in professional tennis are limited. Many young players have visions of becoming professional players, yet far fewer actually turn these visions into reality (Coakley, 2001). In addition to these discouraging odds, professional tennis opportunities are extremely short term. The average tennis career lasts between 3 and 7 years (Coakley, 2001) with a mean of 6.4 years (Otis et al., 2006), leaving a further 30-40 years to the typical retirement age of 65. It is public perception, backed by images portrayed in the media, that players are wealthy. Indeed many are very wealthy and receive massive endorsements from companies. However, salaries vary widely across professional tennis, and the players who receive huge endorsements are the exception rather than the norm. Nevertheless many young players still dream of professional tennis careers.

It is however virtually impossible to nominate a specific age at which players should make the above decisions. As a guide, by the time players reach 15-18 years of age, most experienced 'eyes' and even the players themselves will have a reasonable idea if they have or are likely to have what it takes (physically, technically, tactically, and psychologically) to 'make it'. In general, girls, with their earlier maturation coupled with the characteristics of the women's professional tour, will be able to ascertain their chances of turning professional earlier than boys. Throughout this process, the coach's input, common sense and expertise is all important, especially in the face of over enthusiastic parents eager to see their child turn pro at any cost. Indeed, the coach is likely to have the best understanding of what it takes to be a successful professional player, and may have even confronted similar decisions himself as a player or when coaching other players in the past.

REMEMBER:

It is the coaches' responsibility to provide honest and accurate feedback to players and their parents about the players' prospects of turning professional. In doing so, the coach has to be sure to highlight the pro's and con's of turning professional and other potential options such as combining tennis and study at university (e.g. college tennis in the USA).

PRACTICAL APPLICATION:

Blundell (1995) suggests that in determining whether or not players have what it takes to turn professional, coaches should consider:
- Physical and psychological development of the player.
- Gender of the player.
- Need and potential for technical and tactical improvement.
- Motivation of the player and interest in studies or hobbies other than tennis.
- Economic welfare of the players' parents.
- Available grants: Club, federation, sponsors, etc.

Increasingly astute decisions need to be made with respect to junior players' tournament schedules as they mature.

V. Other important issues

25.3. PERFORMANCE SLUMPS

REMEMBER:

Examples of 'performance slumps' in professional tennis are not uncommon. In 1997, after several years ranked among the top 10, Andre Agassi ended the year with a ranking of 122. He then went onto climb back up to 6 in 1998, before reaching number 1 in 1999. Within years of reaching number 1, Marat Safin and Juan Carlos Ferrero fell to 86 and 98 respectively.

All competitive players, regardless of playing level are likely to have experienced a performance slump. Slumps can be defined as inexplicable drops in performance that extend longer than would be expected from the normal ups and downs of competition (Taylor, 1991). They tend to disrupt arousal levels, intensify feelings of worthlessness and guilt, and produce strong negative thinking and emotions; all of which help to maintain the slumps, and can be draining physically and emotionally. From a psychological standpoint, this negative chain-reaction needs to be overcome before players are able to regain their pre-slump performance levels.

IDENTIFYING A SLUMP

The nature of tennis competition implies that players' performances will fluctuate during the season. As sustaining peak performance week-in week-out is essentially impossible, most declines in performance are to be expected. But whether these decines manifest into slumps can be identified through:

REMEMBER:

It takes time to get into a slump and it takes time to get out of one! As a result, players and coaches must be prepared to put in the necessary time and effort for the players to return to their previous level of performance.

— **Comparing a player's average current level of (and variation in) performance to that of past seasons / years.** If current performance is consistently poor, it may be a slump.

— **Recognising if the causes of the problem are predominantly technical, tactical, physical or psychological.** Often players have difficulty in determining the cause of the problem. This doubt creates uncertainty as to which training intervention / strategy to use and as a result, the changes needed to improve their performance are not made.

CAUSES OF SLUMPS

Loehr (1991) suggests that performance slumps can be brought on by:

PRACTICAL APPLICATION:

For many coaches and players, technical problems are easier to accept than psychological ones. These problems are often seen as a sign of weakness. In fact, psychological problems occur as players do not possess the necessary psychological coping skills.

— **Physical factors:** fatigue, minor injuries, health problems, poor diet, and lingering illness have been associated with persistent performance problems.

— **Technical factors:** modifications to technique can often produce temporary performance slumps. As much as possible, these modifications should be made during breaks from competition where players may be more receptive to skill learning and frustration reduced.

— **Equipment factors:** changes to the player's equipment, particularly racquets and strings, can trigger a decline in performance, leading to a slump.

— **Psychological factors:** long slumps are primarily psychological in nature. Players may fall into a negative 'spiral' of low self-confidence and heightened tension and arousal. Nideffer (1992) suggests that chances are the problem is psychological if:

  - Mistakes tend to occur more frequently under pressure.

  - Players find themselves having a large number of negative thoughts or feelings when competing.

  - A breakdown in one area leads to other problems as well.

When in doubt as to whether the problem is technical or psychological, it may be preferable to initially make a technical adjustment. Then, if the problem is indeed psychological, the refined technique will likely work well in practice, but poorly in matches. Subsequent interventions will then be psychological.

Similarly, the initial onset of a slump may be associated with injuries, or poor health. However, if neither continue to exist and performance remains poor, the primary problem will often be psychological. Also, the root of problem may lie outside the court and be independent of tennis (i.e. family difficulties, financial concerns...).

— **Natural learning plateaus.** Plateaus are unpredictable learning periods in which even though the player may be training hard, there is no observable progress in performance. They can be considered as periods of new learning, but they can also contribute to the occurrence of performance slumps.

— **Increased awareness.** Learning of mental skills awareness (muscle tension, arousal levels, negative attitudes, etc.) can also result in players finding it difficult to perform at their best and potentially in performance slumps.

RECOMMENDATIONS FOR PREVENTING SLUMPS

The best way to deal with slumps is to prevent them from happening! Slumps can be prevented by paying careful attention to their causes and putting in place measures to avoid them.

— **Physical.** Monitor physical condition (players who are well-conditioned will be less susceptible to fatigue, injury, and illness), ensure rest (days off, regeneration activities), reduce the quantity and increase the quality of training, optimise and periodise competition schedules (play meaningful events), and schedule time-off to help ensure a high level of performance.

— **Technical.** Technique is best developed during the off-season and these slumps may be prevented by minimising the technical work that needs to be undertaken during the competitive season (i.e. develop and / or maintain sound technique in the off-season). Working on technique may not only disturb good technique, but it may also reduce confidence and distract concentration. A video library of good technique may be appropriately accessed by players and coaches from time to time.

— **Technological.** The best way to prevent technologically-related performance slumps is to maintain equipment in excellent condition and avoid equipment changes during the competitive season.

— **Psychological.** To prevent slumps triggered by psychological issues related to tennis performance, it is important to have players engaged in a regular mental training programme.

REMEMBER:

The best way to reduce the likelihood of a slump due to physical causes is for players to listen to their bodies. They need to acknowledge fatigue, injury, and illness and when any are evident, they should be dealt with immediately. Simply put, players must learn to work hard and rest hard (Taylor, 1991).

PLAN FOR ELIMINATING SLUMPS

In the event that players are suffering performance slumps, it becomes important to address them in the following systematic way.

Ackowledgement and commitment

First and foremost, players need to accept the fact that they are in a slump and that its cause should be identified. Players may also need to commit to renewing their enthusiasm and excitement for the game. In like kind, coaches should also accept that players are in a slump and make a committment to help them.

IV. Other important issues

It is advisable for players to list the attitudes, beliefs and thoughts that may have contributed to the slump such that they have a better understanding of its potential causes and the process they need to go through to return to pre-slump levels of performance.

Time out

Once players and coaches accept the presence of a slump, players likely need to take some time away from training and competition. This will provide a change of scenery and people, allow them to recover and to 'recharge their batteries', give them the opportunity to view their slump objectively, and ultimately devise an organised plan to overcome the slump.

Goal-setting

Critical to recovering from a slump is the reviewing of personal goals and objectives. The motivation and high energy required to break through the slump can be provided through the setting of new goals:

- **Return-to-form goals** indicating the level of performance to which the player wants to return.
- **Daily training goals,** which are both realistic and challenging.
- **Daily performance goals** that inspire the player and have a reward attached to them. Such goals should be completed in small steps above the current slump level.

PRACTICAL APPLICATION:

If it is necessary to keep competing while trying to come out of the slump, the player should choose to do so at a lower level.

Train physically

Players may benefit from increasing their level of physical conditioning as there is a qualitative link between strong physical and mental performances.

Train mentally

Loehr (1991) calls this a 'comprehensive mental recycling training programme' which consists of:

- 10-15 minutes twice daily.
- Mentally reconstructing attitudes, beliefs and thoughts.
- Sessions characterised by:
    - 5-7 minutes of relaxation.
    - 5-7 minutes of visualisation in which players will visualise themselves breaking through, achieving new and exciting levels of performance, and using self-talk to re-capture the winning feelings and moments.

Patience

Players should not force the process nor place pressure on themselves to come out of the slump. The break-through will occur naturally when their outlook and skills are ready.

Counselling

Players in severe slumps may benefit from individual and group counselling. Individual counselling enables players to air their thoughts and feelings to the counsellors so that coping skills can be developed to assist players better deal with the anxiety and concerns of being in a slump. Group counselling enables players to share their 'slump' experiences within a supportive social network to alleviate any feelings of loneliness or isolation that may otherwise present. These sessions also provide players a forum through which they can share their ideas about how they may get out of a slump.

in following these recommendations, players should be able to minimise the number of slumps they experience throughout their tennis careers. Conversely, when slumps do arise, coaches and players will be replete with the neccesary knowledge and skills to ensure they are as short-lived as possible.

25.4. PSYCHOLOGY OF THE INJURED PLAYER

In spite of improvements in racquets, courts, coaching techniques and conditioning programmes, the incidence of tennis injuries is high. Regardless of experience or ability, no player is immune to injury. And along with physical injury comes its psychological effects. The initial emotional response, the approach to the recovery process, and the residual psychological effect it may have on future performance all vary from individual to individual. Indeed, for elite players, Quinn (2001b) considers dealing with injury as one of the toughest opponents they will face!

Among the professional tennis playing population, any significant injury is likely to be perceived as a traumatic life event. The accompanying emotional stress does not come from the injury itself, but rather from the interruption to participation. For some competitors, an injury causes a severe disruption to their lifestyles, and for others, it may even end their tennis careers. It is thus imperative for coaches to understand why and how players react to injury as well as the psychological factors that may influence the recovery process.

REMEMBER:

Injured players may feel confused, even obsessed about when they will return to play. Rapid mood swings, exaggeration, withdrawal from others, guilt and denial of recovery are also common psychological reactions to injury (Weinberg and Gould, 1995).

PSYCHOLOGICAL FACTORS THAT MAY PREDISPOSE PLAYERS TO INJURY

Research implicates certain psychological factors as having the potential to contribute to injury and re-injury (Quinn, 1996). Specific personality traits, life stress events, and attentional style are all suggested to play a role in predisposing some players to injury (Quinn, 2001b). For example, Rotella and Heyman (1986) reported that frequently injured players are more tender-minded and introverted, and possess a larger number of psychological traits indicative of less-than-desirable psychological adjustment than players injured less frequently. Similarly, those individuals who are subject to a higher number of general stresses (e.g. death of family members, changes in residence, divorce, school graduation, financial difficulties), tennis specific stressors (e.g. trouble with coaches, being dropped to a lower team), and / or day to day stressors, are believed to have their previously established equilibrium offset, thus predisposing them to injury (Feltz, 1986).

Anxiety-related problems such as impaired attention / concentration and heightened muscle tension are also associated with increased stress and injury risk (Blackwell and McCullagh, 1990; Quinn, 2001b), while inappropriate training expectations (e.g. "no pain, no gain") have been empirically linked to injury.

PSYCHOLOGICAL RESPONSES TO INJURY

Leddy et al. (1994) investigated the psychological consequences of injury in tennis players among other sportspersons. Data revealed that when compared to non-injured players, injured players exhibited greater depression and anxiety, and lower self-esteem immediately following, as well as two months after physical injury. These findings support the general observation that physically injured players experience a period of emotional distress, which may become severe enough to warrant clinical intervention.

Typically however, injured players experience five 'emotional phases' - denial, anger, depression, acceptance, and reorganisation - before feeling ready to re-commence competition. As part of this phasic return to tournament matchplay, competitors will likely to encounter varying levels of identity and confidence loss, fear and anxiety, diminished confidence, and reduced performance (Weinberg and Gould, 1995).

DEALING WITH THE INJURED PLAYER

The work of Gould and Medberry (2000) as well as empirical reports from specialists in the field, recommend that coaches and parents assist injured players by:

— Building a social support system for the injured players.
— Develop massive rapport with the players.
— Fine-tuning the players' stress management and relaxation skills.
— Educating players regarding the different stages they can expect to experience during the recovery process.
— Facilitating players to improve their use of mental skills, especially goal-setting, positive self-talk and visualisation, as they relate to the recovery process.
— Encouraging them to talk to other players who have successfully recovered from injury.
— Helping them resist the temptation to return to competition too early or inappropriately increase their training load in an effort to accelerate their rehabilitation.
— Including players in group and / or cross-training activities where possible and appropriate.

Certain types of personalities and life stressors can predispose players to greater risk of injury.

25.5. PSYCHOLOGY OF THE RETIRING PLAYER

One of the most powerful, significant and potentially traumatic experiences encountered by players is that of their playing careers coming to a close. Moreover, retirement from tennis involves a variety of unique experiences that sets it apart from that of retirement from other professional pursuits. Tennis careers are typically shorter than most other careers or occupations, as most players retire, voluntarily or involuntarily, during their mid to late twenties. Players are then forced to contend with this early age of career termination, as well as the want or need to find another career.

Over the past three decades, considerable interest has been directed toward the issue of retirement among tennis players. In newspapers and popular literature, numerous accounts have chronicled both the traumatic and successful experiences of professional players adjusting to life after tennis.

More recently, awareness of the need for pre-retirement planning and counselling has increased (WTA, 2004), and prompted organisations and academies to provide these services.

PRACTICAL APPLICATION:

Players and coaches should understand the psychology of retirement such that players are more likely to experience positive closure of their tennis careers, and / or foster the development of a new identity to encourage growth in their post tennis life (Taylor and Ogilvie, 2001).

CAUSES OF RETIREMENT AMONG PLAYERS

The typical tennis career draws to a close as a function of four factors: chronological age, deselection, the effects of injury, and independent choice.

Chronological age. The decline in performance due to advancing age (and the associated slow deterioration of the physical capabilities, the loss in motivation to train and compete, and the loss of social status) is largely considered to be a primary cause of retirement. Allison and Meyer (1988) found that 10% of their sample of female tennis professionals retired due to age, while Fisher and Conlee (1979) reported a loss of muscle mass or agility to contribute to career termination in older players.

Deselection. The harsh deselection process (survival of the fittest) common to competitive tennis, is another cause of retirement among tennis players.

Injury. Injuries are a significant cause of retirement. Almost 30% of retired players have identified injury as leading to their retirement (Taylor and Ogilvie, 2001).

Indepentent choice. An often overlooked cause of retirement is that of player choice. That is, when players want to assume a new direction in life, seek out new challenges and sources of satisfaction, spend more time with family and friends, immerse themselves in a new social milieu, or simply find that tennis no longer provides the enjoyment and fulfilment that it once did.

Other reasons for retirement from the game may include problems with coaches or the tennis organisation, as well as financial difficulties.

PRACTICAL APPLICATION:

There is still considerable debate about the proportion of players who experience distress due to retirement and how the distress is manifested. Some researchers argue that there is little evidence to indicate that tennis retirement is traumatic, particularly for amateur players. An opposing view has been presented through the analysis of retiring elite-amateur and professional players (Young et al., 2006).

WHAT RESEARCH TELLS US...
Young et al. (2004) found that two thirds of the sample of former elite Australian female players thought about leaving the circuit prior to their actual departure.

CHARACTERISTICS OF RETIREMENT FROM TENNIS

The retirement process from tennis is characterised by:

— **Transition and life change:** Retirement from tennis is not one transition but many transitions. It is not a singular, abrupt event. After all, player's entire lifestyles change: what they do each day, their identity, their interpersonal relationships, and their goals. This transition can be planned or unplanned, voluntary or not. The feelings that may accompany it will change over time as well as the player's responses to them. This is what makes transition a process as opposed to an event.

— **Individual experience:** While the experience may be similar to that of another player, it will never be exactly the same. Once the applause stops and yes, it does stop... What is going to fill that void? The answer for the player is a personal one. Other factors that will likely determine the individual nature of the response include:

- **Developmental contributors.** The fact that professional tennis places the highest priority on winning, stresses the importance of adopting a more holistic approach to tennis development. This should begin early in the life of the player when parents and coaches involved in youth tennis should understand that long-term personal and social development is more important than short-term tennis success.

- **Self-identity.** Players who have been immersed in their tennis have excluded other activities will have a self-identity that is composed almost exclusively of their tennis involvement. The more central the tennis career was to the player identity, the greater the likely loss of self-identity.

- **Perceptions of control.** Often the causes of retirement are outside the control of the individual player and this may create a situation that is highly aversive and threatening, affecting self-competence and self-confidence.

- **Social identity.** Retirement has been associated with a loss of status and social identity. As a result, retired players may question their self-worth and feel the need to regain the lost public esteem. Players with a broad-based social identity that includes family, friendship, educational, and occupational components demonstrate better adaptation in retirement.

- **Other contributing factors.** Socioeconomic status, minority status, gender, health at retirement, marital status, age, years competing and level of attainment will further contribute to adaptation to retirement.

— **Searching:** Players may have to begin to search for employment, or even a new identity.

— **Takes time and energy:** Just as disengaging from the identity as a player takes time, the search for a new role and identity will take time and energy.

— **Needs patience:** Some players will experience difficulty in displaying the necessary patience to establish new roles and occupations.

— **Discovery:** Players may pursue options such as completing a degree, volunteering for a charity organisation, coaching kids, etc. They will likely discover new things about themselves, and a new direction.

— **Phasic process:** Several models of transition have been proposed, consisting of: (1)

> **REMEMBER:**
> Female tennis players cited a variety of reasons for their retirement including a lack of support from their national association, dissatisfaction with lifestyle and the tournament environment, lack of funds, injury, excessive travel, loneliness, too much pressure, conflict with a coach, a lack of guidance as to tournament scheduling, the development of other interests, the absence of a mentor or coach and a lack of enthusiasm and motivation (WTA, 2004).

WHAT RESEARCH TELLS US...
Before leaving the professional circuit, former tennis players implored, 'giving it everything they possibly could' so that they left with no regrets. Young et al. (2004) indicated that many retiring professionals use the assistance of a sport psychologist to help with their transition.

Immobilisation (shock from the event); (2) Minimisation (negative emotions associated with a loss are downplayed); (3) Self-doubt (self-esteem is threatened and depression may ensue); (4) Letting go (through feelings of loss, anger, and disappointment); (5) Testing out (groundwork for a new direction); (6) Searching for meaning (perspective on difficulties of earlier stages); and (7) Internalisation (acceptance and transition completed).

SKILLS / RESOURCES THAT FACILITATE RETIREMENT

Skills / resources known to influence a player's ability to overcome difficulties that may arise during retirement include coping skills, social support, and pre-retirement planning.

— **Coping skills.** The availability of effective coping skills likely facilitates the retirement process. Players may use cognitive restructuring and mental imagery to re-orient their thinking in a more positive direction, self-instructional training to improve attention and problem-solving, and goal-setting to provide direction and motivation in their post-tennis careers. Anger and anxiety strategies such as time-out, relaxation training, and health and exercise and nutritional counselling can also be used to good effect. Further, behaviour modification techniques such as assertiveness training, time management training, and skills assessment and development can help overcome specific behavioural difficulties.

— **Social support.** Throughout players' careers, the vast majority of their friends, and acquaintances as well as their social activities revolve around their tennis lives. Upon career termination, those friendships and networks are unlikely to exist to the same extent. Significantly, players that best adapt to retirement receive considerable support from family and friends outside tennis, while players who experience more difficult transitions have indicated feelings of loneliness and the desire for greater support (Young et al., 2006.

— **Pre-retirement planning.** A process –that includes continuing education, investment strategies, and social networkig– has perhaps the broadest influence on a player's adaptation to retirement. However, for this to be of maximum benefit, any player reluctance to accept their careers will come to a close and that there is a need to plan for that time, must first be overcome.

PRACTICAL APPLICATION:

Former tennis players advice to the current crop is to ease the transition into retirement by planning for the future (evaluating financial and vocational goals, determining what other skills or study need to be undertaken), while also networking and talking to other players who are going through the same processs.

PRACTICAL APPLICATION:

Tennis organisations should adopt strategies to not only help players fulfil their potential on the circuit but also ease their transition into retirement. These strategies should include: ensuring open channels of communication, educating players on several matters related to retirement, acknowledging past achievements of players, and guiding them as to career future opportunities (Young et al., 2006).

CONCLUSION

Elite players are confronted with a number of financial, occupational, emotional, and / or social adjustments in transitioning to their post-tennis lives and careers. Some players will adapt well, and immediately thrive, while others will experience more difficulties in negotiating any cognitive, emotional or behavioural hurdles. Where coping skills, support networks and career-planning will likely help all players maintain their self-worth as they establish new identities in their retirement, the implementation of cognitive, affective and social support intenventions may be required to reduce depression and anxiety among high-stress players.

25.6. LIFETIME SPORT: PSYCHOLOGICAL AND PSYCHOSOCIAL BENEFITS OF TENNIS

Participation in tennis has been shown to benefit players of all ages and playing standards from psychological and psychosocial standpoints. In support of the notion that tennis is a sport for a lifetime, the paragraphs below detail its psychological and psychosocial benefits.

INCREASING VIGOUR, OPTIMISM, SELF-ESTEEM

Finn et al. (1993) showed tennis players to score higher in vigour, optimism and self-esteem while scoring lower in depression, anger, confusion, anxiety and tension than other athletes and non-athletes.

AVOIDING DEPRESSION AND ANXIETY

Wheelchair tennis players that play frequently have been shown to score lower on depression and trait anxiety and higher on vigour than less frequent or inactive wheelchair athletes (Muraki et al., 2000).

BUILDING PERSONALITY AND MANAGING MISTAKES

Tennis has been reported to outperform golf, inline skating and most other sports in developing positive personality characteristics (Gavin, 1992). It also helps players to realise the value of managing and minimising mistakes... skills transferrable to everyday life.

IMPROVING REACTION TIME

Playing tennis improves your general ability to react to stimuli, helping to minimise the deterioration of reaction time that comes with ageing.

In a study of tennis players and sedentary people of varied age, active older men were shown to possess superior reaction and movement times when compared to sedentary men of the same age (Spirduso and Clifford, 1978).

MAINTAINING COGNITIVE FUNCTION

Tennis requires alertness and tactical thinking, with players continuously challenged to adjust to the opponent (style of play, strategies, gamesmanship, etc.), and the elements (wind, sun, equipment, etc.) while still performing at their best. Indeed, where Groppel (1981) reported that tennis may generate new connections between nerves in the brain, and thus promote a lifetime of continual brain development, Yaffe et al. (2001) revealed playing tennis twice weekly to be associated with decreased risk of cognitive decline.

REDUCING THE RISK OF DEMENTIA

Tennis, among other cognitive and physical leisure activities, has been implicated in the reduction of some causes of dementia such as Alzheimer's disease and vascular dementia (Verghese et al., 2003).

GENDER NEUTRAL

Tennis is a sport that promotes gender integration throughout beginner and adult competition. Consistent with this assertion is the finding that adolescents view tennis, more from a gender stereotype point of view, as neutral when compared to 'feminine' (ballet) and 'masculine' (karate) sports (Alley and Hicks, 2005). Consequently, the participation of adolescents is less likely to be influenced by any societal bias.

FOSTERING POSITIVE PARENTAL INFLUENCE

As elaborated on in Chapter 27, parents play crucial roles in life, in sports and in tennis! They have been shown as the primary reason for a player's introduction to the sport (Baxter-Jones and Maffulli, 2003), and are important in providing players supportive familial and learning environments.

DECREASING WEIGHT CONCERNS IN YOUNG GIRLS

Tennis players aged 5-7 years old have reported less weight, appearance and body shape concerns than girls participating in sports such as dance, gymnastics, swimming, aerobics and figure skating (Davidson et al., 2003).

IT IS ENJOYABLE TO PLAY!

Playing tennis is above all great fun! Players go out on court to have a good time and enjoy the challenges it provides. Indeed, the motives that account for adults' participation in tennis have been shown to predominantly relate to the physical (e.g. keeping fit) and social (e.g. making friends) characteristics of the game (Kolt et al., 2004).

Coaches play an important in ensuring that the game is fun for young players and adults alike.

IV. Other important issues

PSYCHOLOGY FOR THE TENNIS COACHES AND OFFICIALS 26

26.1. PHILOSOPHY OF COACHING AND COACHING GOALS

Tennis coaches have many roles – teacher, friend, mentor, psychologist, etc – and are expected to possess competencies (skills and knowledge) across a number of fields (e.g. technique, tactics, psychology, physical conditioning, methodology, nutrition, first aid, and ethics). Further, some coaches virtually work 24/7 for salaries that are not commensurate with these long hours nor the effort they put into their coaching.

In this book we have discussed the psychological challenges and problems of players at length, but…what of the coaches? Research has shown that they too encounter mental 'ups and downs' and may benefit from psychological help as much as players do (Duda et al., 2003). Consequently, this Chapter sees us outline how coaches can mentally approach their work for maximum fulfilment for both themselves and their players.

At the core of every great coach lies a strong coaching philosophy that guides decision-making and subsequent action. These philosophies are the sum of the coaches' beliefs about life, coaching and tennis, and largely determine their approaches to teaching, motivating and educating their players (Lubbers, 2003). Typically, these philosophies should encompass three broad developmental perspectives: coaching to win, coaching to have fun and coaching to help players develop physically, psychologically and socially. As part of this, coaches should consider themselves, initiators and facilitators of the learning process, and not enforcers of a teaching method or playing style. In this capacity, coaches become a catalyst in helping players to better understand the processes toward tennis mastery.

Borne out of any coaching philosophy will be a coach's goals. While the process coaches go through to set their goals may essentially be the same, goals that are desirable and attainable for some may not be for others. This relates to the fact that there is no single or best way to coach as this depends to a great extent on the goals and characteristics of both player and coach. Nevertheless, coaching goals are generally directed towards:

— **Oneself:** Reaching the top of the profession; maximising one's potential; developing a profitable and healthy business …

— **The players:** Teaching players positive values and nurturing them as human beings; helping players to have fun while learning and practicing tennis; facilitating their path to a certain playing standard or ranking.

Although coaches can set both of the above types of goals, those directed toward the players, and more particularly those directed toward their personal development, should be the priority. This much is reflected in Table 26.1, where if coaches are able to foster sound coach-player relationships as well as player fulfillment, outcomes such as making money and reaching the top may well take care of themselves.

REMEMBER:

The role of tennis coaches is not solely to teach tennis, but rather to help their students learn the game by adapting the appropriate information into applicable, practical concepts to which the players can relate and then apply.

PRACTICAL APPLICATION:

The essence of a sound coaching philosophy is understanding the importance of creating a training environment in which learning, having fun, growing and sharing experiences are the primary objectives ahead of winning and beating others.

MOST IMPORTANT	MODERATELY IMPORTANT	LEAST IMPORTANT
- Player fulfillment. - Intrinsic satisfaction. - Good interpersonal relationships. - Professional development. - Creating positive motivational climates.	- Discipline and work rate of players. - Coaching reputation.	- Winning. - Money. - Publicity.

Table 26.1
The priorities of a coach.

IV. Other important issues

26.2. PSYCHOLOGICAL CHARACTERISTICS AND QUALITIES OF SUCCESSFUL COACHES

PRACTICAL APPLICATION:

Some pertinent questions coaches can ask themselves to assist goal-setting and begin to identify their strengths and limitations are: What standard of players do I prefer and / or feel that I am best at coaching - beginners, intermediate, advanced, professionals? What age of player do I think best fits my coaching skills and personality - young children, juniors, adults or veteran players? Do I feel I am more effective at coaching one of the two genders - male or female? Would I describe myself as an 'all-round coach'? Do I coach players of all standards, ages, genders, etc. without paying any attention to my strengths and weaknesses as a tennis coach?

The qualities that characterise good tennis coaches are well documented (Crespo and Reid, 2004b). In short, they are the ability to discipline and motivate players, to recognise and utilise available talent, to foster enthusiasm, to develop pride, to organise and plan, to play tennis, to be imaginative, and to communicate effectively. Throughout the entire coaching process, good coaches retain their sense of humour, uphold high moral and ethical standards, remain highly dedicated and eager to learn, and are forever conscious of the need to account for individual differences between players. It goes without saying that good coaches also have a reasonable understanding of the game!

RECOGNISING STRENGTHS AND LIMITATIONS

As alluded to in the discussion of coaching philosophies above, the setting of goals is as important for coaches as it is for players. Again, these goals are a likely product of coaches' strengths and limitations personally and professionally, as well as those of the players they coach.

Tennis coaches, like other professionals, often specialise in one area of their profession. For example, some coaches specialise in teaching only mini-tennis, while others will work exclusively with professional players, veterans, males, females or wheelchair players. By doing so, coaches are in effect recognising their strengths and limitations and thus concentrate on improving their skills in working with that tennis playing population. Other coaches however, evolve with time. They may begin coaching young players before progressing to coaching adults or competitive players. Although fewer in number, there are examples of some coaches who start coaching players as beginners and continue to work with them throughout their professional careers.

THE COACH AS A COMMUNICATOR

REMEMBER:

As a coach, you too can have role models, and just as your players may ask you for feedback, you should - if possible - ask it of your role models (Crespo and Reid, 2004b). A strong desire to learn is an important characteristic of great coaches.

While understanding and using specific mental skills training (MST) is essential to optimise coaching, alone it is not enough. The coach needs to possess the necessary communication skills to foster positive coach-player relationships and trust; which are prerequisites to the effective implementation of any MST, and the most significant determinants of the extent to which players, and especially children, enjoy their participation in tennis. These skills also better enable coaches to learn to 'read' players' mood states and personalities and, in turn, individualise MST (Gould, 2001).

Given the credence of communication to coaching success, it's important that coaches are clear – to ensure the message is lucid and unambiguous – and direct – so as to eliminate any 'barriers' between them and their players (Crespo and Balaguer, 1994; Young, 2006). Likewise, coaches should be able to adapt the timing and presentation (verbal vs. non-verbal) of their content to the characteristics (i.e. age, playing ability, gender …) of their players, and be sufficiently open to encourage two-way interaction with their players. To further enhance the prospect of the coach-player relationship being one that bears fruit, coaches should consider the following tips:

— Base your communication on **respect and trust** rather than criticism and control.
— Use a **positive approach** to coaching, where the most important kind of success does not come from winning but from striving to win and trying one's best. Avoid being too critical or using too much sarcasm.
— Research has shown that coaches' perceptions of their own behaviours do not match those of the players' (Crespo, 1995) so **ask players** and fellow coaches for feedback regarding your coaching while also self-evaluating your behaviours and actions.

- Demonstrate **emotional consistency** as players are not likely to respond optimally to excessive or unusually passionate displays (of agitation or aggression) over the long term.
- Be conscious of the appropriateness of both your **verbal and non-verbal** communication.
- Understand and recognise that players learn and process information in different ways so try to match the visual, kinaesthetic and / or auditory cues you use to the **predominant learning style** of each player.
- Use **empathy and inclusion strategies** with your players to stimulate the discussion of mutual interests and goals.
- Be **assertive, positive and honest** in your expression of thoughts and feelings so as to not irreparably damage the self-esteem of players. For example:
  - Explain / describe situations to players: Example: "You were supposed to collect balls after the drill".
  - Explain their effect on the class: "Your classmates had to collect more balls and this took them more time".
  - Outline how you would like it done: "I would appreciate if after the next drill you help collect the balls as then we will have more time to play".
- Try to use **simple and direct** communication styles and avoid inappropriate ordering, warning, commanding, criticising, and berating.
- Use **open-ended questions** (that usually begin with what, how, could or would) to promote two-way communication.
- Employ the '**sandwich**' **method** (first praise, then provide feedback and finally praise again) when providing players with feedback.

THE COACH AS A MOTIVATOR

As outlined in Chapter 2, players' motives for their involvement in the game can be extrinsic or intrinsic in nature. For the tennis coach it becomes important to be able to recognise their players' motives, and then provide for them. Indeed, while many tennis players will possess large amounts of intrinsic motivation, the need for coaches to create positive motivational climates cannot be underplayed. To do so, coaches should take note of and endeavour to provide for the following recommendations in player training:

- Get to know your players and help them to set goals that reflect their motives for play.
- Keep sessions regular and enjoyable. Variety is a great motivator in making sessions more appealing.
- Ensure the group ethos is positive and that the use of feedback / rewards reinforces this.
- Organise competition wisely so all players believe they have a chance of success.
- Use a standard start-train-finish routine to provide for immediate player comfort.
- Incorporate a 'switch-on, switch-off' philosophy where players are encouraged to 'switch off' (e.g. have a chat / drink) between sets before giving you their undivided attention when it's time to work.
- Use examples of role models that are likely inspire players, especially, the youngsters.
- Make it clear to players that effort is more important than outcome, as is commitment.
- Continue to learn and improve your coaching skills.

As referred to in the third bullet point of the previous list, feedback and rewards are among the most important motivational tools coaches can employ. Their appropriate use can increase the intensity of a given behaviour, or facilitate its modification. Rewards, in particular, can be effective in this regard.

PRACTICAL APPLICATION:

Samulski (2004) provides coaches the following tips in establishing an appropriate feedback and reward system with their players:
- Tailor the reward system to the needs of the players, and clearly establish which behaviours will be 'rewarded'.
- Use a simple system of rewards, which acknowledges performance over outcome, as well as the small achievements or landmarks along the way to bigger goals.
- Be consistent with the implementation of the rewards.
- Be sincere and specific when providing feedback.
- Use appropriate verbal and non-verbal praise to reinforce positive behaviour.

WHAT RESEARCH TELLS US...
More successful coaches use management (instructions) and silence (not speaking) behaviours (75% of the time), and ask significantly more questions of their players than less successful coaches (Claxton, 1988). Coaches have also been shown to behave more autocratically when coaching beginner players (Crespo et al., 1993; Prapavessis and Gordon, 1991), while beginner players perceive coaches more positively than the coaches themselves (Balaguer et al., 1990). Interestingly as compared to older players, younger players have been shown as less demanding on their coaches (Allison and Ayllon, 1980; Harries-Jenkins and Hughes, 1993).

> **REMEMBER:**
>
> Negative rewards in the form of punishment can arouse fear of failure and hinder learned skills, so they have to be used with caution. Avoid physical activity as punishment or embarrassing players.

Rewards can be positive or negative, extrinsic or intrinsic. Positive rewards are stimuli that facilitate certain behaviours, while negative rewards can help eliminate behaviours when applied effectively (to the behaviour and not the player). Extrinsic rewards such as money, trophies, and prizes can be helpful in getting players initially interested in the sport, but rewards that are intrinsic (e.g. improvement and self-esteem) are considered more effective in motivating players over the long term (Balaguer and Atienza, 1994). However, as mentioned in Chapter 2, extrinsic rewards that are self-administered, timely and relate to the quality of the performance and not the outcome, can in fact help improve intrinsic motivation. Nonetheless, irrespective of the type of reward, it should always be flexible enough to change according to time and circumstance and from one individual to another.

> **PRACTICAL APPLICATION:**
>
> When giving feedback coaches should consider:
> - Using both verbal and visual feedback.
> - Directing players to observe, and then reproduce, the goal of an action or the movement's end point.
> - Providing instructions as to how a skill should be achieved, instead of verbalising its intended outcome (Reid et al., 2006).

Intrinsic **feedback** is provided as players feel, see or hear the consequence of their action, while information presented in different detail by the coach represents feedback in its extrinsic form. Where some coaches have a tendency to offer feedback that lacks specificity; others suffer from providing it all too frequently. Indeed, too much extrinsic feedback may impair a player's ability to independently process and evaluate information (Williams and Hodges, 2005), manifesting on-court with players becoming perplexed when forced to problem-solve without direct guidance from the coach. By lengthening the interval between the action culminating and feedback provision, players are afforded greater opportunities to intrinsically evaluate their own performance, while also reducing the prospect of undesirable dependencies being developed (Liu and Wrisberg, 1997). Throughout, the use of questions by the coach can further encourage players to review specific performance cues.

Although effective feedback can facilitate learning, guide skill development and maintain or improve a player's motivation (Williams and Hodges, 2005), coaches need to be mindful of the balance between providing too much or too little input. To this end, feedback should be provided more regularly to novice players or when players are learning complex tasks, but less frequently as skills develop (Wulf and Shea, 2004); whereby the role of intrinsic feedback should become more prominent. Comparable shifts in feedback content and precision should also accompany player development such that feedback becomes increasingly descriptive (i.e. players are informed of the error committed rather than how to correct it) and precise with improved performance and/or learning. This evolution will likely facilitate tennis players' aptitude in problem-solving (Wulf and Shea, 2004), as well as expedite skill acquisition.

Coaches need effective communication skills to foster positive coach-player relationships and trust.

> **WHAT RESEARCH TELLS US...**
> Moreno et al. (2001) and Avila and Moreno (2003) studied visual search strategies of tennis coaches during error detection and concluded that expert coaches showed more distributed, longer and fewer visual fixations than novice coaches.

BURNOUT AMONG COACHES

While burnout is largely associated with the tennis playing population, it too is a very real proposition for coaches. The profession is full of potential stressors such as the importance of results, lack of social support, inability to meet personal needs, health related problems, etc. In fact, Duda et al. (2003), in examining the effects of burnout and its predictors among coaches, found their sample to experience low to moderate levels of burnout on a monthly basis. Manifesting as unplanned weight gain or loss, depression, heightened anxiety and susceptibility to injury, poor sleeping patterns and / or suppressed immune systems, burnout was shown to correlate negatively with coaches' levels of self-confidence and positively with somatic and cognitive stress. Furthermore, with tennis coaches shown to suffer from levels of burnout similar to those of other professionals where duty of care is high (e.g., nurses, athletic trainers) (Kelley et al., 1998), those coaches who define personal success in coaching in terms of winning and outdoing others place themselves at greater risk of burnout.

According to Duda et al. (2003), coaches wanting to minimise the prospect of burnout, and therefore alleviate potential sources of stress should:

— Remember to keep it fun!
— Don't ever forget your sense of humour!
— Take a look at what you would like to achieve in coaching, focus on things under your control, and place things that are not into perspective.
— Set goals related to your own coaching performance in areas such as strategising, the effective teaching of skills or techniques, positive thinking, creating a positive motivational climate ...
— Become familiar with and then regularly practice some stress management skills (e.g., negative thought stopping, centered breathing, progressive muscle relaxation) that you can use before, during, and following important matches of players you coach. Competent coping when the 'going gets rough' is a skill!
— Seek out those who sustain, encourage, and bring out the best in you.
— Share your feelings and experiences with other coaches that you trust.
— Tennis is a super game but it's only part of your life ... keep it in perspective, and give yourself the down time to pursue the other things you enjoy in life.

THE COACH AS A LEADER

Leadership is the process of influencing people so that they strive, willingly and enthusiastically, toward the achievement of their goals. More specifically, it relates to motivating, directing, supervising, guiding and evaluating people for the purpose of accomplishing a task.

Coaches need to be good leaders. In general, the characteristics of someone considered a good leader are common to the tennis coach and include: determination, integrity, self-confidence, initiative, perseverance, imagination, energy, humour, tact, breadth of vision, caring nature, motivational ability, wisdom, fairness and knowledge.

A general typology of coaching leadership styles enables us to distinguish between authoritarian, democratic and 'laissez faire' coaches, while Table 26.2 highlights five leadership behaviours that have been shown to be common to the tennis coach (Chelladurai, 1980). In adopting these leadership behaviours or styles, coaches should be ever mindful of the fact that the best coach is the one that is skilled enough to adapt to the characteristics of the players and

REMEMBER:

Leadership comprises a set of personal skills (communication, empathy, motivation, management, etc.) that are applied in specific situations (coaching players, managing a company, etc.). And like all skills, those of leadership can also be learned and developed (Crespo and Balaguer, 1994).

WHAT RESEARCH TELLS US...
Chelladurai (1980) explained leadership in sport through the combination of three types of coach behaviour: required (those needed in certain situations), actual (those displayed by the coach) and preferred (those preferred by the players). However, application of this model to tennis has produced equivocal results, with Crespo (1995) showing that when these three types of behaviours matched, player satisfaction and performance improved, yet Riemer and Toon (2001) found no relationship between the congruence of preferred and perceived leadership behaviour and player satisfaction.

to the situation. For instance, an autocratic style may be required when confronted with an emergency situation on-court, while a democratic approach is likely to be more effective in providing for constructive and enjoyable lessons with advanced players.

COACHING BEHAVIOUR	DEFINITION
Training and instruction	Aimed at improving player performance by emphasising the training, and instruction of the games' skills and strategies. The coach structures and co-ordinates player activities.
Democratic	Provides for player participation in decisions pertaining to class goals, practice techniques, and game strategies and tactics.
Autocratic	Involves independent action, and stresses personal authority and the independent decisions of the coach.
Social support	Characterised by a concern for the welfare of the player. Positive motivational climates and interpersonal relationships are also emphasised.
Positive feedback	Rewards players through the recognition and acknowledgement of good performance.

Table 29.2 Characteristics of leadership behaviours (Chelladurai, 1980).

Coaches interested in becoming better leaders on and off the court, may benefit from the following recommendations pertaining to different leadership skills:

— **Sincerity:** Try to be yourself. Commit to your personal beliefs and do not pretend to be someone you are not.
— **Organisation:** Implies planning ahead. There is nothing worse than attending training sessions that have not been thought out. When the coach is searching for ideas of what to do next; when there is no flow or logical sequence in the activities; when the equipment is inadequate or unsuitable; when activities are meaningless and bear no relevance to the match situation, is to the benefit of no one. Such sessions are largely a waste of time and can easily be avoided with a little forward planning.
— **Set rules:** Goals and procedures should be clear to satisfy players' expectations and to create a healthy performance environment.
— **Flexibility:** Behaviours of successful leaders and coaches lie on a continuum, from rigid authoritarianism (task / performance orientation) to flexible sensitivity (relationship / person orientation). It is the role of the good leader to decide which behaviours best fit the situation, the players' characteristics and the coach's characteristics. This flexibility is not a weakness but rather a strength.
— **Understanding:** Try to seek team leaders from the players who seem to be more socially sensitive individuals. Understand the needs of others (e.g. friends, parents) to best inspire their loyalty and commitment.
— **Time management:** Coaches need to manage their time effectively. Not doing so, will mean that it is virtually impossible to expect to manage and lead others.
— **Administration:** Good administration underpins a coach's ability to carry out all the functions involved in his role as a coach. If the coach is efficient and professional, it is increasingly likely that all parts of the coaching puzzle will be pieced together.
— **Delegation:** This is a must if you want to create independence and responsibility in your players. However, to delegate is not to abdicate. Be responsible for this delegation and provide permanent feedback to improve performance and satisfy players' needs.
— **Adapt to the age of your players:** With children, relationship-oriented behaviours by the coach work best as children's receptivity increases along with friendlier coach-player relationships. With adolescents, on the other hand, it may better for the coach to be more directive and

WHAT RESEARCH TELLS US...
Balaguer et al. (1999) found the relationships between motivational climate and players' goal orientations to the perceived and preferred leadership style of the coach to indicate:
- Players who were in a task-involving environment and were higher in task orientation wanted the coach to exhibit more training and instruction behaviours.
- Players perceiving a task-involving environment who were ego oriented, preferred more social support behaviours from their coach.

Tennis Psychology

task oriented (although never punitive). Then, as players mature, they should be given more autonomy and the coach should become more supportive and, again, relationship oriented.
— **Adapt to the degree of stress:** Weinberg and Gould (1995) have shown that when internal or external stress appears (e.g. during a tournament), coaches should increase the task orientation (authoritarianism) of their behaviours. Alternatively, in the absence of stress, player / relationship-oriented behaviours work best.
— **Combine training and instruction:** Coaching behaviours that combine training and instruction with social support improve player satisfaction (Crespo, 1995).
— **Learn and improve:** Be proactive in your search to foster your leadership behaviours. Try to attend workshops or courses that might prove valuable in doing so.
— **Help your players to be leaders:** The coach can help young players in their development of their leadership skills by giving them responsibilities and placing them in positions that require maturity, problem-solving and decision-making.
— **Improve your communication skills:** This is perhaps the most important factor in providing for improved coach-player interaction.

26.3. PSYCHOLOGY OF OFFICIATING

Players are not alone in facing pressure out on court... the game's officials – chair umpires, linesman, and even referees – are also subject to it! With officials expected to ensure matches proceed harmoniously within the context of the rules of the game, while making potentially crowd- and player-riling decisions, one can begin to appreciate that good officials are equipped with more than just a sound understanding of the game!

Much like players interested in achieving maximum performance, aspiring officials need to train the mental skills that are required to officiate effectively and for long periods (Weinberg and Richardson, 1990). Obviously, the ability to stay 'cool' in pressure situations is one of those skills, while others include:

— **Consistency:** Making the same decisions in similar circumstances and avoiding 'evening things up'.
— **Rapport:** Relating effectively to players and coaches by treating them with courtesy and respect. Being approachable and willing to listen, while at the same time keeping an appropriate distance.
— **Decisiveness:** Deciding concurrent to the action observed.
— **Integrity:** Making calls honestly, and displaying integrity on- and off-court.
— **Judgement:** Using common sense to complement a comprehensive and sound understanding of the rules of the game and their application.
— **Confidence:** Demonstrating an assertiveness that reinforces one's self-belief in performing the task at hand.
— **Enjoyment and motivation:** Having fun and displaying a positive mental attitude.

Officials interested in improving their on-court psychological performance should take part in specific MST programmes. Ultimately however, it may first be necessary to acknowledge that they will make mistakes, and then, approximately 50% of the audience is likely to be unhappy with their decision!

REMEMBER:

Effective officiating is characterised by not being afraid to make unpopular calls, not letting the game get out of hand, and maintaining composure.

PSYCHOLOGY FOR TENNIS PARENTS 27

The family is a very important part of the support team for a developing player. In today's game, the role of family members varies tremendously, yet there is compelling evidence that for a young player to have a healthy approach to competition and training, a parent or significant other typically helps to foster an environment of excellence.

From a coach's perspective, healthy parent-coach-player relationships should be viewed as fundamental to player development success, and thus roles should be clarified and understood. While much has been written about the important role of tennis parents' (Crespo and Miley, 2001; Loehr and Kahn, 1987; 1989; Rowley, 1988; USTA, 2001; 2005), in this Chapter we have endeavoured to assimilate this information to assist coaches in their dealings with parents and their children.

PRACTICAL APPLICATION:

The detachment of children from parents when they go to school is magnified in tennis due to the relative independence of the tennis player on the court. This, coupled with the fact that some parents expect to satisfy their own needs through the performance of their child, leads to excessive pressure on young players. So, entrusting children of all age categories with greater independence, but also responsibility, while maintaining positive parental backing becomes all-important for the development of their personality and social skills.

27.1. THE COACH-PLAYER-PARENT DYNAMIC

Most coaches know that behind almost every player there is a dedicated parent who makes considerable sacrifices to help their child to achieve his dreams. Indeed, research has shown that more often than not parents are a positive influence on their child's tennis (Loehr and Kahn, 1989).

Certainly, parents can be underrated in terms of the tasks and actions they can perform to supplement on-court practice, particularly in the early stages of development. There will undoubtedly be some exceptions, but Harwood (2000) believes this is not reason enough to refrain from making the effort to include parents in the performance environment.

REMEMBER:

Sometimes, parents fall into the trap of expecting a return on their tennis investment. If the expected return is for their child to become a mature adult and be able to use tennis as a school for life, then their approach is the correct one. On the contrary, if they expect a return in the shape of wins, rankings, success and money, their motives are misplaced.

The characteristics of parents, that positively influence their child's development are:

— Provide considerable support and recognise their children's achievements by motivating them in a positive and caring way.
— Provide unconditional love.
— Make decisions based upon their child as a person and not as a player by remembering that tennis is for their child and not for them.
— Understand that tennis is a game and not a job and that becoming a successful professional is a great goal but one that is extremely difficult to be achieved.
— Put tennis in perspective and refrain from placing more importance on it than school work.
— Show empathy and understand the emotional challenges that children may suffer in the pursuit of high performance.
— Promote and instill values of effort, hard work, respect of others, good sportsmanship, independence, taking responsibility for one's actions, and the value of discipline for success.
— Make sacrifices and ensure that they are always available if help or guidance is required.
— Respect coaches and communicate with them clearly.
— Prepare to listen and to learn from their children's tennis experience.
— Focus on long-term health and well-being of their children and not winning or rankings.
— If assuming the role of parent-coach, they make sure that when on-court, they are the coach, and when off-court they are the parent.

IV. Other important issues

> **PRACTICAL APPLICATION:**
>
> Tennis parents have rights with which tennis coaches must be familiar:
> - Parents pay bills and have a right to be involved.
> - Parents have an ethical and legal responsibility to protect the safety of their child.
> - Parents have the right to select the coach of their child.
> - Parents have the right to decide on the role that tennis plays in their child's life.
> - Parents are parents of their children for their whole life, whereas the coach may assume the coaching mantle for a period of time... so "the parent stays... and the coach goes".

PARENTS' ROLES

The roles that parents can play can be summarised as follows:

— **Initial involvement**:
  - Baxter-Jones and Maffulli (2003) found that parental influence (57%) and self-motivation (27%) are primarily responsible for bringing young players into the game. They also reported that young players' initial involvement in high level sport is heavily dependent on their parents.

— **Emotional support**:
  - Being supportive, interested, encouraging and caring, and in the process helping to provide their children with a sense of achievement, competence and self-worth, is the foremost role of tennis parents.

— **Financial support**:
  - Parents cover the expenses associated with their child's involvement in tennis programmes (coach, equipment, etc.) and competitions (travels, fees, etc.).

— **Logistical / organisational support**:
  - Parents are also responsible for locating coaches, clubs and tennis programmes, as well as transporting their children to and from practice and competition.

PROBLEMS WITH PARENTS

> **REMEMBER:**
>
> Parents know their child much better than the coach does and may therefore be the source of valuable information to assist coaches more effectively cater for their child's development.

Unfortunately, Gould and Lauer (2005) have indicated that increasing numbers of coaches are finding it difficult to work with the parents of certain players. In general, 'problem' parents can be identified by:

— Living through their child's tennis.
— Basing their worth as a parent on their child's success.
— Trying to coach when they are not trained to do so.
— Interfering with their child's lessons.
— Pushing their child such that they become uptight and de-motivated (i.e. 'pushy' parent).
— Seemingly being overly involved in all aspects of their child's tennis.

Why do these problems arise?
— Misplaced understanding of parental roles.
— Insufficient specific tennis knowledge.
— Desire to help but not knowing how to do so.
— Poor communication between parents and coach.
— Frustration related to their own playing careers.

How to these problems manifest?
— Inappropriate perspectives.
— Overemphasis on winning and rankings.
— Undermine long-term tennis and child development.
— Unrealistic expectations.
— Irrational behaviour (by parent and / or player).
— Poor parent-player relationships.
— Player burnout.

> **WHAT RESEARCH TELLS US...**
> DeFrancesco and Johnson (1997) have shown that incongruences between the perceptions of parents and children regarding parental involvement in coach-player relationships are common. González et al. (1999) reported that players sometimes feel that their parents embarrass them while they compete, and that negative behaviour most frequently displayed by parents includes yelling at players and walking away from the court.

Tennis Psychology

27.2. POSITIVE PARENTING PRACTICES

Parents are naturally interested and want to play an important role in their children's tennis. They usually have doubts as to how best to help their children and want to maximise their contribution whilst at the same time ensure that they, as well as their children, enjoy their involvement in tennis.

Indeed studies have shown that most parents do not encourage their children to begin tennis with the intent of having them develop an elite player, but rather for them to be active, have fun and learn a lifetime sport. While this desire for their children to enjoy themselves is unlikely to change, their parental role will vary as their children's tennis progresses (Loehr and Kahn, 1987). To this end, Gould and Lauer (2005) summarise optimal parenting practices throughout player development:

— **Introductory phase** (up to approximately 10 years old):
  - Provide opportunities for children to play tennis and help make it a fun and successful experience in which they can dream big.
  - Allow children to participate in extra-curricular activities outside tennis, limit excessive tennis practice.
  - Focus on the positive (do not put pressure on winning / rankings), hard work, developing a good person through good behaviour and sportsmanship.
  - Provide unconditional love and support by believing in your child.
  - Allow the coach to do his job and if possible be available to play tennis with your child.

— **Transition** (approximately 10-14 years old):
  - Continue what has been mentioned in the Introductory phase.
  - Alleviate pressure by keeping winning in perspective, but provide an optimal push if the child wants to play competitive tennis.
  - Encourage your child to give 100% effort... and to win.
  - Increase your financial and time commitment to tennis, but also plan and perform non-tennis family activities.
  - Make your child more responsible for their tennis preparation and involve them in any decisions to be made.
  - Learn not to judge or link parenting to your child's play or success.

— **High-performance** (from approximately 15 years old on):
  - Continue doing what has been mentioned in the earlier phases.
  - Lessen parental push as players learn to push themselves.
  - Provide honest feedback to your child.
  - Do not change by virtue of any success experienced by your child.
  - Provide off-the-court support (dealing with finances / talking to sponsors).
  - Serve as a 'sounding-board' in the decision-making process but let your child arrive at the final decision.

Positive parenting practices can also be classified according to the different scenarios in which parents, coaches and players are involved:

> **WHAT RESEARCH TELLS US...**
> Former pro players have indicated that they had both 'pushy' and positive parents, but Gould and Lauer (2005) reported that the players developed in more positive manners presented with less psychological problems than those with 'pushier' parents. In fact, players who have experienced high parental support tended to enjoy tennis more, view it as a more important part of their lives, and maintain their rankings better than players who reported a lower parental support (Hoyle and Leff, 1997).

- **At home**:
    - Refrain from talking tennis all the time.
    - Do not ignore other children in the family.
    - Organise family activities other than tennis.

- **During practices**:
    - Take your child to practices and be on time.
    - Ensure your child is ready to take part in the practice (e.g. with food, water, equipment, etc.).
    - Encourage your child to practice without pressuring him.
    - Be familiar with the concepts of overtraining and burnout.
    - Make sure the coach is sufficiently qualified to coach your child.
    - Discipline your child when necessary (e.g. bad behaviour, lack of effort).
    - Periodically attend practices as an interested observer and not as a 'pseudo-coach'.
    - Ensure your child showers, rests and recovers after practices.
    - Get to know other parents and share your experiences with them.

- **Before matches**:
    - Take your child to matches and be on time.
    - Ensure your child is ready and equipped to play the match.
    - Check your child's performance goals for the match.

- **During matches**:
    - Be an educated spectator.
    - Do not coach your child.
    - Help when asked by an official.
    - Support your child but do not attend every match.
    - Control your emotions and your behaviour.
    - Be generous in your applause for both players and in recognising the good play of your child's opponent.

- **After matches**:
    - Ensure your child showers, rests and recovers.
    - Try to avoid "Did you win?" questions.
    - Try to avoid "We won or we/you lost" statements.
    - Provide your child some time before asking as to their match peformance.
    - Discipline your child when necessary (e.g. bad behaviour, dissent...).
    - Check with your child regarding his 'aches and pains' to make sure there is nothing more serious.

Positive parenting practices should prevail throughout the entirety of a player's career.

27.3. GUIDELINES FOR COACHES WORKING WITH PARENTS

Most effective coaches have been successful in facilitating a positive parent-coach partnership (Loehr and Kahn, 1987). How can this be done? Well, coaches should endeavour to inform parents of related parenting research, while also considering the following recommendations:

— **Define parental roles and responsibilities**:
  - Organise a pre-season meeting with parents that will inform them about your coaching philosophy and will describe the roles and responsibilities of parents, coach and players (Loehr and Kahn, 1989).
  - Work together with parents (as a team) to maximise their child's benefit.
  - Set and convey standards and expectations on what will and will not be tolerated relative to parental behaviour.
  - Hold parents accountable.

— **Try to understand parents**:
  - Be aware that even the best parents are going to make some mistakes.
  - Try to be empathetic and see things from the parents' perspective.
  - Give appropriate time and energy to 'high maintenance' parents.
  - Recognise positive efforts and reinforce desirable parental behaviours.
  - Do not generalise the poor behaviour of a few, to all parents.

— **Establish two-way communication**:
  - Be honest and open.
  - Work hard at listening.
  - Agree with parents as to the best times to communicate with you.

— **Educate and inform parents on**:
  - Knowing what they want from their child's tennis (fun, development).
  - Knowing what their child wants from their tennis experience.
  - Examining their tennis parenting behaviours.
  - Displaying positive parenting behaviours.
  - Fostering positive motivational climates.
  - The Rules of tennis and tournament regulations.
  - The Code of Conduct.
  - The ITF Anti-doping programme.
  - Nutrition, hydration and recovery guidelines.
  - Developing sportsmanship.
  - Understanding the value of discipline.
  - Emotional control techniques before, during and after the match (Loehr and Kahn, 1989).
  - Supporting the game development of their child.
  - The appropriateness of their reactions to their child's winning and losing;
  - How to cope with the 'ups and downs' of their child's tennis life. If they cannot do this... How can they expect it of their child?
  - Putting their child's tennis, and winning into perspective.

WHAT RESEARCH TELLS US...
Monsaas (1985) found that parents of world class players played a major role in their careers. They highly valued and emphasised tennis as well as hard work and doing well, but also winning. They invested a great deal of time in their child's tennis including driving them to lessons, practice and tournaments, finding the best coaches, and spending hours practicing tennis with their child.
Wolfenden and Holt (2005) found six categories associated with adult influence on talent development in tennis (emotional support, tangible support, informational support, sacrifices, pressure, and relationships with coaches). In their study, parents appeared to fulfill the most significant roles by providing emotional and tangible support, and were perceived as a source of pressure when over-involved in competitive settings. They concluded that involvement in elite junior tennis is a team effort whereby players, parents, and coaches fulfill specific roles and are required to make sacrifices.

- Helping their children learn the basics of tennis if they are teaching them.
- The benefits of playing other sports apart from tennis.
- The criteria they may have to follow to find the right coach and to make sure that this coach is qualified to work with their children.
- How to behave as a good parent, and not as a coach, during matches.
- Competitive tennis pathways.
- The different stages of player development.
- Helping their children set appropriate tennis goals.
- Fostering independence in their children.
- How to encourage their children to play tennis without putting pressure on them.

— **Formulate a problem parent strategy**:
- Develop an action plan to deal with problem parents.
- Seek support from other parents and coaches.
- Clearly communicate the parental actions you will, and will not tolerate.

27.4. SUMMARY

In closing, it is important to emphasise that parents play a definitive role in character forming. That is, whether they realise it or not, factors such as their way of life, their attitude towards the child, and especially their behaviour will all affect their offspring's psychological and emotional development.

Similarly, the role of parents in junior tennis is central to player development, and coaches frequently find themselves searching for the best way to interact with parents and to reinforce their important contribution to this process.

Interested readers are referred to the ITF book, *How to be a better tennis parent*, or to *www.itftennis.com/coaching* for additional information on the role of parents in tennis.

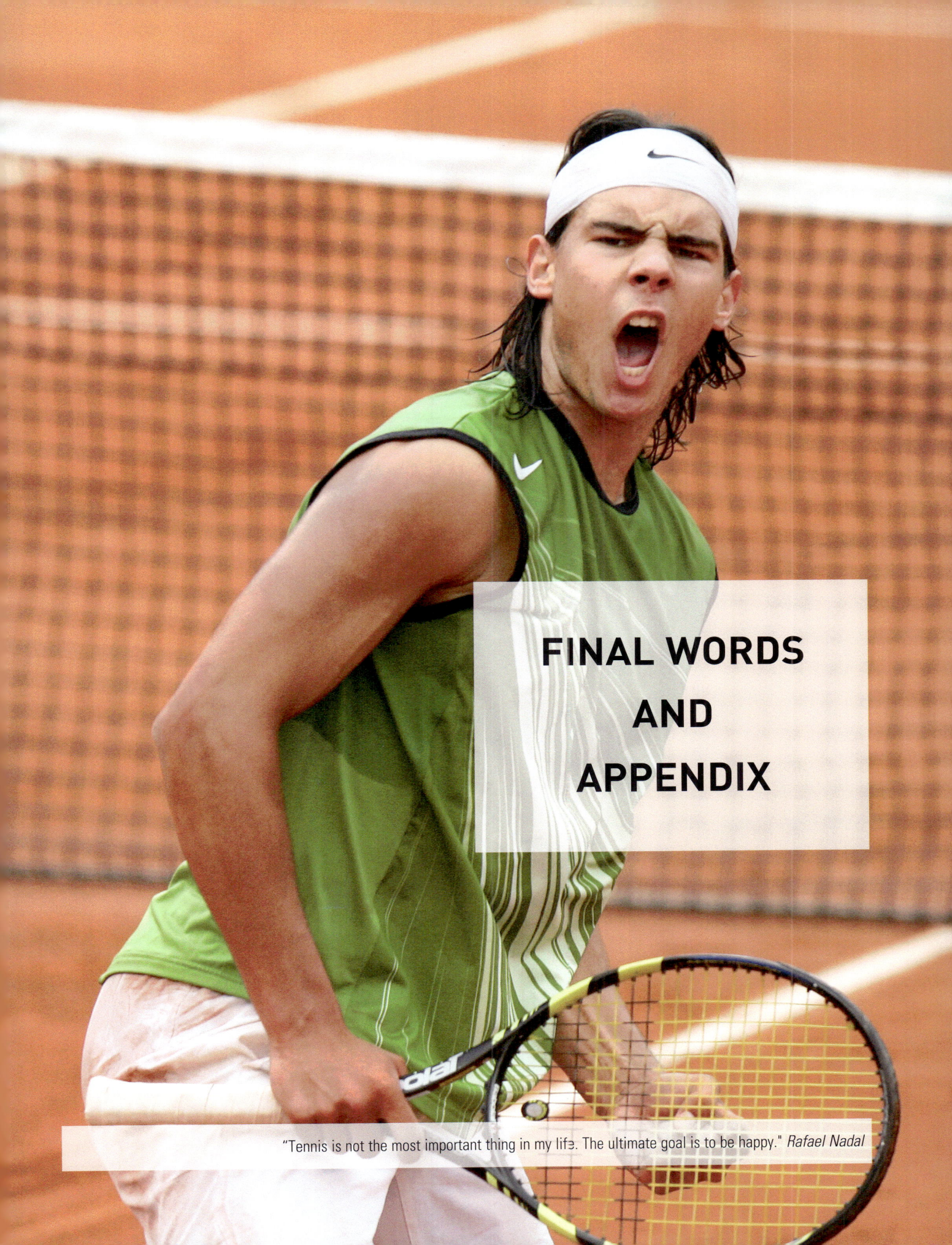

FINAL WORDS AND APPENDIX

"Tennis is not the most important thing in my life. The ultimate goal is to be happy." *Rafael Nadal*

FINAL WORDS

Recent research examining the state of mental skills training (MST) in coaching has revealed that more concrete, 'hands-on' MST examples and activities are needed for coaches to more effectively integrate it into everyday training (Gould et al., 1999a). Well, the purpose of this book has been to provide just that! That is, in an effort to remedy this lack of practical MST information, we have compiled specific and easy-to-implement MST drills that coaches can use with tennis players of all ages and playing levels. This, in turn, places the theory of sports psychology that the book also provides into applied contexts that lend themselves to more immediate and seamless integration into player training.

Most tennis players practice everyday. Indeed, to become mentally consistent means following a psychological training programme daily. Simply exposing one's players to these mental drills and activities on a single occasion is not enough. Certainly, an initial talk, exercise or drill needs to be conducted, but equally important is follow-up and reinforcement of the skill taught throughout the season. Mental skills are like physical skills; they must be practiced, reinforced, and repeatedly challenged under competitive conditions.

The use of sport psychology may extend far beyond MST. For example, problems such as growth and development issues, academic stress, strained relationships, time management, family conflict, and financial concerns affect everyone at one time or another. These issues may easily compromise a young player's tennis performance. When such problems arise, it is important to establish open lines of communication, discuss them with your players and parents, and seek professional assistance when needed, as there is much at stake for all involved. Remember that as coaches we are called upon not only to guide our players as competitors, but also to help them develop life skills. Here, the concept of self-coaching applies as one of the outcomes of an appropriate training and competition structure (Lubbers, 2001; Samulski, 2006).

Finally, players cannot get physically fit in a weekend or dramatically improve their forehand in a session. It follows that significant commitment is required to best develop their mental muscle! Success depends on specific, spaced repetition and regular immersion... 'make good habits and they will make you'.

APPENDIX

SELF-ASSESSMENTS

As highlighted throughout the book, and discussed in some detail in Chapter 16, specific psychological skills questionnaires or inventories can be used to assess all areas of players' mental 'games'. The questionnaires, like those listed below, have been scientifically validated and tend to be available for commercial purchase. However, their utility is enhanced by qualified sports psychologists, who possess the necessary expertise to best administer the assessments and then interpret their results.

GENERAL
PPI (Psychological Performance Inventory; Loehr, 1986).
PSIS (Psychological Skills Inventory for Sport; Mahoney et al., 1987).
ACSI (Athletic Copying Skills Inventory, Smith et al., 1995).
TOPS (Test of Performance Strategies, Thomas et al., 1999).
PAT (Performance Assessment for Tennis, Rees et al., 2000).

MOTIVATION
COI (Competitive Orientation Inventory, Vealey, 1986).
SOQ (Sport Orientation Questionnaire; Gill and Deeter, 1988).
POSQ (Perception of Success Questionnaire; Roberts and Balagué, 1989).

MOTIVATIONAL CLIMATE
TEOSQ (Task and Ego Orientation in Sport Questionnaire; Duda and Nichols, 1989).
PMCSQ (Perceived Motivational Climate in Sport Questionnaire; Walling et al., 1993).

AROUSAL, ANXIETY, ETC.
STAI (State Trait Anxiety Inventory; Spielberger et al., 1970).
SCAT (Sport Competition Anxiety Test; Martens, 1977).
CSAI (Competitive State Anxiety Inventory; Martens et al., 1990).
CSAI-2 (Competitive State Anxiety Inventory; Martens et al., 1982).

SELF-CONFIDENCE, SELF-EFFICACY, ATTRIBUTION
TSCI (Trait Self-confidence Inventory; Vealey, 1986).
SSCI (State Self-confidence Inventory; Vealey, 1986).
PSE (Physical Self Efficacy Scale; Ryckman et al., 1982).
CDS II (Causal Dimension Scale II; McCauley et al., 1992).
Modified Attributional Style Questionnaire (Prapavessis and Carron, 1983).
SASS (Sport- attributional Style Scale; Hanrahan et al., 1989).
POS (Performance Outcome Survey; Leith and Prapavessis, 1989).
WSARS (Wingate Sport Achievement Responsibility Scale; Tenenbaum et al., 1984).

CONCENTRATION
TAIS (Test of Attentional and Interpersonal Styles; Nideffer, 1976).
T-TAIS (Tennis-Test of Attentional and Interpersonal Styles; Van Schoyck and Grasha, 1981).

PERSONALITY
Eysenk Personality Inventory (Eysenck and Eysenck, 1968).
Cattell 16PF (Cattell, Eber and Tatsuoka, 1983).
MMPI (Minnesota Multiphasic Personality Inventory; Minnesota Univ., 1930).

BURNOUT
ABI (Athletic Burnout Inventory; Eades, 1991).
POMS (Profile of Mood States; McNair et al., 1971).
MBI (Maslach Burnout Inventory; Maslach and Jackson. 1981).

The questionnaires presented in the ensuing pages have not been developed to substitute these scientific inventories. Rather, they are meant as a simple method through which coaches and parents can evaluate their role in player development, while also gaining a bit of an insight into their player or child's psychology. In situations where more comprehensive analyses or additional data are needed, it is recommended that coaches, players, and/or parents contact a qualified sports psychologist.

MENTAL SKILLS IN GAME SITUATION SELF-ASSESSMENT

Serve
Return of serve
Baseline game
Approaching the net and playing at the net
Passing the net player

SELF-ASSESSMENT

Motivation
Stress
Self-confidence
Concentration
Motivational climate
Arousal strategies
Self-confidence strategies
Visualisation
Routines
Cognitive management strategies
Attributional patters
Goal-setting

PROGRESSIVE MUSCULAR RELAXATION (PMR) - JACOBSON SYSTEM

VISUALISATION SCRIPT FOR TENNIS

PLAYER'S PSYCHOLOGICAL MATCH ASSESSMENT

MATCH FLOW SCORE CHART

PARENT PROFILE

MENTAL SKILLS SELF-ASSESSMENT
SERVE

Name of the player: _____ Date: _____

Below you will find some statements regarding the mental skills you may use when **serving**. Read each of the items carefully. Below each statement, circle a number from 1 to 5 that best describes your current feelings. There are no right or wrong answers. Please do not leave any item blank. Your honesty is necessary and will be much appreciated.

1. I look forward to the games in which I serve.

1 Never   2 Seldom   3 Sometimes   4 Often   5 Always

2. Before serving, I have a serve plan (direction, power, spin, etc.).

1 Never   2 Seldom   3 Sometimes   4 Often   5 Always

3. Before serving, I feel in control, relaxed and ready.

1 Never   2 Seldom   3 Sometimes   4 Often   5 Always

4. I have confidence in my serve.

1 Never   2 Seldom   3 Sometimes   4 Often   5 Always

5. Before serving, I concentrate well (focusing on all appropriate cues).

1 Never   2 Seldom   3 Sometimes   4 Often   5 Always

6. Before serving, I think positively about how well I will serve.

1 Never   2 Seldom   3 Sometimes   4 Often   5 Always

7. Before serving, I breathe or move to relax or activate.

1 Never   2 Seldom   3 Sometimes   4 Often   5 Always

8. Before serving, I clearly visualise myself hitting a good serve.

1 Never   2 Seldom   3 Sometimes   4 Often   5 Always

9. Before serving, I go through systematic routines to improve my serve performance.

1 Never   2 Seldom   3 Sometimes   4 Often   5 Always

10. After serving, I realistically assess the effectiveness of my serve.

1 Never   2 Seldom   3 Sometimes   4 Often   5 Always

Scoring: Sum your points: _____

< 25 points:	You need to work on your mental skills used when serving to improve your performance.
25-34 points:	You use mental skills when serving but not always consistently. To better use these mental skills when serving, you would benefit from a mental skills training programme specifically tailored to your needs.
35-43 points:	You use the mental skills needed for the serve efficiently. Some more specific mental skills training will help you identify and apply more effective strategies to this stroke.
44-50 points:	You use of the mental skills wehn serving is very efficient. You should work to maintain, individualise and maximise the benefits of their application to this stroke.

**MENTAL SKILLS SELF-ASSESSMENT
RETURN OF SERVE**

Name of the player: _____ Date: _____

Below you will find some statements regarding the mental skills you may use when **returning serve**. Read each of the items carefully. Below each statement, circle a number from 1 to 5 that best describes your current feelings. There are no right or wrong answers. Please do not leave any item blank. Your honesty is necessary and will be much appreciated.

1. I look forward to the games in which I return.

1 Never   2 Seldom   3 Sometimes   4 Often   5 Always

2. Before receiving, I have a return plan (direction, power, spin, etc.).

1 Never   2 Seldom   3 Sometimes   4 Often   5 Always

3. Before receiving, I feel in control, relaxed and ready.

1 Never   2 Seldom   3 Sometimes   4 Often   5 Always

4. I have confidence in my return.

1 Never   2 Seldom   3 Sometimes   4 Often   5 Always

5. Before receiving, I concentrate well (focusing on all appropriate cues).

1 Never   2 Seldom   3 Sometimes   4 Often   5 Always

6. Before receiving, I think positively about how well I will return.

1 Never   2 Seldom   3 Sometimes   4 Often   5 Always

7. Before receiving, I breathe or move to relax or activate myself.

1 Never   2 Seldom   3 Sometimes   4 Often   5 Always

8. Before receiving, I visualise myself hitting a good return.

1 Never   2 Seldom   3 Sometimes   4 Often   5 Always

9. Before receiving, I follow systematic routines to help my return.

1 Never   2 Seldom   3 Sometimes   4 Often   5 Always

10. After receiving, I realistically assess the effectiveness of my return.

1 Never   2 Seldom   3 Sometimes   4 Often   5 Always

Scoring: Sum your points: _____

< 25 points: You need to work on your mental skills when returning to improve your performance.

25-34 points: You use mental skills when returning but not always consistently. To better use these mental skills in the return, you would benefit from a mental skills training programme specifically tailored to your needs.

35-43 points: You use the mental skills needed for the return efficiently. Some more specific mental skills training will help you identify and apply more effective strategies to this stroke.

44-50 points: Your use of the mental skills when returning is very efficient. You should work to maintain, individualise and maximise the benefits of their application to this stroke.

MENTAL SKILLS SELF-ASSESSMENT
BASELINE GAME

Name of the player: _____ Date: _____

Below you will find some statements about the mental skills you may use in your **baseline game.** Read each of the items carefully. Below each statement, circle a number from 1 to 5 that best describes your current feelings. There are no right or wrong answers. Please do not leave any item blank. Your honesty is necessary and will be much appreciated.

1. I like playing from the baseline during matches.

    1 Never   2 Seldom   3 Sometimes   4 Often   5 Always

2. When playing from the baseline, I have a point plan.

    1 Never   2 Seldom   3 Sometimes   4 Often   5 Always

3. When playing from the baseline, I feel in control, relaxed and ready.

    1 Never   2 Seldom   3 Sometimes   4 Often   5 Always

4. I have confidence in my baseline game.

    1 Never   2 Seldom   3 Sometimes   4 Often   5 Always

5. When playing from the baseline, I concentrate well (on the 'here and now').

    1 Never   2 Seldom   3 Sometimes   4 Often   5 Always

6. When playing from the baseline, I think positively about how well I am playing.

    1 Never   2 Seldom   3 Sometimes   4 Often   5 Always

7. When playing from the baseline, I breathe or move to relax or activate.

    1 Never   2 Seldom   3 Sometimes   4 Often   5 Always

8. I can visualise myself hitting good groundstrokes.

    1 Never   2 Seldom   3 Sometimes   4 Often   5 Always

9. I control anger and frustration after making mistakes during baseline rallies.

    1 Never   2 Seldom   3 Sometimes   4 Often   5 Always

10. I am realistic and rational when assessing the effectiveness of my baseline game.

    1 Never   2 Seldom   3 Sometimes   4 Often   5 Always

Scoring: Sum your points: _____

< 25 points:	You need to work on your mental skills when playing from the baseline to improve your performance.
25-34 points:	You use mental skills when playing from the baseline but not always consistently. To better use these mental skills when rallying, you would benefit from a mental skills training programme specifically tailored to your needs.
35-43 points:	You use the mental skills needed for successful baseline play, efficiently. Some more specific mental skills training will help you identify and apply more effective strategies to these strokes.
44-50 points:	Your use of the mental skills needed for successful baseline play is very efficient. You should work to maintain, individualise and maximise the benefits of their application to these strokes.

MENTAL SKILLS SELF-ASSESSMENT
APPROACHING THE NET AND PLAYING AT THE NET

Name of the player: _____ Date: _____

Below you will find some statements about the mental skills you may use when **approaching the net and playing at the net**. Read each of the items carefully. Below each statement, circle a number from 1 to 5 that best describes your current feelings. There are no right or wrong answers. Please do not leave any item blank. Your honesty is necessary and will be much appreciated.

1. I like approaching and playing at the net during matches.

    1 Never   2 Seldom   3 Sometimes   4 Often   5 Always

2. When approaching and playing at the net, I have a point plan.

    1 Never   2 Seldom   3 Sometimes   4 Often   5 Always

3. When approaching and playing at the net, I feel in control, ready and relaxed.

    1 Never   2 Seldom   3 Sometimes   4 Often   5 Always

4. I have confidence in my approach and net game.

    1 Never   2 Seldom   3 Sometimes   4 Often   5 Always

5. When approaching and playing at the net, I concentrate well.

    1 Never   2 Seldom   3 Sometimes   4 Often   5 Always

6. When approaching and playing at the net, I am positive about how well I am playing.

    1 Never   2 Seldom   3 Sometimes   4 Often   5 Always

7. When approaching and playing at the net, I handle pressure well.

    1 Never   2 Seldom   3 Sometimes   4 Often   5 Always

8. I can visualise myself hitting a good approach shot, volley or smash.

    1 Never   2 Seldom   3 Sometimes   4 Often   5 Always

9. I control my anger and frustration after making a mistake with my approach or at the net.

    1 Never   2 Seldom   3 Sometimes   4 Often   5 Always

10. I am realistic when assessing the effectiveness of my approach and net game.

    1 Never   2 Seldom   3 Sometimes   4 Often   5 Always

Scoring: Sum your points: _____

- **< 25 points**: You need to work on your mental skills to more effectively execute your approach shots and net game.
- **25-34 points**: You use mental skills when approaching, volleying and smashing but not always consistently. To better use these mental skills when approaching, volleying and smashing, you would benefit from a mental skills training programme specifically tailored to your needs.
- **35-43 points**: You use the mental skills needed for the approach and net game efficiently. Some more specific mental skills training will help you identify and apply more effective strategies to these strokes.
- **44-50 points**: Your use of the mental skills needed for the approach and net game is very efficient. You should work to maintain, individualise and maximise the benefits of their application to these strokes.

MENTAL SKILLS SELF-ASSESSMENT
PASSING THE NET PLAYER

Name of the player: _____ Date: _____

Below you will find some statements about the mental skills you may use when **passing the net player**. Read each of the items carefully. Below each statement, circle a number from 1 to 5 that best describes your current feelings. There are no right or wrong answers. Please do not leave any item blank. Your honesty is necessary and will be much appreciated.

1. I like playing against opponents when they are at the net.

    1 Never   2 Seldom   3 Sometimes   4 Often   5 Always

2. When passing the net player, I have a point plan.

    1 Never   2 Seldom   3 Sometimes   4 Often   5 Always

3. When passing the net player, I feel in control, ready and relaxed.

    1 Never   2 Seldom   3 Sometimes   4 Often   5 Always

4. I have confidence in my passing game (passing-shots, lobs).

    1 Never   2 Seldom   3 Sometimes   4 Often   5 Always

5. When passing the net player, I concentrate well (in the 'here and now').

    1 Never   2 Seldom   3 Sometimes   4 Often   5 Always

6. When passing the net player, I am positive about how well I can play.

    1 Never   2 Seldom   3 Sometimes   4 Often   5 Always

7. When passing the net player, I control the pressure of the situation effectively.

    1 Never   2 Seldom   3 Sometimes   4 Often   5 Always

8. I can visualise myself hitting a good passing-shot or lob.

    1 Never   2 Seldom   3 Sometimes   4 Often   5 Always

9. I control my anger and frustration well after making a mistake with my passing-shot or lob.

    1 Never   2 Seldom   3 Sometimes   4 Often   5 Always

10. I am realistic when assessing the effectiveness of my passing-shots and lobs.

    1 Never   2 Seldom   3 Sometimes   4 Often   5 Always

Scoring: Sum your points: _____

< 25 points:	You need to work on your mental skills when passing the net player to improve your performance.
25-34 points:	You use mental skills when playing passing-shots and lobs but not always consistently. To better use these mental skills in the passing-shots and lobs, you would benefit from a mental skills training programme specifically tailored to your needs.
35-43 points:	You use the mental skills needed for the passing game efficiently. Some more specific mental skills training will help you identify and apply more effective strategies to these strokes.
44-50 points:	Your use of the mental skills needed for the passing game is very efficient. You should work to maintain, individualise and maximise the benefits of their application to these strokes.

TENNIS MOTIVATION SELF-ASSESSMENT

Name of the player: _____ Date: _____

Below you will find some statements about your **motivation and commitment** to tennis. Read each of the items carefully. Below each statement, circle a number from 1 to 5 that best describes your current feelings. There are no right or wrong answers. Please do not leave any item blank. Your honesty is necessary and will be much appreciated.

1. I am very committed to tennis.

    1 Never   2 Seldom   3 Sometimes   4 Often   5 Always

2. I try hard and give 100% effort to my tennis.

    1 Never   2 Seldom   3 Sometimes   4 Often   5 Always

3. I persist in playing tennis despite failures, problems, or inconveniences.

    1 Never   2 Seldom   3 Sometimes   4 Often   5 Always

4. I enjoy and have fun playing tennis.

    1 Never   2 Seldom   3 Sometimes   4 Often   5 Always

5. I love tennis and I am passionate about it.

    1 Never   2 Seldom   3 Sometimes   4 Often   5 Always

6. I practice and play with as much intensity as I can.

    1 Never   2 Seldom   3 Sometimes   4 Often   5 Always

7. I have the drive and the determination to reach my goals in tennis.

    1 Never   2 Seldom   3 Sometimes   4 Often   5 Always

8. I am disciplined in playing tennis to the best of my ability.

    1 Never   2 Seldom   3 Sometimes   4 Often   5 Always

9. I am very 'hungry' to play tennis.

    1 Never   2 Seldom   3 Sometimes   4 Often   5 Always

10. I accept and enjoy the challenge of playing competitive tennis.

    1 Never   2 Seldom   3 Sometimes   4 Often   5 Always

Scoring: Sum your points: _____

- **< 25 points**: You need to work on your motivation and commitment to tennis to better enjoy the game and avoid burnout or a lack of motivation.
- **25-34 points**: At times you are motivated but this is not always consistent. To ensure more enjoyment and success, you would benefit for working with your coach and team members to develop strategies to ensure you have more fun.
- **35-43 points**: You are motivated and committed to the game but will benefit from specific mental skills programmes targeted at improving enjoyment, fun and love of the game while also reducing the risk of burnout.
- **44-50 points**: You are highly motivated and very committed to the game. You should work on maintaining your love of the game, have fun and enjoy playing!

TENNIS STRESS SELF-ASSESSMENT

Name of the player: _____   Date: _____

Below you will find some statements about your **arousal, anxiety, pressure and stress feelings** in tennis. Read each of the items carefully. Below each statement, circle a number from 1 to 5 that best describes your current feelings. There are no right or wrong answers. Please do not leave any item blank. Your honesty is necessary and will be much appreciated.

Before, during or after competition…

1. I feel stressed, nervous, anxious, pressured, angry, frustrated and/or afraid.

    1 Never   2 Seldom   3 Sometimes   4 Often   5 Always

2. I feel that my body and muscles become tense, tight and rigid.

    1 Never   2 Seldom   3 Sometimes   4 Often   5 Always

3. My heart rate and breathing become accelerated, shallow and/or irregular.

    1 Never   2 Seldom   3 Sometimes   4 Often   5 Always

4. I doubt my performance, and worry that I will lose or choke.

    1 Never   2 Seldom   3 Sometimes   4 Often   5 Always

5. My mind races and I have problems in focussing and thinking clearly.

    1 Never   2 Seldom   3 Sometimes   4 Often   5 Always

6. I feel slow and heavy, with little energy.

    1 Never   2 Seldom   3 Sometimes   4 Often   5 Always

7. I lose my patience and temper; I feel that nothing I do works.

    1 Never   2 Seldom   3 Sometimes   4 Often   5 Always

8. I have no enthusiasm; I feel bored and do not care about what happens.

    1 Never   2 Seldom   3 Sometimes   4 Often   5 Always

9. My timing gets worse, my anticipation disappears and I get distracted easily.

    1 Never   2 Seldom   3 Sometimes   4 Often   5 Always

10. I encounter problems in eating or sleeping.

    1 Never   2 Seldom   3 Sometimes   4 Often   5 Always

- -

Scoring: Sum your points: _____

< 25 points:	You show balanced reactions to match stress. You should work on maintaining the efficiency and appropriateness of your responses to ensure you optimise your arousal control before, during or after match play.
25-34 points:	Well done. You manage your stress well. The key now is to maintain your skills so as to ensure you continue to manage any stressful responses you may experience. Keep up the great work and have fun and enjoy your tennis!
35-43 points:	You react reasonably to match stress to reduce your pressure and anxiety levels. However, you would benefit from specific mental skills training programmes to enhance your arousal control and avoid experiencing anger, fear, tanking, choking, exploding, or rushing before, during or after match play.
44-50 points:	You need to work on your stress management techniques to reduce match pressure and anxiety; to avoid anger, fear, tanking, choking, exploding, or rushing; and therefore to improve your arousal control before, during or after match play

TENNIS SELF-CONFIDENCE SELF-ASSESSMENT

Name of the player: _____ Date: _____

Below you will find some statements about your **self-confidence, self-efficacy, self-image and attribution skills** in tennis. Read each of the items carefully. Below each statement, circle a number from 1 to 5 that best describes your current feelings. There are no right or wrong answers. Please do not leave any item blank. Your honesty is necessary and will be much appreciated.

1. I think I am mentally tough and see myself as a fighter.

    1 Never   2 Seldom   3 Sometimes   4 Often   5 Always

2. I have a positive attitude towards improving myself and my game.

    1 Never   2 Seldom   3 Sometimes   4 Often   5 Always

3. I am confident in my technical skills (strokes, movements, etc.).

    1 Never   2 Seldom   3 Sometimes   4 Often   5 Always

4. I am confident in my tactical and strategical skills (match plan, etc.).

    1 Never   2 Seldom   3 Sometimes   4 Often   5 Always

5. I am confident in my physical skills (speed, power, endurance, etc.).

    1 Never   2 Seldom   3 Sometimes   4 Often   5 Always

6. I am confident in my mental skills (motivation, focus, emotional control).

    1 Never   2 Seldom   3 Sometimes   4 Often   5 Always

7. I think I am self-disciplined, train hard but smart and plan competition well.

    1 Never   2 Seldom   3 Sometimes   4 Often   5 Always

8. I believe in myself and have high expectations of my performance.

    1 Never   2 Seldom   3 Sometimes   4 Often   5 Always

9. I think match outcomes depend mostly on my performance and effort.

    1 Never   2 Seldom   3 Sometimes   4 Often   5 Always

10. I like tough matches and see pressure and adversity as a challenge.

    1 Never   2 Seldom   3 Sometimes   4 Often   5 Always

- -

Scoring: Sum your points: _____

< 25 points: You need to work on your confidence and composure so that your self-esteem, self-efficiency, self-image and attributional patterns improve. This will help ensure you maintain positive attitudes before, during and after match play.

25-34 points: You have satisfactory self-confidence, self-esteem, self-efficiency and self-image. However, you would benefit from specific mental skills training programmes to improve your self-confidence so that your state-of-mind and performance becomes more consistent and positive before, during and after match play.

35-43 points: Your self-confidence, and the way you feel about yourself and your tennis is quite good. With a little more specific work on some mental skills this can be further improved to make you feel great, so positive and confident in what you can do on and off the court.

44-50 points: You display high self-confidence and sound composure. You should work on maintaining these qualities to ensure positive performances and outlooks before, during and after match play.

TENNIS CONCENTRATION SELF-ASSESSMENT

Name of the player: _____   Date: _____

Below you will find some statements about your **concentration skills** in tennis. Read each of the items carefully. Below each statement, circle a number from 1 to 5 that best describes your current feelings. There are no right or wrong answers. Please do not leave any item blank. Your honesty is necessary and will be much appreciated.

Before, during or after competition…

1. I know the cues (ball, opponent) on which to focus in each situation.

    1 NEVER   2 SELDOM   3 SOMETIMES   4 OFTEN   5 ALWAYS

2. I can change focus from one relevant cue to another as I need to.

    1 NEVER   2 SELDOM   3 SOMETIMES   4 OFTEN   5 ALWAYS

3. I focus on the 'here and now', not on past or future events.

    1 NEVER   2 SELDOM   3 SOMETIMES   4 OFTEN   5 ALWAYS

4. My emotions (anger, fear) do not interfere with my ability to concentrate.

    1 NEVER   2 SELDOM   3 SOMETIMES   4 OFTEN   5 ALWAYS

5. My thoughts (doubts, boredom) do not interfere with my ability to concentrate.

    1 NEVER   2 SELDOM   3 SOMETIMES   4 OFTEN   5 ALWAYS

6. My physical condition (being tired) does not interfere with my concentration.

    1 NEVER   2 SELDOM   3 SOMETIMES   4 OFTEN   5 ALWAYS

7. External distractions (noise, line calls) do not interfere with my concentration.

    1 NEVER   2 SELDOM   3 SOMETIMES   4 OFTEN   5 ALWAYS

8. I am able to direct my focus internally (analysis, visualisation of myself).

    1 NEVER   2 SELDOM   3 SOMETIMES   4 OFTEN   5 ALWAYS

9. I am able to focus on external cues (environment, ball, opponent).

    1 NEVER   2 SELDOM   3 SOMETIMES   4 OFTEN   5 ALWAYS

10. I concentrate on one thing at a time.

    1 NEVER   2 SELDOM   3 SOMETIMES   4 OFTEN   5 ALWAYS

- -

Scoring: Sum your points: _____

- **< 25 points:** You need to work on your concentration skills to enhance your ability to attend and focus before, during and after match play.
- **25-34 points:** You have satisfactory concentration skills. However, you would benefit from specific mental skills training programmes to minimise your distractibility and avoid concentration lapses. This will help ensure that you are able to optimally focus before, during and after match play.
- **35-43 points:** Your concentration skills are quite good. Further developing more specific mental skills will benefit you even more to ensure you remain focused in tough and stressful situations and keep your thoughts in the present to play your best tennis.
- **44-50 points:** You possess very good concentration skills. You should work on maintaining them to ensure focus can be maintained before, during and after match play.

TENNIS MOTIVATIONAL CLIMATE ASSESSMENT

Name of the player: _____ Date: _____

Name of the coach: _____

Below you will find some statements about **the atmosphere or climate that you experience in your tennis training sessions or matches**. Read each of the items carefully. Below each statement, circle a number from 1 to 5 that best describes your current feelings. There are no right or wrong answers. Please do not leave any item blank. Your honesty is necessary and will be much appreciated.

In practice or matches, my coach…

1. Gives praise, rewards and pays attention to all players.

    1 NEVER   2 SELDOM   3 SOMETIMES   4 OFTEN   5 ALWAYS

2. Helps all of us to improve our strengths and weaknesses.

    1 NEVER   2 SELDOM   3 SOMETIMES   4 OFTEN   5 ALWAYS

3. Rewards personal effort, commitment and interest.

    1 NEVER   2 SELDOM   3 SOMETIMES   4 OFTEN   5 ALWAYS

4. Asks us to help each other rather than compete against each other.

    1 NEVER   2 SELDOM   3 SOMETIMES   4 OFTEN   5 ALWAYS

5. Emphasises the idea that we are a team.

    1 NEVER   2 SELDOM   3 SOMETIMES   4 OFTEN   5 ALWAYS

6. Does not get angry or punish players when we make mistakes.

    1 NEVER   2 SELDOM   3 SOMETIMES   4 OFTEN   5 ALWAYS

7. Rewards all players, not just the best ones.

    1 NEVER   2 SELDOM   3 SOMETIMES   4 OFTEN   5 ALWAYS

8. Wants us to improve and learn new things in each practice or match.

    1 NEVER   2 SELDOM   3 SOMETIMES   4 OFTEN   5 ALWAYS

9. Wants us to try our best, show good behaviour and enjoy the experience.

    1 NEVER   2 SELDOM   3 SOMETIMES   4 OFTEN   5 ALWAYS

10. Is more concerned about the performance than about the score.

    1 NEVER   2 SELDOM   3 SOMETIMES   4 OFTEN   5 ALWAYS

- -

Scoring: Sum your points: _____

< 25 points:	You perceive an ego-oriented motivational climate in which winners and results are rewarded, mistakes punished and competition among players fostered. The coach should change this climate to become more task-oriented to ensure that all players are given praise and rewards performance improvement and not results are emphasised, and mistakes are considered as part of the learning process.
25-34 points:	You perceive a motivational climate oriented satisfactorily to the task. However, the coach may need to adjust certain practices to ensure that all players are given praise and rewards performance improvement and not results are emphasised, and that mistakes are considered as part of the learning process.
35-43 points:	You perceive a good task-oriented motivational climate. To further improve this, the coach may need to give even more praise and reward whilst focusing on the improvement of each players performance.
44-50 points:	You perceive an excellent task-oriented motivational climate. The coach should work on maintaining this climate to ensure that all players are praised and rewarded performance improvement and not results, continues to be emphasised, and that mistakes are still considered part of the learning process.

TENNIS AROUSAL STRATEGIES SELF-ASSESSMENT

Name of the player: _____ Date: _____

Below you will find some statements about your **arousal, anxiety, pressure and stress management strategies** in tennis. Read each of the items carefully. Below each statement, circle a number from 1 to 5 that best describes your current feelings. There are no right or wrong answers. Please do not leave any item blank. Your honesty is necessary and will be much appreciated.

1. I control pressure well before, during and after matches.

    1 Never   2 Seldom   3 Sometimes   4 Often   5 Always

2. I use breathing or close my eyes to control stress and release tension.

    1 Never   2 Seldom   3 Sometimes   4 Often   5 Always

3. I relax muscles to prepare between points and during changeovers.

    1 Never   2 Seldom   3 Sometimes   4 Often   5 Always

4. I control anger and frustration after making mistakes.

    1 Never   2 Seldom   3 Sometimes   4 Often   5 Always

5. I know how to control my heart rate when under pressure.

    1 Never   2 Seldom   3 Sometimes   4 Often   5 Always

6. I keep my concentration in most stressful situations.

    1 Never   2 Seldom   3 Sometimes   4 Often   5 Always

7. I eat and sleep well, before and after difficult matches.

    1 Never   2 Seldom   3 Sometimes   4 Often   5 Always

8. I listen to music, practice yoga or visualisation to manage anxiety.

    1 Never   2 Seldom   3 Sometimes   4 Often   5 Always

9. I bounce up and down between points to activate myself if I need to.

    1 Never   2 Seldom   3 Sometimes   4 Often   5 Always

10. I smile and use humour to overcome stressful situations.

    1 Never   2 Seldom   3 Sometimes   4 Often   5 Always

Scoring: Sum your points: _____

- **< 25 points**: You need to work on your stress management techniques to alleviate pressure and anxiety, to avoid you experiencing anger, fear, tanking, choking, exploding, or rushing, and to best approximate optimal arousal control before, during or after match play.

- **25-34 points**: You use satisfactory stress management strategies to reduce your anxiety levels. However, you would benefit from specific mental skills training programmes to improve your performance; to avoid anger, fear, tanking, choking, exploding, or rushing; and to optimise arousal control before, during and after match play.

- **35-43 points**: Your use of stress management techniques is quite good and helps you reduce the tension, negative emotions, and pressures felt before, during and after matches. To be even more effective and to ensure optimal arousal control practice a few times a week the specific stress management strategies you need.

- **44-50 points**: Your use of stress management techniques is very effective. You should work on maintaining the use of these techniques to ensure optimal arousal control before, during and after match play.

TENNIS SELF-CONFIDENCE STRATEGIES SELF-ASSESSMENT

Name of the player: _____   Date: _____

Below you will find some statements about your **self-confidence strategies** in tennis. Read each of the items carefully. Below each statement, circle a number from 1 to 5 that best describes your current feelings. There are no right or wrong answers. Please do not leave any item blank. Your honesty is necessary and will be much appreciated.
During matches and practices…

1. I use self-talk and control it depending on the situation.

   1 Never   2 Seldom   3 Sometimes   4 Often   5 Always

2. I speak positively to myself to motivate, activate, fight or improve.

   1 Never   2 Seldom   3 Sometimes   4 Often   5 Always

3. I use positive self-talk to improve my concentration and confidence.

   1 Never   2 Seldom   3 Sometimes   4 Often   5 Always

4. I use positive self-talk to control fear, choking, anger and frustration.

   1 Never   2 Seldom   3 Sometimes   4 Often   5 Always

5. I have a success file that includes my best performances and aspirations.

   1 Never   2 Seldom   3 Sometimes   4 Often   5 Always

6. My body (head, eyes, face, chest, back, arms) shows how positive I am.

   1 Never   2 Seldom   3 Sometimes   4 Often   5 Always

7. I like to behave like the champion I am.

   1 Never   2 Seldom   3 Sometimes   4 Often   5 Always

8. I like to dress like a pro player.

   1 Never   2 Seldom   3 Sometimes   4 Often   5 Always

9. I try to quickly counter negative or irrational beliefs that arise.

   1 Never   2 Seldom   3 Sometimes   4 Often   5 Always

10. I like to positively question myself and assess myself to improve my game.

    1 Never   2 Seldom   3 Sometimes   4 Often   5 Always

- -

Scoring: Sum your points: _____

< 25 points:	You need to work on better using self-confidence improvement techniques to enhance your positive thinking and self-belief, while also negating any negative thoughts, anger, fear, tanking, choking, exploding, or rushing, before, during and after match play.
25-34 points:	You use self-confidence techniques appropriately. However, you would benefit from specific mental skills training programmes to improve your self-confidence and positive thinking as well as to reduce any irrational thoughts and actions before, during and after match play.
35-43 points:	Your self-confidence skills are good. When you use self-confidence strategies, you see the benefits in how you feel, look, act and play. The key is to consistently employ these techniques so that you feel confident all the time, before, during and after your matches.
44-50 points:	You employ confidence techniques very effectively to help you perform at your best. You should work on maintaining the use of these techniques to optimise your levels of self-confidence before, during and after match play.

TENNIS VISUALISATION SELF-ASSESSMENT

Name of the player: _____ Date: _____

Below you will find some statements about your **visualisation skills** in tennis. Read each of the items carefully. Below each statement, circle a number from 1 to 5 that best describes your current feelings. There are no right or wrong answers. Please do not leave any item blank. Your honesty is necessary and will be much appreciated.

Before, during or after competition…

1. I use visualisation to improve my tennis (strokes, tactics, etc.).
 1 Never   2 Seldom   3 Sometimes   4 Often   5 Always

2. I see myself playing perfect tennis or winning my favourite tournament.
 1 Never   2 Seldom   3 Sometimes   4 Often   5 Always

3. I visualise myself internally (see myself with my own eyes).
 1 Never   2 Seldom   3 Sometimes   4 Often   5 Always

4. I see myself externally as if I am watching a DVD and I am on the screen.
 1 Never   2 Seldom   3 Sometimes   4 Often   5 Always

5. I visualise things or situations –moving statically/dynamically- with vividness.
 1 Never   2 Seldom   3 Sometimes   4 Often   5 Always

6. I use all my senses (sight, smell, sound, touch, and taste) to visualise.
 1 Never   2 Seldom   3 Sometimes   4 Often   5 Always

7. When I visualise I feel it helps me to reduce anxiety.
 1 Never   2 Seldom   3 Sometimes   4 Often   5 Always

8. Visualisation improves my anticipation, concentration and confidence.
 1 Never   2 Seldom   3 Sometimes   4 Often   5 Always

9. When I visualise I can control the images I see.
 1 Never   2 Seldom   3 Sometimes   4 Often   5 Always

10. I can visualise for varying lengths of time (a few seconds, minutes).
 1 Never   2 Seldom   3 Sometimes   4 Often   5 Always

Scoring: Sum your points: _____

- **< 25 points**: You need to work on your visualisation skills to positively benefit from their application before, during and after match play.
- **25-34 points**: You possess satisfactory visualisation skills. However, you would benefit from specific mental skills training programmes to benefit more comprehensively from visualisation's application before, during and after match play.
- **35-43 points**: Your visualisation skills are good, and can be improved with more specific emphasis to make your visualisations even clearer and more beneficial, ensuring you maximise your success.
- **44-50 points**: You have very good visualisation skills. You should work to maintain, individualise and maximise the benefits of their application before, during and after match play.

TENNIS ROUTINES SELF-ASSESSMENT

Name of the player: _____   Date: _____

Below you will find some statements about your **use of routines and rituals** in tennis. Read each of the items carefully. Below each statement, circle a number from 1 to 5 that best describes your current feelings. There are no right or wrong answers. Please do not leave any item blank. Your honesty is necessary and will be much appreciated.

1. I use routines to improve my tennis (preparation, stress control, motivation).

   1 Never   2 Seldom   3 Sometimes   4 Often   5 Always

2. Before matches, I sleep and eat well, and I prepare all that I need.

   1 Never   2 Seldom   3 Sometimes   4 Often   5 Always

3. Before matches, I warm-up physically and mentally and have a match plan.

   1 Never   2 Seldom   3 Sometimes   4 Often   5 Always

4. Before serving, I have a systematic ritual and visualise my perfect serve.

   1 Never   2 Seldom   3 Sometimes   4 Often   5 Always

5. Before receiving, I focus on the server and the ball and have a return plan.

   1 Never   2 Seldom   3 Sometimes   4 Often   5 Always

6. Between points, I relax or activate and get ready depending on the situation.

   1 Never   2 Seldom   3 Sometimes   4 Often   5 Always

7. During change overs, I towel off, relax, drink and maintain game focus.

   1 Never   2 Seldom   3 Sometimes   4 Often   5 Always

8. After matches, I shower, drink, eat, and analyse the match.

   1 Never   2 Seldom   3 Sometimes   4 Often   5 Always

9. After match, I relax, stretch, read, listen to music, or sleep.

   1 Never   2 Seldom   3 Sometimes   4 Often   5 Always

10. I manage time effectively (punctuality, planning).

    1 Never   2 Seldom   3 Sometimes   4 Often   5 Always

Scoring: Sum your points: _____

- **< 25 points**: You need to work on your routines to positively benefit from their application before, during and after match play.

- **25-34 points**: You use routines satisfactorily. However, you would benefit from specific mental skills training programmes to optimise your routine use before, during and after match play.

- **35-43 points**: You use routines very well in some situations, but not as effectively as you could all the time. You would benefit more from practicing specific mental routines for all situations before, during and after match play, and thus really optimise your routines.

- **44-50 points**: You employ routines very effectively. You should work to maintain, individualise and maximise the benefits of their application before, during and after match play.

TENNIS COGNITIVE MANAGEMENT STRATEGIES SELF-ASSESSMENT

Name of the player: _____   Date: _____

Below you will find some statements about your **cognitive management strategies** in tennis. Read each of the items carefully. Below each statement, circle a number from 1 to 5 that best describes your current feelings. There are no right or wrong answers. Please do not leave any item blank. Your honesty is necessary and will be much appreciated.

1. I like solving the tactical 'problems' that match situations create.
   1 NEVER   2 SELDOM   3 SOMETIMES   4 OFTEN   5 ALWAYS

2. I achieve stability and control my thoughts through positive thinking.
   1 NEVER   2 SELDOM   3 SOMETIMES   4 OFTEN   5 ALWAYS

3. I use thought-stopping techniques to let negative thoughts and mistakes go.
   1 NEVER   2 SELDOM   3 SOMETIMES   4 OFTEN   5 ALWAYS

4. Relaxation helps me to reduce pressure.
   1 NEVER   2 SELDOM   3 SOMETIMES   4 OFTEN   5 ALWAYS

5. I replace negative thoughts, feelings and actions with positive ones.
   1 NEVER   2 SELDOM   3 SOMETIMES   4 OFTEN   5 ALWAYS

6. I assess my errors and use key words to reinforce my positive behaviour.
   1 NEVER   2 SELDOM   3 SOMETIMES   4 OFTEN   5 ALWAYS

7. I am realistic and rational when I assess my skills and plan my development.
   1 NEVER   2 SELDOM   3 SOMETIMES   4 OFTEN   5 ALWAYS

8. I take responsibility for my practice and matches (times, equipment, partners).
   1 NEVER   2 SELDOM   3 SOMETIMES   4 OFTEN   5 ALWAYS

9. Success is performing well and displaying 100% effort, not only winning.
   1 NEVER   2 SELDOM   3 SOMETIMES   4 OFTEN   5 ALWAYS

10. I use meditation, yoga or other techniques to focus my mind when needed.
    1 NEVER   2 SELDOM   3 SOMETIMES   4 OFTEN   5 ALWAYS

Scoring: Sum your points: _____

- **< 25 points**: You need to work on your use of cognitive management strategies to benefit from their application before, during and after match play.

- **25-34 points**: You use cognitive management strategies satisfactorily. However, you would benefit from specific mental skills training programmes to best use them before, during and after match play.

- **35-43 points**: You use good cognitive management strategies. Some more specific mental skills training will help you identify and apply more effective strategies before, during and after match play.

- **44-50 points**: You possess and use very good cognitive management strategies. You should work to maintain, individualise and maximise the benefits of their application before, during and after match play.

TENNIS ATTRIBUTIONAL PATTERNS SELF-ASSESSMENT

Name of the player: _____   Date: _____

Below you will find some statements about your **attributional patterns** in tennis. Read each of the items carefully. Below each statement, circle a number from 1 to 5 that best describes your current feelings. There are no right or wrong answers. Please do not leave any item blank. Your honesty is necessary and will be much appreciated.

When I have played a match and I have…

1. Won, I think it is mostly due to my technical and tactical skills.

    1 Never   2 Seldom   3 Sometimes   4 Often   5 Always

2. Won, I think it is mostly due to the fact that I practice hard.

    1 Never   2 Seldom   3 Sometimes   4 Often   5 Always

3. Won, I think it is mostly to the fact that I give 100% when I play.

    1 Never   2 Seldom   3 Sometimes   4 Often   5 Always

4. Won, I think it is mostly due to my physical skills.

    1 Never   2 Seldom   3 Sometimes   4 Often   5 Always

5. Won, I think it is mostly due to my mental skills.

    1 Never   2 Seldom   3 Sometimes   4 Often   5 Always

6. Lost, I think it is mostly due to the superior skills of my opponent.

    1 Never   2 Seldom   3 Sometimes   4 Often   5 Always

7. Lost, I think it is mostly due to the superior effort of my opponent.

    1 Never   2 Seldom   3 Sometimes   4 Often   5 Always

8. Lost, I try not to think that it is due to my bad luck.

    1 Never   2 Seldom   3 Sometimes   4 Often   5 Always

9. Lost, I try not to think that it is due to the bad calls of the umpire.

    1 Never   2 Seldom   3 Sometimes   4 Often   5 Always

10. Lost, I avoid thinking that it is due to my lack of effort.

    1 Never   2 Seldom   3 Sometimes   4 Often   5 Always

- -

Scoring: Sum your points: _____

< 25 points: You need to change your attributional patterns to optimise your performance potential.

25-34 points: You possess satisfactory attributional patterns. However, you may benefit from specific mental skills training programmes to enhance the consistency of your attributions and performance.

35-43 points: You display good attributional patterns. A mental skills training programme specifically tailored for you will further help you to realise your performance potential.

44-50 points: You display excellent attributional patterns. You should work on maintaining them so as to enhance your chances of realising your performance potential.

TENNIS GOAL-SETTING SELF-ASSESSMENT

Name of the player: _____ Date: _____

Below you will find some questions that will help you set your tennis **goals** for the upcoming season. Read each of the questions carefully. Answer each of them honestly. There are no right or wrong responses. Please do not leave any question unanswered.

1. CURRENT SITUATION. What is your current playing situation? Where do you stand?
....
....

2. LONG-TERM (DREAM) GOAL. What is your ultimate goal as a player? What do you want to achieve as a player?
....
....

3. DREAM GOAL FOR THE SEASON. What is your 'dream' goal for this season? What would you like to achieve if you play your best tennis?
....
....

4. REALISTIC GOAL FOR THE SEASON. What is your 'realistic' goal for this season? What would you like to achieve if things all go well?
....
....

5. PURPOSE. What will achieving your 'realistic' goal do for you? Why is it important to you?
....
....

6. MEANS. What do you need to reach your 'realistic' goal? How can you reach your 'realistic' goal?
....
....

7. OBSTACLES. What could prevent you from achieving your 'realistic' goal?
....
....

8. SOLUTIONS. How can these obstacles be overcome?
....
....

9. SHORT-TERM GOALS. List monthly or weekly goals that will help you achieve your 'realistic' goal for this season?

Monthly: ....
....

Weekly: ....
....

10. DEADLINE. Give yourself a deadline by which you would like to achieve your 'realistic' goal for this season?
....
....

PROGRESSIVE MUSCULAR RELAXATION (PMR) - JACOBSON SYSTEM

A Modified Approach (Loehr, 1991)

Jacobson's training procedures involve alternate muscle tensing and relaxing with the intention of developing an acute awareness of the difference. The technique, players will find, is surprisingly simple, and should take approximately ten minutes to complete.

Note: Before practicing PMR, you should consult your physician if you have a history of serious injuries, muscle spasms, or back problems, because the deliberate muscle tensing of the PMR procedure could exacerbate any of these pre-existing conditions.

1. Select a comfortable chair, preferably a reclining one.
2. Find a quiet room.
3. Close both eyes take two deep breaths and try to feel yourself 'let go'.
4. Extend both arms (in front of you) and clench your fists... gradually increase the tension until all of the muscles in your fingers and hands are contracted... then relax...let your arms drop naturally. Be aware of the difference between feeling 'tense' and 'relaxed'.
5. Extend both arms again, tensing the muscles of your lower arm...hold it, become aware of the feeling... now relax...letting your arms drop naturally to your side.
6. Tense the muscles of your forehead by frowning... hold it, become aware of the feeling... now relax... letting all the muscles of your forehead lengthen.
7. Tense the muscles in your face... grimace... hold it, become aware of the feeling... now relax.
8. Tense the muscles of your neck... hold it, become aware of the feeling... now relax.
9. Tense the muscles of the shoulders... hold it, become aware of the feeling... now relax.
10. Tense the muscles of the back, first the upper back and then the lower back... hold it, become aware of the feeling... now relax.
11. Tense the muscles of your chest hold it, become aware of the feeling... now relax.
12. Tense the muscles of your stomach hold it, become aware of the feeling... now relax.
13. Tense the muscles of your upper leg... hold it, become aware of the feeling... now relax.
14. Tense the muscles of your lower leg... hold it, become aware of the feeling... now relax.
15. Tense the muscles of your feet and toes... hold it, become aware of the feeling... now relax.
16. Now concentrate on relaxing all of the muscles of your body. Become aware of any areas that might still be tense in any way, and try to relax them. Try to maintain this state of total muscle relaxation for at least two to three minutes.
17. Open your eyes, stretch and feel refreshed... go about your business!

Shortened form of PMR

Follow steps 1 to 3 above.

4. Tense the muscles of your legs, feet and toes... hold it, become aware of the feeling... now relax.
5. Tense the muscles of your abdomen, stomach, back and chest... hold it, become aware of the feeling... now relax.
5. Tense the muscles of your arms, shoulders and neck... hold it, become aware of the feeling... now relax.
6. Tense the muscles of your face... hold it, become aware of the feeling... now relax.

Follow steps 16 and 17.

VISUALISATION SCRIPT FOR TENNIS

(Adapted from Weinberg, 2002)

Note: Perform some progressive muscle relaxation before commencing this visualisation exercise.

BEFORE THE MATCH

Imagine yourself as you arrive at the tennis club...see people playing...feel the air, the environment...hear the sounds of balls and racquets...feel the sun on your back...enjoy anticipating the match...experience the feeling in your stomach and in your body...you are a little nervous but very ready...remembering that these are common feelings before you play a match....

DURING THE WARM-UP

You step out on the court to warm-up and your feet feel light and bouncy. Your groundstrokes are fluid and easy, yet powerful. You feel the short backswing and nice follow-through of your shots. You are moving around the court freely and effortlessly, getting to all of your opponent's shots. You warm-up your volley and overhead and everything feels good. Your contact point on your volleys is out in front of you and you are anticipating well. You feel a nice stretch on the back of your arm and in your lower back as you go back to hit some overheads. They are clean and right in the centre of the racquet. As you warm-up your serve you feel that your motion is fluid, your ball toss is consistent and that you are really reaching up and transferring your weight into the ball. The ball is hitting the spots in the service box that you are aiming for, using a variety of serves, spins and speeds.

In hitting the final strokes of the warm-up... remember some of your affirmations... encourage yourself after a good shot: 'I am a positive person', 'I am a confident player', 'I believe in myself and my abilities', 'I play each shot in the moment and I am very focussed as I play', 'I am in control of my temper and am free of anger and resentment'.

DURING THE MATCH

You now see yourself starting the match serving and getting right into the flow of the match. You visualise some strong serves where your opponent can only just send the ball back to the mid court and you decisively put the ball away with short, topspin, angled strokes. Your next point is a long rally from baseline to baseline. You see yourself keeping the ball deep and hitting it firmly but yet with a good margin for error. Finally, your opponent hits a short ball and you come in and slice it deep to the backhand corner. Your opponent tries a down the line passing shot but you anticipate correctly and are right there to hit a short cross court volley winner. You finish the game with a big ace down the middle of the 'T'. This game gets you off to a fast start and gets your adrenaline flowing and your concentration on the march.

The match has now started...you are moving well, you are light and quick...you are focussed...as the ball comes to you on each shot, you concentrate perfectly on the ball...you establish a rhythm of bounce, hit, bounce, hit...hitting with power and accuracy...as you hit each ball, you see it going over the net exactly where you want it to go...you hear the sound of the ball hitting your racquet in the right spot...you are glad to be out on this beautiful day playing...and playing well...you feel relaxed...loose.

You continue to see yourself getting into position...the ball coming to your forehand, you hit it and watch it go directly to where you wanted to hit it...the ball returns...you hit a backhand crosscourt...a forehand straight down the line...deep in the corner, a winner. A serve comes to your backhand, you stroke perfectly, hitting it down the line...another winner...another serve to you, coming to your forehand, you hit a nice drop shot just over the net...your opponent scrambles to get it and hits a high lob...you settle into position and quickly execute an overhead smash...you receive another serve...to your backhand and execute a deep backhand crosscourt shot, you feel powerful and controlled...experience your bodily sensations of relaxation and quickness. You are hitting each stroke with power, accuracy, and control...if you miss a shot, you notice what you did in error, make the necessary adjustments, and let it go...coming back to the present moment for the next point...all that exists is one shot at a time...one point at a time.

With the match drawing to a successful close, experience the power you feel as a good and competent player...a player who wins...a player who gives everything...you have achieved your goals...you have played well and feel proud and complete...allow yourself to have it all as you slowly let go of the image...let it float away and leave your mind...come slowly back to your physical space...reconnect with your breathing and the feel of the chair or floor beneath you...move your toes and then your fingers...breathe...when I count to three you may open your eyes...one...two...three....

PLAYER'S PSYCHOLOGICAL MATCH ASSESSMENT

Name of the player: _____   Date: _____

1 Never   2 Seldom   3 Sometimes   4 Often   5 Always

SKILL	The player usually…	1	2	3	4	5
PRE-MATCH	Analyses and reacts positively to potential stressors (match history, spectators, family, etc.)					
	Uses efficient mental routines					
	Has a satisfactory match plan (tactical, technical, physical and mental)					
	Conducts a thorough mental warm-up					
MOTIVATION	Accepts the challenge, is committed					
	Thrives when under pressure					
	Is mainly performance-oriented					
	Seems to have fun even in difficult circumstances					
	Gives 100%, chases every ball					
EMOTIONAL CONTROL	Refrains from irrational behaviour					
	Does not get upset easily or show poor body language					
	Does not curse					
	Uses breath appropriately					
	Relaxes arms, neck, hands…					
	Endeavours to optimise arousal (not too tight or too sloppy)					
	Tries to pump up when appropriate					
	Reacts positively and effectively against gamesmanship from the opponent					
	Reacts effectively / positively in key moments: forced / unforced errors, bad calls, wind, break points, etc.					
CONTROL OF THOUGHTS	Displays positively, goes for it					
	Uses positive self-talk					
	Seems self-confident					
	Projects a strong image (head ahead, eyes, shoulders and back straight, pumped fist, racquet head up…)					
	Uses power walk to move around the court					
	Visualises appropriately					
	Displays game intelligence (analyses personal and opponent performance)					
CONCENTRATION	Controls eyes (racquet, strings, inside court…)					
	Seems focussed on relevant cues (ball)					
	Sustains concentration over time					
	Varies focus according to the situation					
	Uses and maintains routines between points					
	Performs mental work / rituals during changeovers					
	Sends a strong mental message to the opponent					
	Distracts easily					
POST-MATCH	Follows a routine					
	Reacts positively and constructively					
	Analyses the match appropriately					
	Displays correct attributions regarding the outcome					
	Understands and learns from the outcome					
	Prepares well for the next match (if needed)					

RANKING OF PSYCHOLOGICAL ASPECTS TO IMPROVE:

1. What_____. How_____. When_____

2. What_____. How_____. When_____

3. What_____. How_____. When_____

MATCH FLOW SCORE CHART
(Higham and Harwood, 2002)

Player: _____ Opponent: _____

Round: _____ Final score: _____

Game flow:

```
                                    6-7         7-6
                                          6-6
                            5-7                       7-5
                                    5-6         6-5
                            4-6           5-5         6-4
                      3-6         4-5           5-4         6-3
                2-6         3-5         4-4           5-3         6-2
          1-6         2-5         3-4           4-3         5-2         6-1
    0-6         1-5         2-4           3-3         4-2         5-1         6-0
          0-5         1-4           2-3         3-2         4-1         5-0
                0-4         1-3           2-2         3-1         4-0
                      0-3         1-2           2-1         3-0
                            0-2         1-1           2-0
                                  0-1         1-0
                                        0-0
```

SET FLOW:

```
                        1-2         2-1
                  0-2         1-1         2-0
                        0-1         1-0
                              0-0
```

Instructions: Start at the bottom. Join the scores to show the match flow. Circle key games. Make notes in the margins to document what happened mentally and tactically during the key games.

PARENT PROFILE

Name of the parent: _____ Date: _____

Below you will find some statements regarding yourself as **a parent of a tennis player**. Read each of the items carefully. Below each statement, circle a number from 1 to 5 that best describes your current feelings. There are no right or wrong answers. Please do not leave any item blank. Your honesty is necessary and will be much appreciated.

1. I know that my role as a parent of a player is different to that of the coach.

   1 Never   2 Seldom   3 Sometimes   4 Often   5 Always

2. I think my child, the coach and myself, share common healthy goals for my child's tennis.

   1 Never   2 Seldom   3 Sometimes   4 Often   5 Always

3. I am not an additional source of pressure (i.e. to win) on my child.

   1 Never   2 Seldom   3 Sometimes   4 Often   5 Always

4. I am not pushy, critical and over involved in my child's tennis.

   1 Never   2 Seldom   3 Sometimes   4 Often   5 Always

5. I support, encourage and reinforce my child's involvement in tennis.

   1 Never   2 Seldom   3 Sometimes   4 Often   5 Always

6. I understand the pressures that competitive tennis can present for my child.

   1 Never   2 Seldom   3 Sometimes   4 Often   5 Always

7. I look positive and calm when my child is losing or plays poorly.

   1 Never   2 Seldom   3 Sometimes   4 Often   5 Always

8. I value the good behaviour of my child more than the match result.

   1 Never   2 Seldom   3 Sometimes   4 Often   5 Always

9. I do not make my child guilty when he/she loses a match.

   1 Never   2 Seldom   3 Sometimes   4 Often   5 Always

10. After the match, I treat my child the same no matter the result.

    1 Never   2 Seldom   3 Sometimes   4 Often   5 Always

Scoring: Sum your points: _____

< 25 points: You need to work on several key issues to better fulfil the role of a parent of a tennis player.

25-34 points: Your performance as a tennis parent tends to be good, but is not always consistent. In order to improve, you would benefit from constructive and relevant advice from other parents, your child's coach or a tennis psychologist, or a mental skills training programme specifically tailored to your needs as a tennis parent.

35-43 points: You are generally a very good tennis parent. Some more specific guidelines will further help you identify and apply even more effective tennis parenting strategies.

44-50 points: You consistently display very good tennis parenting skills. You should work to maintain and maximise the benefits of your behaviours to help yourself and your child's tennis.

REFERENCES

Alley, T., & Hicks, C. (2005). Peer attitudes towards adolescent participants in male- and female-oriented sports, *Adolescence*, Summer.

Allison, M.G., & Ayllon, T (1980). Behavioral coaching in the development of skills in football, gymnastics and tennis, *J. App. Behav. An.*, 13, 297-314.

Allison, M.T., & Meyer, C. (1988). Career problems and retirement among elite athletes: the female tennis professional, *Sociology Sport J.*, 5, 212-222.

Anderson, L.R. (1982). Sex differences on a conjunctive task: mixed doubles tennis teams. *Personality and Social Psych. Bull.* 8, 2: 330-335.

Anshel, M. H. (1990). Toward validation of a model for coping with acute stress in sport. *Int. J. Sport Psych.* Jan-Mar, 21,1: 58-83.

Anshel, M. H., & Wrisberg, C.A. (1993). Reducing warm-up decrement in the performance of the tennis serve. *J. Sport & Ex. Psych.*, 15, 3: 290-303.

Aronson, W.R. (1986). Pre-season and pre-match stress levels of women intercollegiate tennis players. *MS Thesis*. Springfield College.

Atienza F.L., Balaguer I., & Garcia-Merita M.L. (1998). Video modeling and imaging training on performance of tennis service of 9- to 12-year-old children, *Per., & Mot. Skills*, Oct; 87, 2 :519-29.

Australian Tennis Magazine (2005). *Interview with Maria Sharapova*, July.

Avila, F., & Moreno, F.J. (2003). Visual search strategies elaborated by tennis coaches during execution error detection processes. *J. Hum. Mov. Studies*, 44, 209-224.

Balaguer, I., & Atienza, F.L. (1994). Principales motivos de los jóvenes para jugar al tenis. *Apunts*, 31, 285-299.

Balaguer, I. (1998). *Psicología del tenis. Curso de Profesor Nacional.* ENMT-RFET. Madrid.

Balaguer, I. (1993). Entrenamiento psicológico con tenistas. In M. Crespo (Coord.) *Tenis II* (pp. 273-292). COE.

Balaguer, I., Atienza, F.L., Guallar, A., & Crespo, M. (1990). Discrepancia perceptiva de la conducta de los entrenadores de tenis entre los jugadores y los propios entrenadores. *III C. N. Psic. Soc.* Santiago, Septiembre.

Balaguer, I., Duda, J.L., & Crespo, M. (1999). Motivational climate and goal orientations as predictors of perceptions of improvement, satisfaction and coach ratings among tennis players. *Scan. J. Medi & Sci. Sports*, 9: 381-388.

Balaguer, I., Guallar, A, Atienza, F.L., Pastor, Y., Alberca, S., & Tebar, M.P. (1993). Atribuciones en tenistas de competición en función del resultado y de la percepción subjetiva del mismo. 2nd *Int.Confer. Psychological Intervention & Hum. Dev: Educat., & Comm. Intervent.*Valencia, July.

Balaguer, I., Guivernau, M., Duda, J. L., & Crespo, M. (1997). Analisis de la validez de constructo y de la validez predictiva del Cuestionario de Clima Motivacional Percibido en el deporte (PMCSQ-2) con tenistas españoles de competición. *Rev. Psicol. Deporte*, 11, 41-59.

Bandura, A. (1977). Self-efficacy: Toward a unifying theory of behavioural change. *Psychol. Rev.*, 84, 2: 191-215.

Barling, J., & Abel, M. (1983). Self-efficacy beliefs and tennis performance. *Cogn. Ther. Res.*, 7, 265-272.

Barrell, G.V., & Trippe, H.R. (1975). Field dependence and physical ability, *Per., & Mot. Skills*, 41, 216 - 218.

Baxter-Jones A.D.G., & Maffulli, N. (2003). Parental influence on sport participation in elite young players. *J. Sports Med., & Phys. Fit.*, 43:250-55.

Beck, A.T. (1963). Thinking an depression I. Idiosyncratic content and cognitive distorsion. *Arch. Gen. Psychiatrics*, 2, 324-333.

Berlant. A.R., & Weiss, M.R. (1997). Goal orientation and the modeling process: an individual's focus on form and outcome. *RQES*, 68, 4: 317-30.

Blackwell, B., & McCullagh, P. (1990). The relationship of athletic injury to life stress, competitive anxiety and coping resources, *Athl. Training*, 25: 23-27.

Bloom, B. S. (1985). *Developing Talent in Young People*. Balantine Books, NY.

Blundell, N. (1995). *So you want to be a tennis pro?* Lothian. Victoria, Australia.

Bouchard L.J., & Singer, R.N. (1998). Effects of the Five-step Strategy with videotape modeling on performance of the tennis serve. *Percept. Mot. Skills*, Jun; 86, 3 Pt 1: 739-46.

Boutcher, S.H. (1992). Attention and athletic performance: An integrated approach. In T.S. Horn (Ed.). *Advances in Sport Psychology* (pp. 251-266). Champaign, Il. Human Kinetics.

Brabenec, J. (1981). *Tennis: The decision making sport*. Hancok House. Canada.

Braden, V., & Burns,B. (1996). *Win and laugh at doubles*. Little Brown. Boston.

Brown, J. D. (1988). *The effects of cooperative and individualistic goal structures on the learning domains of beginning tennis students*. PhD Diss. Texas A&M Univ.

Buckolz, E., Prapavessis, H., & Fairs, J. (1988). Advance cues and their use in predicting tennis passing shots, *Can. J. Sport Sci.*, 13, 1, 20-30.

Butler, R. J. (1996). *Sport Psychology In Action*. Butterworth-Heinemann: Oxford, England.

Butler, R. J., & Hardy, L. (1992). The performance profile: Theory and application. *The Sport Psychologist*, 6, 253-264.

Burke, K. L. (1988). *The effect of a perceptual cognitive training program on attention/concentration style and performance of the tennis serve.* PhD Diss. Florida State Univ.

Burke, K.L., Edwards, T., Weigand, D.A., & Weinberg, R.S. (1997). Momentum in sport: a real or illusionary phenomenon for spectators, *Int. J. Sport Psych.*, 28, 1, 79-96.

Butt, D.S., & Cox, D.N. (1992). Motivational patterns in Davis Cup, University and recreational tennis players. *Int. J. Sport Psych.*,23, n° 1, 1-13.

Carron, A. (1982). Cohesiveness in sports: Interpretations and considerations. *J. Sport Psych.*, 4 , 123-138.

Cascales, A.M. (2001). The road to the top: from beginner to Davis Cup Champion. In M. Crespo, M. Reid & D. Miley (Eds.). *Tennis Player Development* (pp.95-100). London. ITF Ltd.

Castellani, A. (2001). *L'allenamento del tennista di alto livello*. DVD.

Castiello, U., & Umiltà, C. (1988). Atenzione e tennis. *Scuola dello Sport. Rivista di Cultura Sportiva*, VII, 13, 28-33.

Cattell, R.B., Eber, D., & Tatsuoka, M. (1970). *Handbook of 16PF*. Champaign, Il.

Caycedo, A. (1973). *Sofrología Médica. Oriente-Occidente.* Aura. Barcelona.

Cayer, L. (1991). International Doubles. *Presentation ITF Worldwide Coaches Workshop*. Dublin.

Cervelló, E., Santos-Rosa, F.J., Jiménez, R., Nerea, A., & García, T. (2002). Motivación y ansiedad en jugadores de tenis. *Rev. Motricidad*, 9, 141-161.

Claxton, D.B. (1988). A systematic observation of more and less successful high school tennis coaches. *J. Teaching Phys. Ed.*, 7, 302-310.

Claxton, D.B., & Lacy, A.C. (1986). A comparison of practice field behaviours between winning high school football and tennis coaches, *J. App. Res. Coaching & Athletics*, 1, 188-200.

Coackley, L. (1992). Burnout among adolescent athletes: a personal failure or social problem. *Sociology Sport J.*, 9, 271-285.

Coackley, L., & Terry, P. (1994). A comparison of the effectiveness of four intervention strategies in reducing state anxiety among elite junior tennis players. *J. Sports Sci.*, 13, 186.

Coakley, J. J. (2001). *Sport in Society*. Boston: McGraw-Hill.

Collins, S. W. (1990). *The role of anger among male college level tennis players*. PhD Diss. U. So. Mississippi.

Conforto, C., & Marcenaro, M. (1979). Psychometric and psychodinamic investigation of the personality of tennis players. *Int. J. Sport Psychology*. 10, 4, 217-230.

Cormier, S. C. (1982). *The effects of augmented visual cues on the performance of groundstroke consistency for beginning college-age tennis classes*. MS Thesis. U. Arizona.

Covassin, T., & Pero, S. (2004). The relationship between self-confidence, mood state and anxiety among collegiate tennis players. *J. Sport Behavior*. 72, 3, 230-243.

Crespo, M. (1995). *Liderazgo en el tenis*. PhD. Diss. Universitat Valencia.

Crespo, M. (2002). Aspectos psicológicos del jugador de tenis. In J. Maquirriain (Ed.). *Medicina deportiva aplicada al tenis*. Vol. I. (pp. 231-244). Maori. B.As.

Crespo, M., & Balaguer, I. (1994). Las relaciones entre el deportista y el entrenador. In I. Balaguer (Dir.) *Entrenamiento Psicológico en el Deporte* (pp. 17-56). Albatros. Valencia.

Crespo, M., Balaguer, I., & Atienza, F. (1993). Variables influencing leadership styles in tennis coaches. *Proceedings of the 8th World Congress of Sport Psychology*. 205-208. Lisboa. Portugal.

Crespo, M., & Miley, D. (1998). *ITF Advanced Coaches Manual*. ITF Ltd, London.

Crespo, M., & Miley, D. (2001). *How to be a better tennis parent*. ITF Ltd. London.

Crespo, M., & Reid, M. (2004). Learning values through tennis, *Tennis Pro*, XIII, 2, March/April, 23-26.

Crespo, M., & Reid, M. (2004b).Características psicológicas de los entrenadores de tenis exitosos. In J. Maquirriaín, B. Pluim & J.P. Ghisi (Eds.). *Medicina deportiva aplicada al tenis*. Vol. II. (pp. 195-210). Maori. B.As.

Csikszentmihalyi, M. (1990). *Flow: The psychology of optimal experience*. New York: Harper Perennial.

Czajkowski, Z. (1995). Znaczenie pobudzenia w dzialalnosci sportowej. Cz.1 i 2. *Sport Wyczynowy*, 7-8, 9-10.

Chelladurai, P. (1980). Leadership in sports organizations. *Can. J. App. Sport Sci.*, 5: 4, 226-231.

Daino, A. (1985). Personality traits of adolescent tennis players. *Int. J. Sport Psych*. 16, 2, 120-125.

Davidson, K.K., Markey, C.N., & Birch, L. (2003). A Longitudinal Examination of Patterns in Girls' Weight Concerns and Body Dissatisfaction from 5 to 9 Years Old. *Int. J. Eating Dis.*, 33, 320-332.

Davis, K. (1991). A performance enhancement program for a college tennis player. *Int. J. Sport Psy.*,22, 2:140-164.

Davis, K. (1992). A mental trainning program for elite junior tennis players, *Sports Coach*, 15, 3, 34.

Daw, J., & Burton, D. (1994). Evaluation of a comprehensive psychological skills training program for collegiate tennis players, *The Sport Psychologist*, 8, 37-57.

Deci, E.L., & Ryan, R.M. (1985). *Intrinsic motivation and self-determination in human behaviour*. N.Y. Plenum Press.

DeFrancesco, C., & Burke, K.L. (1997). Performance enhancement strategies used in a professional tennis tournament, *Int. J. Sport Psychol.*, 28, 185-195.

DeFrancesco, C., & Johnson, P. (199). Player and parent perceptions in Junior Tennis, *J. Sport Behav.*, 20,1, 29-36.

Dent, P. (2002). Mental skills training. *ITF South and East African Coaches Workshop*, Pretoria, South Africa.

Dorsky, F. (1996). Mental training: a lot like physical training, *ITF CSSR*, 9, 8.

Dube, S.K., & Tatz, S.J. (1991). Audicence effects in tennis preformance. *Per., & Mot. Skills*, 73, 3, 844-846.

Duda, J.L. (2001a). Fostering the ideal performance state in tennis: What does sport psychology tell us? In M. Crespo, M. Reid & D. Miley (Eds.). *Top Tennis Coaching* (pp. 52-55). London. ITF Ltd.

Duda, J.L. (2001b). The implications of the motivational climate in tennis. In M. Crespo, M. Reid & D. Miley (Eds.). *Top Tennis Coaching* (pp. 55-58). London. ITF Ltd.

Duda, J.L., Balaguer, I., & Crespo, M. (2003). Burnout among tennis coaches: What is it, what causes it and what can we do about it? *ITF CSSR*, 30, 12-13.

Duda, J.L., Balaguer, I., Moreno, Y., & Crespo, M. (2001). *The relationship of the motivational climate and goal orientations to burnout among junior elite tennis players*. Paper presented to AAASP. Orlando.

Duda, J.L., Chi, L., Newton, M.L., Walling, M.D., & Catley, D. (1995). Task and ego orientation and intrinsic motivation in sport, *Int. J. Sport Psychology*, 26, 40-63.

Duda, J.L., & Nichols, J.G. (1989). *The Task and Ego Orientation in Sport Questionnaire*. Unpublished manuscript.

Dunlap, P., & Berne, L. (1991). Addressing competitive stress in junior tennis players, *JOPERD*, 62, 1, Jan, 59-63.

Eades, A. (1991). *An investigation of burnout in intercollegiate athletes: The development of the Eades Athletic Burnout Inventory*. Paper presented at the N .A. Society Psych. Sport & Phys. Act. Nat. Conf.Asilomar, CA.

Efran, J.S., Lesser, G.S., & Spiller. M.J. (1994). Enhancing tennis coaching with youths using a metaphor method. *The sport psychol.*, 8, 4, 349- 359.

Eghan, T. (1988). *The relation of teacher feedback to student achievement in learning selected tennis skills*. PhD Diss. Louisiana State Univ. and Agricultural and Mechanical College.

El Gammal, A.N.I. (1993). Anxiety state of tennis players: a comparative study. In T.Reilly, M.Hughes & A.Lees (Eds.) *Science and Racket Sports*, (pp. 226-227). Blackwell Publishing. London.

Ellis, A. (1955). *Reason and Emotion in Psychotherapy; A Guide to Rational Living*. Prometheus Books.

Emmen, H., Wesseling, L., Bootsma, R., Whiting, H., & Van Wieringen, P. (1985). The effect of video-modelling and video-feedback on the learning of the tennis service by novices. *J. Sports Sc*. 3, 127-138.

Epstein, (1983). Natural healing processes of the mind: Graded stress inoculation as an inherent coping mechanism. In D. Meichenbaum & M. E. Jaremko (Eds.), *Stress reduction and prevention* (pp. 39-66). New York: Plenum Press.

Eraña, I. (2004). Entrenamiento psicológico con tenistas. R. Psicol. Deporte., 13, 2, 263-271.

Ericsson, K. A. (1996). The acquisition of expert performance: an introduction to some of the issues. In K. A. Ericsson (Ed.) *The Road to Excellence: The Acquisition of Expert Performance in the Arts and Sciences, Sports, and Games* (pp. 1-50). Mahwah, NJ: Erlbaum.

Eysenck, H.J., & Eysenck, S.B.G. (1968). Eysenck Personality Inventory Manual. London: Univ. of London Press.

Farouk, K. (2003). Anxiety in Tennis and its effect on performance. In M. Crespo, M. Reid, & D. Miley (Eds). *Applied Sport Science for High Performance Tennis* (pp. 140). London. ITF Ltd.

Farrow, D., Chivers, P., Hardingham, C., & Sachse, S. (1998). The effect of video-based perceptual training on the tennis return of serve, *Int. J. Sport Psychology*, 29, 231-242.

Feltz, D. L. (1986). The psychology of sports injuries. In P. E. Vinger & E. F. Hoerner (Eds.), *Sport injuries: The unthwarted epidemic* (2nd ed., pp. 336-344). Littleton, MA: PSG Publishing.

Finn, J., Axtell, J. R., Kemler, D., & Stofan, J. (1993). *Profile of Mood States among Senior Tennis Players*, USTA National Conference on Sports Medicine and Science in Tennis, Tampa, FL, April 28-May 1.

Fisher, A.G., & Conlee, R.K. (1979). *The complete book of physical fitness* (pp. 119-121). Provo, UT: Brigham Young Univ. Press.

Forsyth, D.R., & Schlenker, B.R. (1977). Attributional egocentricism following performance in a competitive task. *J. Social Psych.*, 102, 215-222.

Forti, L. (1992). *La formación del tenista completo*, Paidos Educación.

Fox, A. (2000). Paranoid? Who's paranoid? *Tennis Match*, 8, 2, 66.

Gallwey, W. T. (1975). *The inner game of tennis*. Pan Books.

Galvan, Z.J., & Ward, P. (1998). Effects of public posting on Inappropriate On-court Behaviors by Collegiate Tennis Players, *The Sport Psychologist*, 12, 4, 419-426.

Garcés de los Fayos, E.J. (1995). Burnout en deportistas. *Revista de Psicologia Social Aplicada*, 5, 3, 5-15.

Garcia Ucha, F. (2001). Atención en el tenis. *Ed. Fisica Rev. Digital*.

Gauron, E.F. (1984). *Mental training for peak performance*, Lansing N.Y.; Sport Science Associates.

Gavin, J. (1992). *The exercise habit*. Champaign, Il. Human Kinetics.

Gibbons, T. (1998). The Development of Excellence. A Common Pathway to the Top in Music, Art, Academics and Sport, *Olympic Coach*, 8, 3.

Gill, D. (1992). Gender and sport behaviours. In T. S. Horn (Ed.) *Advances in Sport Psychology*. (pp. 143-160). Champaing, Ill.: Human Kinetics.

Gill, D.L., & Deeter, T.E. (1988). Development of a Sport Orientation Questionnaire. *RQES*. 59, 191-202.

Girod, A. (1999). Concentration and tennis: mechanisms and exercises, *ITF CSSR*, 17, 4-5.

Girod, A. (2001). Self-confidence, *ITF CSSR*, 25, 9-10.

Girod, A. (2003). Visualisation in tennis, *ITF CSSR*, 30, 7-8.

Girod, A. (2004). On-court psychological training in tennis, *Tennis Europe Coaches Workshop*, Valetta, Malta.

Girod, A. (2005). Tennis and neurolinguistic programming, *ITF CSSR*, 37, 11-12.

González, G, Tabernero, B., & Márquez, S. (1999). Análisis de los motivos para participar en futbol y en tenis en la iniciación deportiva, *Rev. Española Ed. Física y Deportes*. 6, 2, 12-23.

Gould, D. (1997). *Play better tennis under pressure*. Champaign, Il. Human Kinetics Video.

Gould, D., Damarjian, N., & Medbery, R. (1999a). An examination of mental skills training in junior tennis coaches. *The Sport Psychol.*, 13, 2, 127-144.

Gould, D., Dieffenbach, K., Cheung, Y., Lauer, L., Medberry, M., & Darmajian, N. (2001). *The USTA mental toughness skills and drills*. USTA.

Gould D., & Lauer, L. (2005). Maximizing your relationships with players parents. *High performance coaching*. USTA Newsletter, 7, 1.

Gould D., & Medberry, R. (2000). *Psychological Issues*. Amer. Acad. Orthopaedic Surg., & Amer. Acad. Pediatrics.

Gould, D., Medbery, R., Darmajian, N., & Lauer, L. (1999b). A survey of mental skills training knowledge, opinions, and practices of junior tennis coaches, *J. App. Sport Psych.*,11, 1, 28-50.

Gould, D., Udry, E., Tuffey, S., & Loehr, J. (1996a). Burnout in competitive junior tennis players: I. A quantitative psychological assessment, *The Sport Psychol.*, 10, 322-340.

Gould, D., Udry, E., Tuffey, S., & Loehr, J. (1996b). Burnout in competitive junior tennis players: II. Qualitative analysis, *The Sport Psychol.*, 10, 341-366.

Gould, D., Udry, E., Tuffey, S., & Loehr, J. (1997). Burnout in competitive junior tennis players: III. Individual differences in the burnout experience, *The Sport Psychol.*, 11, 257-276.

Goulet, C, Bard, Ch., & Fleury, M. (1988). Analyses des indices visuels prélevés en réception de service au tennis, *Can. J. Sport Sci.*, 13, 1, 79-87.

Goulet, C, Bard, Ch., & Fleury, M. (1989). Expertise differences in preparing to return a tennis serve: a visual information processing approach, *J. Sport & Ex. Psych.*, 11, 382-398.

Greenwood, C. M, Dzewaltowski, D.A., & French, R. (1990). Self-efficacy and psychological well-being of wheelchair tennis participants and wheelchair nontennis participants. *Adapted Phys. Act. Q.*, 7, 1: 12-21.

Greer, H.S., & Engs, R. (1986). Use of progressive relaxation and hypnosis to increase tennis skill learning. *Percept., & Mot. Skills*, 63, 1, 161-162.

Griffiths, G.W. (2003). Eye Dominance in sport - a comparative study. *Optometry Today*, 43,13.

Grinder, J., & Bandler, R. (1976). *Frogs into Princes: Neuro Linguistic Programming*. Science and Behavior Books.

Groppel, J.L. (1981). *Why play tennis?* USTA.

Guallar, A, Balaguer, I., Atienza, F.L., Blasco, P., Castillo, I., & Fuentes, I. (1993). Expectativas, emociones y atribuciones en tenistas de competición en función del resultado y de la percepción subjetiva del mismo. In S. Barriga & J.M. León (Eds.). *Aspectos psicosociales del ambiente, la conducta deportiva y el fenómeno turístico* (pp 201-213) Sevilla. Eudema.

Guallar, A., & Balaguer, I. (1994). Percepción e interpretación del éxito y del fracaso. In I. Balaguer (Dir.). *Entrenamiento psicológico en el deporte. Principios y aplicaciones* (pp.91-134). Albatros, Valencia.

Guallar, A., & Pons, D. (1994). Concentración y atención en el deporte. In I. Balaguer (Dir.). *Entrenamiento psicológico en el deporte. Principios y aplicaciones* (pp.207-246). Albatros, Valencia.

Gutiérrez, M. (1995). *Los valores sociales y deporte*. Gymmos Ed. Madrid.

Hanin, Y.L. (1993). Individual zones of optimal functioning (IZOF) model: A new approach to performance anxiety. In K. Henschen (ed.). *Sport psychology: An analysis of player behaviour*. (pp.103-119) 3rd Movement Publ. Ithaca, NY.

Hanraban, S.J., Grove, J.E., & Hattie, J.A. (1989). Development of a questionnaire measure of sport-related atibutional style. *I.J. Sport Psych.*, 20, 114-134.

Hardy, L. (1990). A catastrophe model of performance in sport. In J.C. Jones & L. Hardy (Eds.). *Stress and performance in sport* (pp.81-106). Chichester, England: Wiley.

Hardy, L., Jones, J.G., & Gould, D. (1996). *Understanding Psychological Preparation for Sport: Theory and Practice of Elite Performers*. Chichester: John Wiley.

Haskins, M. (1965). Development of response recognition training films in tennis, *Per., & Mot. Skills*, 21, 207-211.

Harries-Jenkins, E., & Hughes, M. (1993). A computerised analysis of female coaching behavior with male and female players. In T.Reilly, M.Hughes & A.Lees (Eds.) *Science and racket sports* (pp. 238-243). E & FN Spon: London.

Harris, D., & Harris, L. (1984). *The player's guide to sport psychology: Mental skills for physical people*. Human Kinetics, Champaign, Ill.

Harter, S. (1978). Effectance motivation reconsidered, *Human Development*, 21, 34-64.

Harwood, C. (2000). Developing youngsters mental skills…without them realising it!, *ITF CSSR*, 21, 6-7.

Harwood, C., & Biddle, S. (2002). The application of achievement goal theory in youth sport. In I. Coackerill (Ed.).*Solutions in sport psychology* (pp. 58-73). Thompson Learning. London.

Harwood, C., & Dent, P. (2003). Practical mental skills training, *ITF CSSR*, 30, 5-6.

Harwood, C., & Swain, A.B.J. (1998). Antecedents of pre-competition achievement goals in elite junior tennis players, *J. Sports Sci*, 16, 357-371.

Harwood, C., & Swain, A.B.J. (2001). The development and activation of achievement goals in tennis: I. Understanding the underlying factors, *The Sport Psychol.*, 15, 319-341.

Harwood, C.G., & Swain, A.B.J. (2002). The development and activation of achievement goals in tennis: II. A player, parent and coach intervention, *The Sport Psychol.*, 16, 111-138.

Haskins, M. (1965). Development of response recognition training films in tennis. Per., & Mot. Skills. 21, 207-211.

Heath, K. F. (1982). *A study of sex role, sex differences, locus of control, and expectancy of success in tennis among college students*. PhD Diss. Univ. of Oregon.

Heckel, R.V. (1993). Comparison of touching behaviors of winners and losers in racquetball and tennis. *Per., & Mot. Skills*, 77, 3, 1392-1394

Hedrick, B. (1984). The effects of wheelchair tennis & mainstreaming upon the perceptions of physically disabled adolescents, *Therapeutic Recreation J.*, 19, 2, 34-46.

Heider, F. (1958). *The psychology of interpersonal relations*. New York: John Wiley & Sons.

Heller, R. (2001). Some cautions on the coaches role in managing anxiety related problems in junior players, *ITF CSSR*, 25, 15.

Henneman, M.C., & Keller, D. (1983). Preparatory behaviour in the execution of a sport related movement: the return of service in tennis. *Int. J. of Sport Psychology*. 14, 149-161.

Hewitt, J., & Jackson, S. (1986). Differential attributions for winn-loss in competitive tennis. *Per., & Mot. Skills*, 63, n°1, 970.

Higger, Y. (2002). Physical training for tennis - the need for a better integration, *ITF CSSR*, 26, 13-14.

Higham, A. (1994). Know the flow. *Coaching Excellence*, 6, 6-8.

Higham, A. (2000). *Momentum: the hidden force in tennis*. Meyer & Meyer Sports. Aachen.

Higham, A., & Harwood, C. (2002). *Match flow score chart*. Unpublished document.

Hoyle, R.H., & Leff, S.S. (1997). The role of parental involvement in youth sport participation and performance. *Adolescence*, 32, 125, 233-243.

Houston, J.M., Carter, D., & Smith, R.D. (1997). Competitiveness in elite professional players. *Per., & Mot. Skills*, 84 (3 Pt 2) 1447-1454.

Hunfalvay, M. (2004). *Characteristics of Expert Wheelchair Tennis Players According to Visual Selective Attention Preference*. AAHPERD National Convention.

ITF (1994). Using napping as a refresher, *ITF CSSR*, 4, 11.

Jackson, S., & Csikszentmihalyi, M. (1999). *Flow in sports: the keys to optimal experiences and performances*. Champaign, IL: Human Kinetics.

Jacobson, E. (1938). *Progressive relaxation*. Chicago: University of Chicago Press.

Jaenes, J.C. (1995). Analisis de la ansiedad y autoconfianza en tenistas jovenes. In J.C. Caracuel, J.C. Jaenes, L. Linares, A. Oña, & E.A.Perez (Eds.) *Psicologia del Deporte en Andalucia*, (pp.145-150). Edinford: Malaga.

Jaenes, J.C. (2001). Un caso de intervención en tenis. *Rev. Psicol. del Deporte*, 10, 2, 307-313.

Johnston, T. M. (1994). *The effects of verbal labeling on the performance of the forehand groundstroke in tennis*. MS Thesis. C SU, Fullerton.

Jones, G., Hanton, S., & Connaughton, D. (2002). What is this thing called mental toughness? An investigation of elite sport performers, *J. App. Sport Psych.*, 14, 3, 205-218.

Jones, C.M., & Miles, T.R. (1978). Use of advanced cues in predicting the flight of a lawn tennis ball. *J. Human Mov. Studies*, 4, 231-235.

Kavussanu, M., & Roberts, G.C. (1996). Motivation in Physical activity contexts: the relationship of perceived motivatonal climate to intrinsic motivation and self-efficacy, *J. Sport & Ex. Psych.*, 18, 264-280.

Kelley, B., Eklund, B., & Ritter-Taylor, M. (1999). Stress and burnout among collegiate tennis coaches. *J. Sport & Ex. Psych.*, 21(2), 113-130

Kessler, L., & Rothstein, A.L. (1981). Videotape replay and the learning of skills in open and closed environments, *RQES*, 52,2, 191-199.

Kim, S. O. (1990). *Self-efficacy and causal attribution of college students in a tennis competition*. PhD. Diss. Univ. Oregon.

Knisel, E. (2001). Stress management in tennis: how to win the big points. In J.Mester, G.King, J.Strüder, E.Tsolakidis & A.Osterburg (Eds.). *Proceedings 6th An. Congr. European College Sports Sci.*, (p.1246).

Knudson, D., & Kukla, D. (1997). The impact of vision and vision training on sport performance. *JOPERD*, 68, 4, 17-24.

Knudson, D., & Morrison, C. (2002). *Qualitative analysis of human movement*. Human Kinetics, Champaign, IL.

Kokkonen, J., Nelson, A.G., & Cornwell, A. (1998). Acute muscle stretching inhibits maximal strength performance. *RQES*, 69(4):411-415.

Kolt, G. S., Driver, R. P., & Giles, L. C. (2004). Why older Australians participate in exercise and sport. *J. Ageing & Physical Activity*, 11, 185-198.

Krahenbuhl, GS. (1971). Stress reactivity in tennis players. *RQES*, Mar;42(1):42-6.

Kriese, C. (1985). *Total tennis training*. Master Press. Michigan.

Kuipers, E. (1996).How much is too much? Performance aspects of overtraining. *RQES*, Sep;67(3 Suppl):S65-9.

Kluka, D.A. (1991). Visual skills: Considerations in learning motor skills for sport. *ASAHPERD J.*, 14(1), 41-43.

Landers, D.M., & Boutcher, S.H. (1986). Arousal-performance relationships. In J.M. Williams (Ed.). *Applied sport psychology: Personal growth to peak performance* (pp.163-184). Palo Alto. CA: Mayfield.

Lawrence, N. (1995). Gaining momentum, *ITF CSSR*, 7, 7.

Leddy, M. H., Lambert, M. J., & Ogles, B. M. (1994). Psychological consequences of athletic injury among high-level competitors, *RQES*, 65, 4, 347-354.

Lee, A.M., Landin, D.K., & Carter, J.A. (1992). Student thougths during tennis instruction. *J. Teaching in Physical Education*, 11, 3, 256-267.

Leitao, M.T., & Do Lago, O.C. (2003). Benefits or practicing tennis for players with mental disability. In M. Crespo, M. Reid & D. Miley (Eds.). *Tennis Player Development* (p. 143). London. ITF Ltd.

Leitao, M.T., & Machado, A.A. (2003). A tennis player with a mental disability: Family interference in the achievement of results. In M. Crespo, M. Reid & D. Miley (Eds.). *Tennis Player Development* (p. 141). London. ITF Ltd.

Leith, L.M., & Prapavessis, H. (1989). Attributions of causality and dimensionality associated with sport outcomes in objectively evaluated and subjectively evaluated sports. *Int. J. Sport Psychology*, 20, 224-234.

Lesko, S. J. (1992). *Perceived competence and intrinsic motivation among junior tennis players*. MS Thesis. Springfield College.

Liggett, D.R. (2000). *Sport Hypnosis*. Champaign, Ill. Human Kinetics.

Liu, J., & Wrisberg, C.A. (1997). The effect of knowledge of results delay and the subjective estimation of movement form on the acquisition and retention of a motor skill. *RQES*, 68: 145-151.

Locke, E. A., & Latham, G. P. (1990). *A theory of goal setting and task performance*. Englewood Cliffs, NJ: Prentice Hall.

Loehr, J. E. (1986). *Mental toughness training for sports: Achieving athletic excellence*. Lexington, MA: Stephen Greene Press.

Loehr, J.E. (1988). The 16 seconds cure. *World Tennis*, September, 80-83.

Loehr, J. E. (1990). *The mental game*. The Steven Greene Press / Pelham books, New York.

Loehr, J. E. (1991). *USPTR Manual on Mental thoughness training*. USPTR: Hilton Head, SC.

Loehr, J.E., & Striegel, D.A. (1994). *The USTA Sport Psychology Guidebook for Coaches*. 2nd Ed. USTA.

Loehr, J. E. (2001) Player Development at the Core. *High Performance Coaching*, Vol 3, No.1.
Loehr, J. E., & Gullikson, T. (2001). Maintaining technique under pressure. In P. Roetert & J. Groppel (Eds.). *World-class tennis technique* (pp. 131-146). Champaing, Il. Human Kinetics.
Loehr, J.E., & Kahn, E.J. (1987). *Net results*. The Stephen Greene Press. Pelham Books. Lexington, Ma.
Loehr, J.E., & Kahn, E.J. (1989). *The parent-player tennis training program*. S. Greene. Pelham Books. Lex., Ma.
Love, B. (1985). Momentum in tennis. *Presentation at the Spanish Coaches Workshop*. Pamplona.
LTA. (2003). *Long Term Player Development*. LTA. London.
Lubbers, P. (2000). On-court Mental Training. *Presentation at the ITF Central American and Caribbean Coaches Workshop*, Weston, Fl.
Lubbers, P. (2001). An Integrated Approach to Mental Training. In M. Crespo, M. Reid & D. Miley (Eds.). *Tennis Player Development* (pp. 37-40). Proceedings of the ITF WWCW, Bangkok Thailand. London. ITF Ltd.
Lubbers, P. (2003). Mental skills training. In M. Crespo, M. Reid & D. Miley (Eds.). *Tennis Player Development* (pp. 75-78). Proceedings of the ITF WWCW, Vilamoura, Portugal. London. ITF Ltd.
Lubbers, P., & Gould, D. (2003). Phases of world-class player development. *ITF CSSR*, 30, 2.
Luis, V., Reina, R., Sanz, D., Fuentes, J., & Moreno, F. (2003). *Análisis del comportamiento visual y de reacción de tenistas de diferente nivel ante la simulación en laboratorio de la situación de aproximación a la red*. Kronos. Madrid.
Maehr, M.L. (1974). Culture and achievement motivation. *American Psychologist*, 29, 887-896.
Mahoney, M.J., Gabriel, T.J., & Perkins, T.S. (1987). Psychological skills and exceptional athletic performance. *The Sport Psychol.*, 1, 181-199.
Mamassis, G., & Doganis, G. (2004). The Effects of a Mental Training Program on Juniors Pre-Competitive Anxiety, Self-Confidence, and Tennis Performance. *J. App. Sport Psych.*, 16, 2, 118 - 137.
Manili, U., & Pase, D. (1986). La scelta spontanea del partner atraverso il sociograma. *Movimento*. 2, n°1. 13-15.
Marrero, G., Martín-Albo, J., & Núñez, J.L. (2000). Perfil de personalidad del tenista. *Rev. Psicología del Deporte*, 9, 1-2, 21-36.
Martens, R. (1976). *Competitiveness in sport*. Paper presented at the Int. Cong. Phys. Act. Sci. Quebec City.
Martens, R. (1977). *Competitive State Anxiety Test*. Champaing, Ill.: Human Kinetics Pub.
Martens, R. (1987). *Coaches Guide to Sport Psychology*. Champaign, Il. Human Kinetics.
Martens, R., Vealey, R.S., & Burton, D. (Eds.). (1990). *Competive anxiety in sport*. Champaign, Il. Human Kinetics.
Martens, R., Vealey, R.S., Burton, D., Bump, L.A., & Smith, D.E. (1982). *Competive state anxiety inventory*. Simposium at the NASPSA meeting, College Park, MD.
Martens-Scholz, H. (2003). Computer based coaching. In S. Miller (Ed.). Tennis Science and Technology (pp. 273-298). London, ITF Ltd.
Maslach, C., & Jackson, S.E. (1981). The measurement of experienced burnout. *J. Occupational Behav.*, 2, 99-113.
McAleney, P.J., Barabasz, A., & Barabasz, M. (1990). Effects of flotation restricted enviromental stimulation on intercollegiate tennis performance. *Per., & Mot. Skills*, 71, 1023-1028.
McAuley, E., & Duncan, T.E. (1990). Cognitive appraisal and affective reactions following physical achievement outcomes. *J. Sport & Ex. Psych.*, 12, 415-426.
McAuley, E., Duncan, T.E., & Russell, D. (1992). Measuring causal attributions: The revised Causal Dimension Scale (CDSII). *Pers., & Soc. Psych. Bull.*, 18, 566-573.
McClelland, D. C. (1961). *The Achieving Society*. New York: Van Nostrand Reinhold.
McLennan, P. (1991). *The effects of biomechanical feedback on the tennis serve*. MA Thesis. Univ. West Florida, Pensacola, FL 32514.
McNair, D.M., Lorr, M., & Droppleman, L.F. (1971). *EDITS manual for POMS*. San Diego, CA: Educational and Industrial Testing Service.
Meichenbaum, D. (1985). Teaching thinking: A cognitive-behavioral perspective. In S.F. Chipman, J.W. Secal & R. Glaser (Eds.), *Thinking and learning skills: Research and open question* (vol. 2, pp. 407-426). Hillsdale, NJ, LEA.
Miller, G., & Gabbard, C. (1988). Effects of visual aids on acquisition of selected tennis skills. *Per., & Mot. Skills*, 67.2, 603-06.
MMPI. (1930). *Minnesota Multiphasic Inventory*. University of Minnesota.
Mitchell, M., & Kernodle, M. (2004). Using multiple intelligences to teach tennis. *JOPERD*, 27, 3, Oct., 75, 8, 27-32.
Monsaas, J.A. (1985). Learning to be a world-class tennis player. In B.S. Bloom (Ed.), The development of talent in young people (pp. 211-269). New York: Ballantine.
Moran, A. (1994). The psychology of concentration in tennis, *ITF CSSR*, 5, 7-8.
Moran, A. (1995a). How effective are psychological techniques used to enhance performance in tennis? The views of some international tennis coaches. In T.Reilly, M.Hughes & A.Lees (Eds.) Science and Racket Sports (pp.221-225). Blackwell Science. London.
Moran, A. (1995b). Dealing with pressure, *ITF CSSR*, 6, 10-12.
Moran, A. (1996). *The psychology of concentration in sport performers: A cognitive analysis*. Psychology Press.
Moreno, F., Avila, F., Damas, J., García, J., Reina, R., Luis, V., & Ruiz, A. (2001). Visual search strategies in experienced and inexperienced tennis coaches. In J.Mester, G.King, J.Strüder, E.Tsolakidis & A.Osterburg (Eds.). *Proc. 6th An. Con. Eur. Col. Sports Sci.*, 546.
Muraki, S., Tsunawake, N., & Hiramatsu S.(2000). The effect of frequency and mode of sports activity on the psychological status in tetraplegics and paraplegics. *Spinal Cord*, May;38(5):309-14.
Nevill. A.M., Holder, R.L., Bardsley, A., Calvert, H., & Jones, S. (1997). Identifying home advantage in international tennis and golf tournaments, *J. Sports Sci.*, 15, 437-443.
Newton, M., & Duda, J.L. (1992). Tennis is not a matter of life and death, it is much more important than that - The relationship between dispositional goal perspectives and effort, interest, involvement and trait anxiety in adolescent tennis players, *RQES*, 63, 1, A81-A82.
Newton, M., & Duda, J.L. (1993). Elite adolescent players' achievement goals and beliefs concerning success in tennis. *J. Sport & Ex. Psych.*, 15, 437-448.
Newton, M., & Duda, J.L. (1995). Relations of goal orientations and expectations on multidimensional state anxiety. *Per., & Mot. Skills*, 81, 3, 2: 1107-1112.
Nichols, M.C. (1988). *The effects of teacher feedback on student achievement in tennis serving*. MA Thesis. Univ. Maryland.
Nideffer, R.M. (1976). *The inner player*. New York: Thomas Crowell.
Nideffer, R.M. (1992). *Psyched to win*. Champaing, Il. Human Kinetics.
Nideffer, R.M. (1993). *The Attentional & Interpersonal Style Inventory (TAIS): Theory and Application*. New Berlin, Wisconsin: ASI Publications.
Noel, R. (1980). The effects of visuo-motor behaviour rehearsal on tennis performance. *J. Sport Psych.*, 2, 221-226.
Ojea, G., & Vicente, J. (2002). The importance of routines in competition, *ITF CSSR*, 26, 6-7.
Orawiec, A., & Danczyk, R. (1994). Temperament a wybrane zdolnosci psychomotoryczne zawodników hokeja na lodzie. *Trening*, 4.
Orlick, T. (1986). *Coaches Training Manual to Psyching for Sport*. Leisure Press. Champaign, Ill.

Otis, C. (2001). Female athlete triad: Too fit to quit or thin to win? In M. Crespo, B. Pluim, M. Reid (Eds.). *Tennis Medicine for Tennis Coaches* (pp. 123-126). London: ITF Ltd.

Otis, C., Crespo, M., Flygare, C., Johnston, P., Keber, A., Lloyd-Kolkin, D., Loehr, J., Martin, K., Pluim, B., Quinn, A., Roetert, P., Stroia, K., Terry, P., & Silva, R. (2006). The Sony Ericsson WTA Tour 10 year age eligibility and professional development review. *Br. J. Sports Med.*, 40: 464-468.

Pantelidis, D., Chamoux, A., Fargeas, M.A., Robert, A., & Lac, G. (1997). Is a 11-year-old tennis player indifferent to competition stress? *Arch Pediatr.* Mar;4, 3:237-42.

Paulhus, D., Molin, J., & Schutchs, R. (1979). Control profiles of football players, tennis players and non players. *J. Social Psych.*, 108, 2: 199-205.

Pérez Recio, G. (1995). Planes de competición. *Rev. Psicol. Gral. Ap.*, 48, 11: 77-94.

Perlstein, S. (1995). *Winning doubles.* Lyons Press.

Perry, J.D., & Williams, J.M. (1998). Relationship of intensity and Direction of Competitive Trait anxiety to skill level and gender in tennis, *The Sport Psych.*, 12, 169-179.

Prapavessis, H. (1993). Concentration skills for returning serve in tennis. *Sports Coach*, Oct.-Dec., 31-34.

Prapavessis, H., & Carron, A.V. (1988). Learned helplesnes in sport. *The Sport Psych.*, 2, 189-201.

Prapavessis, H., & Gordon, S. (1991). Coach/Player relationships in tennis. Canadian J. Sport Sci., 16:3, 229-233.

Puig, J., & Villamarin, F. (1995). *Motivación y autoeficacia durante la iniciación deportiva en tenis* (pp. 103-109). In E. Cantón (comp.). V Congreso Nal. Psicología Act. Física y Deporte. Valencia, March.

Quinn, A. M. (1996). *The Psychological factors involved in the recovery of elite athletes from long term injuries.* Doctoral diss., University of Melbourne, Australia.

Quinn, A. M. (2001a). Believe it and you'll achieve it: 25 ways to increase your player's self-confidence. In M. Crespo, M. Reid & D. Miley (Eds.). *Tennis Player Development* (pp. 81-86). London. ITF Ltd.

Quinn, A. M. (2001b). Psychological factors that predispose players to injury. In M. Crespo, B. Pluim, M. Reid (Eds.). *Tennis Medicine for Tennis Coaches* (pp. 155-159). London: ITF Ltd.

Quinn, A. M. (2003). Prepare your mind to win. In M. Crespo, M. Reid & D. MIley (Eds.). *Applied Sport Science for High Performance Tennis* (pp. 69-74). London. ITF Ltd.

Quinn, A.M. (2004). Off-court psychological activities, *ITF CSSR*, 32, 10-11.

Ransom, K., & Weinberg, R.S. (1985). Effect of situation criticality on performance of elite male and female tennis players, *J. Sport Behav.*, 8, 144-148.

Rees, T., & Hardy, L. (2001). Matching social support with stressors: effects on tennis performance. In J.Mester, G.King, J.Strüder, E.Tsolakidis & A.Osterburg (Eds.). 6th An. Cong. Europ. College Sports Science, 1229.

Rees, T., Hardy, L., & Ingledew, D. K. (2000). Performance assessment in sport: formulation, justification, and confirmatory factor analysis of a measurement instrument for tennis performance. *The Sport Psych.*, 7, 160-172.

Rees, T., Ingledew, D. K., & Hardy, L. (1999) Social support dimensions and components of performance in tennis, *The Sport Psych.*, 6, 253-264.

Reid, M., Quinn, A. & Crespo, M. (2003). (Eds.) *ITF Strength and Conditioning for Tennis.* ITF Ltd. London.

Rhea, D., Mathes, S.A., & Hardin, K. (1997). Video recall for analysis of performance by colegiate female tennis players, *Per., & Mot. Skills*, 85, 3, pt 2: 1354.

Richardson, P.A., Adler, W.A., & Hankes, D. (1988). Game, set, match: psychological momentum in tennis, *The Sport Psych.*, 2, 69-76.

Riemer, H.A., & Toon, K. (2001). Leadership and satisfaction in tennis: examination of congruence, gender, and ability, *RQES*, Sep. 72, 3, 243-56.

Rikli, R., & Smith, G. (1980). *Videotape feedback effects on tennis serving form. Per., & Mot. Skills*, 50, 895-901.

Roberts, G. C., & Balagué, G. (1989). *The development of a social cognitive scale of motivation.* 7th World C. Sport Psychology. Singapore.

Roberts, G. C. (1992). *Motivation in sport and exercise.* Champaign, Ill.: Human Kinetics.

Roberts, G.C., & Pascuzzi, D. (1979). Causal attributions in sport: Some theoretical implications. *J. Sport Psych.*, 1, 203-211.

Roberts,G.C., Kleiber,D.A., & Duda,J.L. (1981). An analysis of motivation in children's sport: The rol of perceived competence in participation. J. Sports Psych., 3, 206-216.

Rota, S., Manili, U., & Baldo, E. (1986). Aspetti psicodinamizi e relazionali nel doppio. *Movimento*, 2, 1. 16-20.

Rotella, R. J., & S. R. Heyman. (1986). Stress, injury, and the psychological rehabilitation of athletes. In J. M. Williams (Ed.), *Applied sport psychology: Personal growth to peak performance* (pp. 343-364). Palo Alto, CA: Mayfield.

Rowley, S. (1988). *Parents are important too!* LTA.

Ryckman, R.M., Robbins, M.A., Thornton, B., & Cantrell, P. (1982). Development and validation of a physical self-efficacy scale. *J. Personality and Social Psychology*, 42 (5), 891-900.

Ryska, T. A. (1992). *The role of perceived coach support on dimensions of pre-competitive anxiety among high school tennis players.* PhD Diss. Univ. of South. California.

Saferstein, D. B. (1989). *Factors affecting competitive trait anxiety in elite junior tennis players.* PhD Diss. Cal. School of Professional Psychology.

Samulski, D. (2004). *¿Cómo motivar a jugadores jóvenes?* Workshop ITF COSAT. Paraguay,15-21 Noviembre.

Samulski, D. (2006). *Tenis: Dicas psicologicas para vencer.* Belo Horizonte Imprensa Universitaria.

Santos-Rosa, F.J., Cervelló, E., Jiménez, R., & García, T. (2004). *Efecto de las claves situacionales en el flow desarrollado por tenistas de competición.* IV Congreso Nacional de tenis, RFET. Sevilla.

Saviano, N. (1999). Establishing a Developmental Plan. *High Performance Coaching*, 1, 1.

Schonborn, R. (1993). Tactics, *ITF CSSR*, 1, 10.

Schubert, J., & Vanfraechem-Raway, R. (1986). Approche a la personalite des joueurs de tennis. *Int. J. Sport Psych.*, 17, n°5, 375-389.

Schultz, J., & Luthe, W. (1959). *Autogenic Training: A Psychophysiological Approach in Psychotherapy.* New York: Grune & Stratton.

Schwartz, S. (1992). Universals in the content and structure of values: theoretical advances and empirical tests in 20 countries. In M. Zanna, *Advances in Experimental Social Psychology*, vol 25, p.1.

Scott, D., Scott, L., & Howe, B.L. (1998). Training anticipation for intermediate tennis players. *Behav. Modif.*, 22, 3: 243-261.

Shim, J., Carlton, L.G., Chow, J.W., & Chae, W.S. (2005). The use of anticipatory visual cues by highly skilled tennis players. *J. Mot. Behav.*, Mar; 37(2):164-75.

Silva, J.M. (1994).Sport performance phobias. *Int. J. Sport Psych..* 25, 100-118.

Silva, J.M., Hardy, C.J., & Grace, R.K. (1988). Analysis of psychological momentum in intercollegiate tennis, *J. Sport & Ex. Psych.*, 10, 3, 346-354.

Singer, R.S. (1969). Personality differences between and within baseball and tennis players. *RQES*, 40, 3, 582-588.

Singer, R.N., Cauraugh, J.H., Chen, D., & Slenbey, S. (1994). Training mental quickness in beginning intermediate tennis players. *The Sport Psych.*, 8, 305-318.

Singer, R., Cauraugh, J., Chen, D, & Steinberg, G. (1996). Visual search, anticipation and reactive comparisons between highly-skilled and beginning tennis players, *J. App. Sport Psych.*, Mar. 8 (1). 9-26.

Singh, K. (2003). Yoga and tennis, *ITF CSSR*, 30, 8-9.
Slaikeu, K., & Trogolo, R. (1998). *Focused for tennis*. Human Kinetics, Champaign, Ill.
Slder, J. (1996). *Psychology of tennis*. Unpublished document.
Slder, J. (2001). Psychological development for juniors. In M. Crespo, M. Reid & D. Miley (Eds.). *Tennis Player Development* (pp. 41-44). Proceedings of the ITF WWCW, Bangkok Thailand. London. ITF Ltd.
Smeeton, N.J., Williams, A.M., Hodges, N.J., & Ward, P. (2005). The relative effectiveness of various instructional approaches in developing anticipation skill. *J. Exp. Psych. App.*, 11, 98-110.
Smith, R.E. (1986). Toward a cognitive-affective model of athletic burnout. *J. Sport Psych.*, 8, 36-50.
Smith, R.E., Schultz, Smoll, & Ptacek, (1995). Development and validation of amultidimensional measure of sport-specific psychological skills. The Athletic Coping Skills Inventory-28. *J. Sport & Ex. Psych.*, 17, 379-387.
Solanellas, F., Font, J., & Rodríguez, F. (1996). Prevalencia del estilo atencional en la población catalana de tenistas, *Ap. E.F. Esport*, 44-45, 154-165.
Solberg, E.E., Halvorsen, R., Sundgot-Borgen, J., Ingjer, F., & Holen, A. (1995). *Br. J. Sports Med.* 29:255-57.
Solmon, M.A., & Boone, J. (1993). The impact of student goal orientation in physical education classes. *RQES*, Dec, 64, 4: 418-424
Sosa, C. (2005). *Herramientas para el entrenamiento psicológico deportivo*. Piscis: Buenos Aires.
Southard, D., & Amos, B. (1996). Rhytmicity and preperformance ritual: stabilizing a flexible system. *RQES*. 67, 3, 288-296.
Spielberger, C.D. (1966). Theory and research on anxiety. In C.D. Spielberger (Ed.). *Anxiety and behaviour* (pp. 3-22). New York. Academic.
Spielberger, C.D., Gorsuch, R.L., & Lushene, R.E. (1970). *STAI Manual for the State-trait anxiety inventory (self-evaluation questionnaire)*. Palo Alto, California: Consulting Psychology Press.
Spink, K. S., & Roberts, G. C. (1980). Ambiguity of outcome and causal attributions, *J. Sport Psych.*, 2, 237-244.
Spirduso, W.W., & Clifford, P. (1978). Replication of age and physical activity effects on reaction time movement time, *J. Gerontology*, 33, 23-30.
Steinberg, G.M., Chaffin, W.M., & Singer, R.N. (1998). Mental quickness training, *JOPERD*, 69, 7-41.
Surburg, P.R. (1968). Audio, visual and audio-visual instruction with mental practice in developing the forehand tennis drive, *RQES*, 39, 728-734.
Taylor, J. (1991). Career direction, development, and opportunities, *The Sport Psych.*, 5, 266-280.
Taylor, J. (1996). Pre-match routines, *ITF CSSR*, 9, 4.
Taylor, S. S. (1992). *Stimulus cueing versus visualisation in tennis*. PhD Diss. Hofstra Univ.
Taylor, J., & Ogilvie, B.C. (2001). Career termination among athletes. In R. Singer, H. Hausenblas, & C. Janelle (Eds.). *Handbook of Sport Psychology*, (2nd Ed.), (pp. 672 – 691). New York, NY: Wiley & Sons.
Tenenbaum, G., Furst, D., & Weingarten, G. (1984). Attribution of causality in sport events: Validation of Wingate Sport Achievement Responsibility Scale. *J. Sport Psych.*, 6, 4, 430-439.
Terry, P. (1994). Mental trainning for junior tennis players resident at the Rover LTA school Bisham Abbey 1987-1993: Issues of delivery and evaluation. In T.Reilly, M.Hughes & A.Lees (Eds.) *Science and Racket Sports*, 212-220. Blackwell: London.
Terry, P., Coakley, L., & Karageorghis, C. (1995). Effects of intervention upon precompetition state anxiety in elite junior tennis players: The relevance of the matching hypothesis, *Per., & Mot. Skills*. 81, 287-296.
Terry, P., Cox, J., Lane, A., & Karageorghis, C. (1996). Measures of anxiety among tennis players in singles and doubles matches, *Per., & Mot. Skills*. Oct. 83, 2: 595-603.
Theodorakis, Y. (1996). The influence of goals, commitment, self-efficacy and self-satisfaction on motor performance, *J. App. Sport Psych.*, 8, 2, 171-183, Sept.
Theodorakis, Y., Bagiatis, K., Madis, K., & Papakonstantinou, B. (1993). *Effects of self-efficacy and goals on motor performance*. Int. Congress Sport Psych. Lisbon, 894-897.
Thomas, P, Murphy, S.M., & Hardy, L. (1999). Test of Performance Strategies: Development and preliminary validation of a comprehensive measure of athletes' psychological skills, *J. Sport Sci.*, 17, 697-711.
Thorpe, J.A. (1967). Intelligence and skill in relation to success in singles competition in badminton and tennis. *RQES*, Mar; 38, 1:119-25.
Unierzyski P. (1996) *Morfologiczne, motoryczne i psychiczne uwarunkowania poziomu sportowego we wczesnym okresie uprawiania tenisa ziemnego*. Doctoral Dissertation. AWF Poznan.
Unierzyski, P., & Gracz, J. (2002). Temperament and achievement motivational-critical permanent psychological factors in tennis. *Studies in Physical Culture and Tourism*, 9, 125-131.
USTA. (1994). *Player competencies*. USTA. NJ.
USTA. (2001). *USTA Guide for parents*. USTA Publ.
USTA. (2003). *Tennis participation research*. Taylor Research Group. USTA-TIA.
USTA. (2005). *Parenting my tennis champion*. USTA High Performance.
Van Aken, I. (2004). Mental skills to teach at young age. 12th *ITF Asian Coaches Workshop*. Delhi, India, October.
Van Noord, N. L. (1984). *Development and evaluation of a self-talk assessment instrument for tennis players*. PhD Diss. Michigan State Univ.
Van Raaltke, J.L., Brewer, B.W., Rivera, P.M., & Petitpas, A.J. (1994). The relationships between observable self-talk and competitive junior tennis players' match performance, *J. Sport & Ex. Psych.*, 16, 400-415.
Van Schoyck, S.R., & Grasha, A. (1981). Attentional style variations and athletic ability: the advantages of a sport-specific test, *J. Sport Psych.*, 3, 2, 149-165.
Van Wieringen, H., Emmen, R. Bootsma, R., Hoogesteger, M., & Whiting, H. (1989). The effect of video-feedback on the learning of the tennis service by intermediate players, *J. Sports Sci.*, 7, 153-162.
Vealey, R.S. (1986). Conceptualization of sport-confidence and competitive orientation. Preliminary investigation and instrument development, *J. Sport Psych.*, 8, 221-246.
Verghese, J., Lipton, R. B., Hall, C. B., Kuslansky, G., & Katz, M. J. (2003).Low blood pressure and the risk of dementia in very old individuals, *Neurology*, 61:1667-1672.
Villamarín, F., Mauri, C., & Sanz, A. (1998). Competencia percibida y motivación durante la iniciación en la práctica del tenis. *R. Psicol. Deporte*, 13, 41-56.
Vom Hofe, A., & Fery, A. (1991). Attentional demands of a temporal prediction task: the trajectory of a tennis ball, *Per., & Mot. Skills*, 73, 1235-1243.
Walling, M.D., Duda, J.L., & Chi, L. (1993). The Perceived Motivational Climate in Sport Questionnaire: Construct and predictive validity. *J. Sport & Ex. Psych.*, 15, 172-183.
Ward, P., Williams, A.M., & Bennett, S.J. (2002). Visual search and biological motion perception in tennis, *RQES*, 73, 1, 107-112.
Weinberg, R.S. (1988). *The mental advantage*. Leisure Press. Champaign, Ill.
Weinberg, R.S. (2002). *Tennis: Winning the mental game*. H. Zimman, Inc. Oxford. Ohio.
Weinberg, R.S. (2003). Effective goal-setting for tennis players and coaches, *ITF CSSR*, 30, 3-4.

Weinberg, R.S., Burke, K., & Jackson, A. (1997) Coaches' and players' perceptions of goal-setting in junior tennis: an exploratory investigation, *The Sport Psych.*, 11,4, 426-440.

Weinberg, R.S., Grove, R., & Jackson, A. (1992) Strategies for building self-efficacy in tennis players: a comparative analysis of Australian and American coaches, *The Sport Psych.*, 6, 3-13.

Weinberg, R.S., & Gould, D. (1995). *Foundations of sport and exercise psychology*. Champaign, Ill. Human Kinetics.

Weinberg, R.S., Gould, D., Jackson, A., & Barners, P. (1980). Influence of cognitive strategies on tennis serves of players of high and low ability. *Per.& Motor Skills*, 50, 663-666.

Weinberg, R.S., & Jackson, A. (1989). The effects of psychological momentum on male and female tennis players revisited, *J. Sport Behav.*, 12, 3, 167-179.

Weinberg, R.S., & Jackson, A.J. (1990). Buiding self-efficacy in tennis players: a coaches' perspective, *J. App. Sport Psych.*, 2, 164-174.

Weinberg, R.S., Richardson, P.A., & Jackson, A.J. (1981). Effect of situation criticality on tennis performance of male and female tennis players, *Int. J. Sport Psych.*, 12, 253-259.

Weinberg, R.S., & Richardson, P.A. (1990). *Psychology of officiating*. Human Kinetics. Champaign, Ill.

Weiner, B. (1985). *An attributional theory of achievement motivation and emotion*. New York: Springer Verlag.

Whittaker, S.A. (1980). *Nonverbal of winning and losing behaviour in tennis*. PH.D. Diss., Univ. Washington, Dec.

Whittaker, S.A. (1983). An identification of the components of nonverbal winning and losing behaviour in tennis. In T. Orlick, J.T. Partington & J. Salmela (eds), *Mental training for coaches and players* (pp.120-123)Ontario. Coaching Ass. Canada.

Whittam, P. (1994). *Tennis talk: Affirmations for mental fitness in tennis*. Sapphire Pub. Corp. Bahamas.

Wilkinson, S. (1996). Visual Analysis of the overarm throw and related sport skills: Training and transfer effects. *J. Teaching in Phys. Ed.*, 16, 66-78.

Williams, J.M. (1986). *Applied sport psychology: Personal growth to peak performance*. Palo Alto. CA: Mayfield.

Williams, L. (1994). Goal orientations and players' preferences for competitive information sources. *J. Sport & Ex. Psych.*, 16, 416-430.

Williams, A.M., & Hodges, N.J. (2005). Practice, instruction and skill acquisition in soccer: Challenging tradition. *J. Sports Sci.*, 23, 6: 637-650.

Williams, A.M., Ward, P., Knowles, J., & Smeeton, N. (2002). Anticipation skill in a real-world task: Measurement, training, and transfer in tennis. *J. Exp. Psych. App.*, 8, 4, 259-270.

Wilson, D. (2001). Key behavioural characteristics of successful juniors, *ITF CSSR*, 25, 2-3.

Wolfenden, L.E., & Holt, N.L. (2005)l. Talent development in elite junior tennis: Perceptions of players, parents and coaches. J. App. Sport Psych., 17, 108-126.

Wolpe, J. (1958). *Psychotherapy by reciprocal inhibition*. Stanford Univ.Press.

Woods, R.B. (2001). Children development: Its impact on the young tennis player. In *USA Tennis Parent's Guide* (pp.16-22). USTA. Key Biscayne, Fl.

WTA. (2004). *Age Eligibility Panel Review*. Unpublished manuscript.

Wughalter, E., & Gondola, J.C. (1991). Mood states of professional female tennis players, *Per., & Mot. Skills*. 73, 1, 187-190.

Wulf, G., McNevin, N., Fuchs, T., Ritter, F., & Toole, T. (2000). Attentional focus in complex skill learning, *RQES*. 71, 3, 229-239.

Wulf, G., & Shea, C.H. (2004). Understanding the role of augmented feedback: The good, the bad, and the ugly. In A.M. Williams & N.J. Hodges (Eds.). *Skill acquisition in sport: Research, theory and practice (pp.* 121-144). London: Routledge.

Yaffe, K., Grady, D., Pressman, A., & Cummings, S. (2001). A prospective study of physical activity and cognitive decline in elderly women. *Arch. Inter. Med.*, 161: 1703-1708.

Yi-Hsu, W., Chien-Chih, C., Mei-Yao, H., Kuo-Chuan, T., & HuiMei, L. (2005). *The effects of different tennis teaching models on perceptions of learning environment and learning outcomes of tennis in college physical education*. AAHPERD National Convention and Exposition.

Yoo, J. (2003). Motivational climate and perceived competence in anxiety and tennis performance, *Per.& Mot. Skills*. 96, 2: 403-13.

Young, J. (1998). *The Mind: The Weapon of Champions*, Australian Tennis. October.

Young, J. (2000). In the zone, *ITF CSSR*, 20, 10-11.

Young, J. (2003). Improving concentration, *ITF CSSR*, 30, 10-11.

Young, J. (2006). Keys to effective communication with players, *ITF CSSR*, 38, 3-5.

Young, J.A., Kane R, & Pain, M.D. (2004). Elite Female Past Players' Experiences in Leaving the Professional Tennis Circuit. *STMS J.*, 9, 3-4.

Young, J., Pearce, A., Kane, R., & Pain, M.D. (2006). Leaving the professional tennis circuit: exploratory study of experiences and reactions from elite female athletes. *Br. J. Sports Med.*, 40: 477-483.

Zajonc, R.B. (1965). Social facilitation, *Science*, 149, 269-274.

Zanolli, S., Faccini, P., & Dal Monte, A. (1990). L'allenamento specifico alla concentrazione. Scuola dello sport. *Riv. di Cultura Sportiva*, 18-22.

Zlesak, F. (1995). Building up a professional attitude, *ITF CSSR*, 7, 10.

BIOGRAPHIES OF THE AUTORS

MIGUEL CRESPO

Miguel is the Research Officer for the Tennis Development Department of the International Tennis Federation (ITF). Based in Spain, Miguel is responsible for the ITF Coaches Education Programme and has been involved in the writing, co-authoring or editing of many of the ITF's coach education publications. Some of these books have been published in more than ten languages. He also travels the world conducting coaches' workshops, presenting at international conferences, and reporting on the latest developments in the field of sports science applied to tennis coaching. He is co-editor of the ITF's *Coaching & Sports Science Review*, the official coaching publication of the ITF, which is published in English, French and Spanish, and coordinates the different research and publication grants offered by the ITF.

Miguel has a Doctorate on the psychological constructs of Leadership in Tennis and a B.A. in Philology. He is former Director of the National Coaching School for the Royal Spanish Tennis Federation and was coach and captain of Spanish National Junior Teams. Miguel has taught coaches at all levels and has written articles and books for coaches, players and officials of the game.

Miguel is member of the "Children, Adolescents and Sport" Working Group of the Sport Medical Commission of the International Olympic Committee, the ITF Coaches Commission, and is the ITF representative on the Editorial Board of the STMS newsletter "Medicine and Science in Tennis".

MACHAR REID

Machar was the Assistant Research Officer for the International Tennis Federation from 2000-2004, where his brief included touring as a coach with the ITF Junior 'A' Team, co-editing ITF Coaching & Sport Science Review, conducting research, and tutoring ITF Level II and III Coaching Courses. During this time, he also filled the role of strength and conditioning advisor to ATP player, Greg Rusedski. More recently, he has consulted to Tennis Australia as a Sport Science and Coaching Consultant and assisted the Chinese Tennis Association in the physical preparation of their top 100 female players.

In Australia, Machar has complemented a strong background in sport science, featuring a comprehensive course of under- and post-graduate study, with a scholarship coaching post at the Australian Institute of Sport Tennis programme. A regular presenter at international workshops and contributor to peer-reviewed scientific journals, Machar is currently completing his Ph.D. and working as an Associate Lecturer in Biomechanics at the University of Western Australia.

ANN QUINN

Renowned peak performance specialist Dr Ann Quinn has helped many of Australia's top athletes attain outstanding success from tennis players Pat Cash and Pat Rafter to World Champions and Olympic medallists in more than 10 sports. From 1998-2002, she was the National Director of Coach Education for Tennis Australia and is now the Director of Quinnessential Coaching in Melbourne, Australia where she consults to clients ranging from young athletes to world-class champions, from emerging leaders to corporate CEO's. She also teaches Performance Psychology at Melbourne University and consults and lectures all over the world.

Ann travelled the tennis circuit for more than 10 years working with many top players on both the physical and mental aspects of the game. She was also formerly Health and Fitness Director of the Nick Bollettieri Tennis Academy in Florida. Ann has been honoured with many awards including the National Strength and Conditioning Association Strength and Conditioning Coach of the Year, Australian Sports Medal, Professional Tennis Registry Plagenhoef Sport Science Award, and the International Tennis Federation (ITF) Award for services to the game in coaching.

Ann has a Ph.D. in Psychology, (Melbourne) M.Sc. in Biomechanics, (Illinois) Ba.App.Sc in Human Movement, (RMIT) Dip Ed., (Melbourne) and Dip Nutr. (London). She is a member of the ITF Coaches Commission and the Sony Ericsson Women's Tennis Association Professional Development Advisory Panel. Ann has also written, co-authored and edited several coaching publications and has been a keynote presenter at tennis conferences all over the world (www.annquinn.com).

Miguel Crespo (left), Ann Quinn (centre), and Machar Reid (right).

USEFUL CONTACTS

INTERNATIONAL TENNIS FEDERATION
BANK LANE
ROEHAMPTON
LONDON SW15 5XZ
ENGLAND

TEL 44 (0) 208 878 6464
FAX 44 (0) 208 878 7799

itf@itftennis.com

ITF TENNIS DEVELOPMENT DEPARTMENT

Development
Tel: 44 (0) 208 392 4703 - 09
Fax: 44 (0) 208 392 4742
E-mail: development@itftennis.com

Coaching
Tel./Fax.: 34 96 348 61 90
e-mail: coaching@itftennis.com
www.itftennis.com/coaching

Juniors
Fax: 44 (0) 208 392 4735
E-mail: juniors@itftennis.com

Vets
Fax: 44 (0) 208 392 4737
E-mail: vets@itftennis.com

Wheelchair
Fax: 44 (0) 208 392 4741
E-mail: wheelchairtennis@itftennis.com

PUBLICATIONS
- ITF Coaching and Sports Science Review.
- ITF This Week.
- Take Two.
- E-mail Monthly newsletter for tennis coaches.